ADDITIONAL PRAISE FOR *THE SUGAR KING*

There are two great icons in the history of Louisiana over the last century and a half, Leon Godchaux and Samuel Zemurray. No other individuals have been more prominent. Zemurray's ("Sam the Banana Man") story, twined with the founding of the United Fruit Company, is well known. In contrast, Godchaux's extraordinary achievements and life story have been both forgotten and in many respects until now all but unknown. The Sugar King fills that gap in a lively narrative filled with new information and fascinating detail.

Bill Goldring – New Orleans native, business leader and philanthropist. Chairman, Sazarac Company, Inc. Founder of the Goldring/Woldenberg Institute of Southern Jewish Life. Chairman Goldring Family Foundation and the Woldenberg Foundation.

ADDITIONAL PRAISE FOR *THE SUGAR KING*

"Finally, an in-depth, well-researched biography of one of the most remarkable individuals in Louisiana history. Peter Wolf's The Sugar King: Leon Godchaux tells the incredible story of a poor immigrant peddler of French Jewish origins who, in a complex decades-long business relationship with a Creole of color named Joachim Tassin, became a leading clothier in New Orleans, a major manufacturer and merchant, a builder of railroads, and mostly importantly, the "Sugar King of Louisiana," revolutionizing the growing and processing of the region's most important crop. Leon Godchaux's legacy lives on today, through his philanthropy and through his progeny, among them Peter Wolf himself— great-great-grandson of the Sugar King, who here writes "a life story that begged to be told.""

Richard Campanella, author, geographer, associate dean for research at Tulane University School of Architecture. Author of Bienville's Dilemma: A Historical Geography of New Orleans.

· ·

ADDITIONAL PRAISE FOR *THE SUGAR KING*

"There are Horatio Algers, and then there is Leon Godchaux, a French Jew who strapped on a peddler's backpack upon arriving in pre-Civil War New Orleans penniless and unlettered and walked his way into history. Fifty years on, Godchaux had become not only the city's clothing baron but Louisiana's sugar king. (He left his mark on its railroads, too.) Peter Wolf, an urbanist and well-known writer, has done a masterful job unraveling the strands of his great-great grandfather's stunning ascent from rags to riches. There are eye-openers in nearly every chapter, none more surprising than the saga of the mixed-race Joachim Tassin. Everyone who has visited this subject in the past has gotten it wrong. Wolf's dogged effort to get to the bottom of Tassin's biography is alone worth the price of the book. It's a book that specialists and general readers alike will profit from."

Lawrence N. Powell, Professor Emeritus, Department of History, Tulane University. Author of The Accidental City

Also by Peter M. Wolf

THE SUGAR KING:
LEON GODCHAUX

A New Orleans Legend,
His Creole Slave,
and His Jewish Roots

Peter M. Wolf

Bayou Editions
P.O. Box 135 Lake George, New York

To order additional copies of this book, contact:
peter@petermwolf.com
Xlibris
844-714-8691
www.Xlibris.com
Orders@Xlibris.com
837225

Your local bookseller or Amazon.com

CONTENTS

ILLUSTRATIONS

To Godchaux descendants; to the Tassin
family; and to Betsy Davidson.

"When Leon Godchaux died on May 18, 1899, his obituary crowded the news of the day aside in the newspapers. The dramatic incidents of his career were telegraphed to the East and West and the far Pacific slope."

—*The New Orleans Item*

Fig. 1. Leon Godchaux ca. 1890, courtesy of Carrie Godchaux Wolf.

Author's Note

Leon Godchaux maintained no journal, wrote no diary, submitted to no interviews, commissioned no biography, and rarely allowed his picture to be taken. His granddaughter believes he could neither read nor write.

Godchaux, an illiterate immigrant child to New Orleans, brilliantly managed his affairs through brutal financial panics. He refused to take commercial advantage of the ignominious institution of slavery. He imagined his way through the Civil War. During Reconstruction, he exempted himself from the insidious stains of White supremacy sentiment and from the violent fury in memory of the Lost Cause. He built large enterprises so fair to employees that they were not targets of the contentious beginning of the American labor movement. He was the steward of exceptionally large stretches of productive land. Alas, after his and his children's stewardship, under new owners, much of it became both suburban sprawl and some of the most noxious property in America, polluting air, water, and lives.

Leon Godchaux rose to become one of the most respected merchants in New Orleans, the largest taxpayer in the state, and the acknowledged Sugar King of Louisiana. He was my great-great grandfather.

In reconstructing Leon's story, from time to time I have taken my best guess as to a particular conversation or state of mind while remaining faithful to events as they actually happened.

FOREWORD

by Calvin Trillin

According to the "dictum of first effective settlement," propounded by the distinguished cultural geographer Wilbur Zelinsky, if, say, the first people to establish a viable settlement in an American county have traditionally had a serious devotion to wine, the county is never likely to vote for Prohibition laws no matter how many Southern Baptist teetotalers show up later.

I like to apply the dictum, with a few adjustments here and there, to some individuals whose upbringings were the equivalent of that first settlement—to Peter Wolf, for instance, who has spent most of his adult life in New York but was born and raised in New Orleans. In the foreword to his memoir, *My New Orleans, Gone Away,* I wrote that "the years he spent at an Eastern boarding school seemed to have had no more impact on his cultural core than living for a decade in Midland, Texas, had on George H. W. Bush, of Greenwich, Connecticut."

The strength of Peter's attachment to his home territory has to do partly with family. His family's history has been rooted in New Orleans since 1837, when his great-great grandfather Leon Godchaux (then known as Lion Godchot)—a five foot five inches tall penniless, illiterate Jewish teenager from a small village in Alsace-Lorraine—arrived in the city. By the time Godchaux died, in 1899, he was the owner of, among other holdings, the dominant department store in New Orleans, the largest sugarcane refinery in the country, and vast acreages of sugarcane land whose initial parcel was one of the plantations he had called on as a teenager carrying a peddler's pack. Apparently, he accomplished all that without learning how to read or write.

As if that journey doesn't seem remarkable enough, his most trusted ally along the way was a preternaturally talented biracial man, Joachim Tassin, whose life reflected the complicated standing of southern Louisiana's free people of color in the nineteenth century. Tassin was thought to be an immigrant from Jamaica.

In six American decades, there seemed to be hardly any commercial activity in southern Louisiana that did not include Leon Godchaux. He founded a railroad. He led the effort to shore up levees as the great flood of 1893 approached. He modernized the local clothing industry with the help of an early Singer sewing machine. But his greatest impact was on the sugar industry. He came to be known as the Sugar King of Louisiana.

Peter Wolf did not inherit any of Leon Godchaux's sugarcane land. But as a great-great grandson who happened to be steeped in the lore of the family and of the family's home territory, he was left a valuable bequest by the Sugar King: a life story that begged to be told.

1

The Jewish Immigrant

When Lion Godchot arrived at the port of New Orleans in 1837 on packet boat *Indus*, according to gossip, obituaries, and over 150 years of published accounts, he was accompanied by a young mulatto boy named Joachim Tassin. (*Mulatto* denotes a person of mixed White and Black ancestry.)

Tassin, a thin, light-skinned West Indian freeman of color, had signed on *Indus* at Jamaica to work in the ship's galley. As their packet boat made its laborious way through the rough waters and doldrums of the Caribbean on its last stop before New Orleans, the boys became friendly. When *Indus* docked at New Orleans, Tassin jumped ship to team up with his new fast friend. The native Jamaican and the French Jew soon became a "two-man store on legs," peddling their "first scant stock of goods up and down the winding River Road to small farmers and plantation workers." They went on to establish a small store in Convent, Louisiana, before opening their clothing business in New Orleans.

This irresistible story of their touching bond, forged during the darkest days of slavery between a Caribbean-born freeman of color and a thirteen-year-old French-born Jewish White illiterate immigrant, served for a century and a half as an inspiring tale of interracial friendship and mutual interdependence.

The facts, however, do not support this story. In his early childhood in Lorraine, Lion had known the adversity of being a hand-to-mouth itinerant peddler selling yarn and scraps to nearby villages. He had walked for days on end, alone a week at a time, on narrow byways across fields between villages, carrying a pack that held his food, clothes, and whatever he could glean from elsewhere to sell in more remote villages. Lion trudged through rain and bruising wind, his food meager, his lodging uncertain, and sometimes none at all. He struggled hungry and poor to help his family survive.

Lion Godchot—thin, short, impoverished, and yes, illiterate—stepped off the *Indus*'s gangplank on February 20, 1837, at the foot of Canal Street in New Orleans. He stepped onto the delicate, perpetually threatened tiny knoll of elevated terrain that was New Orleans, tenuously visible just above sea level, at the edge of a vast and vicious river, in the midst of a disease-laden swamp. He carried no more than a bar of soap, knitted underwear, a homespun shirt or two, all wrapped in a checkered scarf woven by his mother on her own loom. Lion was in fact alone.

Four months earlier, the boy had left home. At the shabby town square of his native village of Herbéviller, his weeping widowed seamstress mother had waved goodbye as his carriage disappeared, headed west. Gathered around Michelette, who was then forty-six, were Lion's five siblings dressed in tattered hand-me-downs. The family had been poor ever since Paul Godchot, the village butcher, had died when Lion was seven years old.

In the 1840s, steamship agents stationed throughout Alsace-Lorraine were in business to sell cheap, belowdecks passage on the busy seaway from Le Havre to New Orleans. Targeted customers were would-be immigrants, many of them young, discontent, and ambitious Jews from poor families—families that had long clustered near the Rhine on the western edge of the former Holy Roman Empire.

Using hard-earned family savings, Lion traveled for several days by stagecoach to Paris and from there to the port of Le Havre, where he arrived in October of 1836. He secured passage belowdecks on *Indus*, a freight packet steamer headed across the Atlantic through the Caribbean—destination New Orleans. He weathered that crossing of the seemingly illimitable Atlantic squeezed belowdecks with hundreds of other immigrants. "We think he left home because there was not enough food for all of the children," his grandson Walter Jr. has recorded. "When my grandfather arrived, he had no money and did not know anyone in New Orleans. We don't know why he picked New Orleans. Perhaps it was the only ship he could find."

When young Lion arrived and stepped away from *Indus*, he left his last home, one filled with migrants whose background he understood. Suddenly, he was surrounded by all that was utterly unfamiliar. He had almost no money and was unable to read or to write in French or in English, much less speak a word of English. He had abandoned his known world: his mother, now so very far away, so too his tiny village where his Orthodox Jewish family had lived for generations. Young Lion had the instinct of an adventurer and on that first day proved sturdy enough to find his way into the vast uncertainties of his future.

* * *

When Lion left home, his Jewish heritage was a factor. The Jews of France had been emancipated for only forty-five years. In the outwash of the French Revolution, emancipation had freed the Jews to travel freely in and out of France. But Lion possessed no skill to enable him to enter a new trade in his home country. Neither his small rural hamlet nor the larger cities in France offered promise he could imagine.

Like most Jews in rural Alsace-Lorraine, Lion Godchot was Orthodox. His family would have kept kosher; worn yarmulkes; spoken Yiddish; and identified more as members of a beleaguered tribe than as citizens of the French state. Lion would have been painfully aware of how often the Jewish people in and around his homeland had been persecuted, abused, and even murdered over the past centuries. During his hardscrabble childhood, his parents, both born in Herbéviller, had surely taught him a basic fact of life: survival for a Jew was perennially perilous, forever at the mercy of fluctuating local, national, and geopolitical whims.

He would have heard stories—passed down to his parents from their parents, and to them from their ancestors, who had sheltered in the West for centuries—about all those years during the Holy Roman Empire when Jews in his native land, at one time or another, had endured pogroms, the Crusades, discriminatory laws, imposed dress codes, punitive taxes, and forced relocations.

Alsace-Lorraine had been governed for hundreds of years by laws of the Holy Roman Empire, going all the way back to Charlemagne. That all changed in Lion's parents' lifetime when Napoleon defeated Francis II of Austria at the Battle of Austerlitz, in 1806, the decisive event that ended the Holy Roman Empire. A mere thirty-one years later, young Lion Godchot was fleeing Europe and on his way to becoming Leon Godchaux in New Orleans.

Lion's immediate family origins in Alsace-Lorraine are reliably dated to the first quarter of the eighteenth century, in the person of his great grandfather, born 1725, whose last name was probably spelled Godechaux. His only child, Mayer, Lion's grandfather, was born near Herbéviller in 1752. Mayer became a butcher and died in Herbéviller in 1812. Mayer's son Paul, also a butcher in Herbéviller, was Lion's father. Where their ancestors came from before France is shrouded in uncertainty. According to some of the stories passed down through Lion's family (and supported by modern evidence), it was originally from Israel, followed by centuries of voluntary and involuntary westward migration. (I will argue in a subsequent book that they—like the ancestors of thousands of American Jewish families—spent centuries before France on Sardinia.)

* * *

To better understand my great-great-grandfather's childhood, I visited Herbéviller, driving by car from Paris, a dot on even the large-scale Michelin map. The village center, ten blocks long and two blocks deep, is somber. Beyond the tight assortment of low-slung buildings, cleared fields encircle the village, some planted with crops, others dotted with grazing dairy cattle. At the end of those ten blocks, the main street resumes its role as a modest departmental highway.

The huddled, clustered village is composed of a spare assortment of narrow streets, lined by a continual wall of one- and two-story houses, pushed up against a slim sidewalk. Leon (he would come to be known as "Leon" once settled in New Orleans. I call him Leon when he is known as Leon) described his hometown to his granddaughter Elma Godchaux as a place where "small houses set along a narrow street, [were] cobbled with stone." Not much had changed in nearly two hundred years. The stucco that sheathed the houses is painted a monotonous blend of brown, tan, or gray, that reminded me of camouflage, creating the portrait of a drab, forlorn townscape.

In Lion's day, Herbéviller was a farming village of some 600 residents; by the time I got there, the population had shrunk to a tiny hamlet of about 215 people. Leon's description of his house and his village, as reported by

Elma, became vivid while I stood on what might have been his street; before what might have been his house, "there was a square dresser, a mirror hung by wire, the loom and a chair beside it. In the yard there was a manure pile where the flies hung all summer long. There was a cow and an old tired horse that dragged the plow. There were chickens too and a lamb petted by the children."

Fig. 2. Lion Godchot's presumed family home façade, ca. 1880s, Herbéviller, Loraine, France. Photographer unknown. Courtesy of the Leon Godchaux Collection, Record Group 496, the Louisiana Historical Center.

I looked for people to ask about the Godchot family presence, what might have happened to them during the war, and where they lived. But no one was evident on any street in town, and no stores or cafés were open. What I did see as I walked around Herbéviller was stunningly close to Godchaux's description of his village told to another granddaughter, Justine Godchaux McCarthy, and later reported from a private interview in 1997 with Justine McCarthy by the scholar Laura Renée Westbrook: "All of the houses were small and low, with thick stone walls and plain but serviceable furnishings. Each household included a fireplace that allowed for open-hearth cooking and served as the heat source. Family farms and grazing land were on the periphery of town; livestock pens for sheep and cattle were next to the houses."

After a short stroll on the main street, I walked onto the land beyond the village perimeter. I imagined following the path out of the village on which young Lion had departed for his weekly peddling excursions. Starting to work at the age of ten to help his nearly impoverished family, Lion staked out a territory of three to five miles' distance from home, which he could cover by foot. Alone, often hungry, away from his family most of the week, the young waif of a boy peddled his wares in the surrounding villages of Domévre, Verdenal, Réclonville, Ogéviller, and Fréménil. There were few opportunities for a young ambitious boy, especially an illiterate one.

Elma Godchaux, by then a well-known author, published in 1940, the year before she died, an article in the New Orleans *Times-Picayune* newspaper that reported in his own words, as best as she could recall, young Lion's experience just before he left: "1836 was a mere 21 years after the battle and defeat at Waterloo. People talked . . . about the upstaged glorious emperor and the restoration of the Bourbons. . . . Also, Germany had surged across the Rhine. There was a feeling of defeat in France. . . . There was a feeling that the wars would always be, that they always had been, and a man would be a soldier and work himself out within a little space."

*   *   *

Lion's unpremeditated timing proved to be propitious for a white European Jew. Thirty-four years before he landed, Louisiana was still a French territory: residents were subject to the French legislative act of 1724 called *Le Code Noir*, legislation that reflected pervasive anti-Semitic sentiment in France. Though the legislation was primarily focused on management of enslaved blacks, it forbade practice of any religion other than Catholicism and specifically prohibited Jews from living in Louisiana.

Nevertheless, limited Jewish settlement occurred in Louisiana during the French period. Some eighteenth-century Jewish immigrants dared to defy *Le Code Noir*. Not until 1803, when President Thomas Jefferson negotiated the Louisiana Purchase with Napoleon and Louisiana came under American jurisdiction, did Jews acquire the right to legally inhabit what nine years later would become the eighteenth state in the Union. Thereafter, the sparse community of fewer than two thousand Jews in Louisiana were, at least theoretically, protected by the concept of religious freedom promised by the Constitution.

In the first half of the nineteenth century, during the period in which Lion arrived, European Jewish immigration to New Orleans remained sparse. Western European Jews like Lion, trickled in, a family and individuals a few at a time. Because their numbers were small, the Jewish population in New Orleans remained relatively inconspicuous and therefore more palatable to the dominant Catholic and growing Protestant population.

Following midcentury, the sparse Jewish community gave way to a Jewish cohort of substantial size. Once large-scale Jewish group migration from Central and Eastern Europe arrived in the later years of the nineteenth century, attitudes toward Jews stiffened in Louisiana. Jews were excluded from the elite social clubs and with a few exceptions from Mardi Gras krewes. In Shreveport, the influx of Jews provoked an 1873 ordinance that forbade Jews from opening their stores on Sunday. By the early twentieth century, some 7,500 Jews inhabited Louisiana, two thirds living in New Orleans, which by then had become home to the largest Jewish population in the South.

2

1837: Rowdy, Polyglot New Orleans

When Lion walked down that gangplank, standing there, marveling at the Mississippi River's broad southward flow past the ever-vulnerable city, alone on the bank, he surely felt fearful, unsettled—uncertain how he would survive. He also would have felt wonder at this awesome body of water against whose mighty current *Indus* had struggled one hundred miles upriver as it maneuvered its way from the Gulf of Mexico to the port of New Orleans.

New Orleans was a logical destination for the boy. French was spoken, and frequent cheap passage was available from French ports. In most years between the 1830s and 1860, New Orleans held pride of place as the leading immigration port in the South and second only to New York in the nation. The port of New Orleans, crucial to Lion's eventual success, was the fourth most active in the *world*, eclipsed only by those of London, Liverpool, and New York.

Fig. 3. Nouvelle-Orléans Port of New Orleans at Jackson Square, ca. 1840. New Orleans waterfront and St. Louis Cathedral at about the time Lion Godchot arrived. Lithograph by L. Lebreton. Courtesy of the Historic New Orleans Collection, acc. no. 00.36.

The Mississippi River, the driving force in the city's growth and commerce, was a portal to the world while at the same time the port's docks, and warehouses, and labor pool enabled it to serve the vast lands of the Louisiana Purchase, the newly acquired interior of America, the Mississippi River watershed.

Fig. 4. New Orleans levee scene, ca. 1880s. Cotton bales in the foreground, barrels of sugar nearer the Mississippi at the port that had been the fourth most active in the world prior to the Civil War. Watercolor and gouache by Peter Karl Frederick Woltze. Courtesy of the Historic New Orleans Collection, Gift of Mr. Williams Solomon, in honor of James and Carolyn Solomon, acc. no. 2015.145.

Lion arrived at a rowdy, emerging polyglot and predominantly Catholic city. New Orleans had been an American town with its own charter for only thirty-two years. Louisiana had been the eighteenth state for a mere twenty-five years. The city, unlike anyplace else in the country, possessed a long history of both French and Spanish rule.

When Lion arrived, New Orleans was the most heterogeneous city in the country. It teemed with denizens of every background, religion, and nationality—African, French, German, Spanish, Caribbean, and Native American. Long-standing ethnic and economic diversity had created an environment of religious and social tolerance for free people that was not to be found elsewhere in America.

New Orleans was also the epicenter of one of the largest and most active slave markets in the nation. It was surrounded by and dependent upon a slave-powered agricultural economy based on cotton and sugar. Steps from Canal Street, at the intersection of the river and the Esplanade (both streets will figure prominently in Leon's life), there were slave auction pens. The enormous New Orleans commerce in slaves began in 1808, when transatlantic slave importation had been outlawed in the United States, though smuggling continued. Thereafter, most slave inventories had to be continually refreshed domestically, supplied by professional traders based in the upper South and the East who transported slaves into the New Orleans market. The traders specializing in the resale of human beings needed to supply labor to the expanding Deep South sugar and cotton fields.

*   *   *

Once on firm ground, carrying his small pack, Lion began to walk. He walked on a riprap of boulders put in place to harden the meager levee, to help contain the river, to protect the city. He gazed past the boulders out into the lumbering river. He would have watched the fast-flowing water lapping against the rock-reinforced bank, gnawing at it but unable to gain a purchase.

Beyond the rocky escarpment, Lion would have gazed with wonder at the diversity of workers—slaves, Whites,

French, Creole, Spanish, free people of color—hauling cotton bales and stacking sugar bags, and stevedores provisioning the dense flock of impatient steamships crowding the dock. (Though not the only and certainly not the most restrictive definition of the term, I use *Creole* in this book as an inclusive noun or adjective to refer to a locally born person of mixed race with a hereditary background of Black, free person of color, French, Spanish, Caribbean, and/or Native American mixed with White.) Lion saw both free and enslaved Africans toiling at every task imaginable. Because of rising unemployment during the depression of the period, many more men of every nationality were walking the streets, idle, seeking work.

Yet work was taking place everywhere around him. More than 4,000 slaveholders—a privileged coterie of prominent Whites, free people of color, banks, businesses, churches, and convents—owned more than 20,000 slaves. The rest of the city's population of just over 100,000 (in 1840) was composed of roughly 60 percent Whites (including French, Spanish, Irish, and German) and nearly 20,000 inhabitants called by Anglos "free people of color" and by the French community *gens de couleur libres.*

* * *

The *gens,* soon to become a community twined into Lion's life, constituted a diverse influential population that included manumitted Africans and a wide variety of people of mixed-race African, Caribbean, and European descent integral to the culture and commerce of the city. Many of the men—and more of the women than is generally recognized—owned their own businesses; others held important jobs in all aspects of construction, trade, retail, crafts, the arts, music, science, and real estate. Some were long-established landowners and residents who had lived in New Orleans since as far back as the early eighteenth century. New Orleans was home to more than a quarter of all the freemen and -women of color in the nation. Some were slave owners.

The record-breaking proportion of free people of color living in New Orleans hearkened back to colonial days when interracial unions were so pervasive that French and Spanish civil codes recognized three distinct populations: Europeans, slaves, and free people of color. After Louisiana became part of the United States, this tripartite legal and social segmentation was significant enough, and free people of color powerful enough, to be retained, at least for a while. At midcentury, the free Black and Creole minority in New Orleans, though never entirely exempt from prejudice and harassment by the White majority, enjoyed the status of a relatively privileged and respected subculture.

* * *

Lion's first steps into the city were in search of a particular address, the only address he knew. He walked along muddy, fetid Old Levee Street (now Decatur), darkened by coal exhaust from arriving and departing oceangoing and river-running steamships. Railroads had not yet arrived. Lion negotiated streets whose open gutters and channels were hard-pressed to carry off the accumulation of rainwater, human waste, and refuse. Sewage from open drains poured into the unpaved streets. The mortality rate in New Orleans was twice that of cities of comparable size. Its inhabitants were devastated by periodic epidemics of typhoid, cholera, malaria, and, most often and most dreaded, yellow fever (both the climate and the ecological habitat of New Orleans were sickeningly hospitable to the *Aedes aegypti* mosquito). In 1837, the year Lion arrived, the yellow fever scourge claimed more than two thousand lives.

In the closing light of that first day, Lion proceeded beyond the river, through the French Quarter, into the nearby area filled with teeming warehouses. The low-slung commercial brick buildings were like those he knew back in France. Inside their wide-open doors, he saw stands of produce from near and far, bales of cotton from the southern uplands, bags of sugar destined for upriver and Europe.

Lion was in search of a particular street, a particular address, the warehouse where Leopold Jonas conducted his trade. He probably had a letter of introduction to Jonas, one he had carried across the sea, his most treasured, nearly his only possession.

Jonas, a Jewish immigrant wholesale merchant from Lorraine, probably expected Lion, though he had no idea when the boy might appear. A letter from a Godchot family friend had likely arrived weeks before. At first sight, Jonas would have been shocked: the boy was so small and so young, his matted thick brown hair unkempt, his pasty white skin betrayed weeks and months belowdecks, while his sparkling blue eyes suggested energy and determination. After a brief greeting, he would have fed Lion and offered the exhausted child a space to sleep in a back room of his warehouse.

*   *   *

In the first days that followed, Jonas showed Lion around the bustling city. Lion would say very little, exhausted, and disoriented. Jonas would have cautioned, "There is rampant disease here, a scourge is striking, the city in the grip of a hard time."

In those first two weeks, Jonas probably helped the boy learn rudimentary words in English. He instructed Lion Godchot to creolize his name, to call himself Leon Godchaux, so that he would fit in with the dominant French community. He offered to loan the boy enough money to outfit a peddler's pack. He explained that New Orleans was in the throes of a nationwide financial panic, and with it the collapse of cotton and sugar prices that were demolishing the New Orleans economy. Prospects in the city for an illiterate small young boy were meager. He told the now and forever after Leon where to start out peddling, how to construct his route through the countryside, and assured him a place to stay when he returned. Still overwhelmed, the newly minted Leon could likely say little more than "*Merci, Monsieur Jonas. Merci.*" Jonas urged Leon to leave quickly, to avoid becoming infected, new as he was to the area, with no local immunities. Leon set out on the route

Jonas had proscribed. He resumed the one and only thing he knew how to do—peddle scraps of clothing and notions outside of town.

*　　*　　*

With that first infusion of capital—a backpack stocked with pins, needles, ribbons, yarn, mirrors, combs, and other small household items—Leon took to the road. He walked out of town. The road that lay before him was a rutted one: the plantations along the Mississippi and its tributaries and feeder bayous were linked to one another and to the city by mud-covered wagon trails, the most heavily traveled being the River Road that ran at the base of the Mississippi River levee and connected many of the plantations.

When Leon returned to New Orleans from that first trip upriver, his pack empty, he promptly repaid Jonas. According to Leon's grandson Walter Godchaux Jr., "He asked Mr. Jonas to send his profit to his mother in France . . . this established his credit. He got another pack and prospered and later was able to buy a mule and wagon." Once in possession of a wagon, Leon was able to increase his carrying capacity and his service territory. In a short while, he managed to gain command of sufficient rudimentary English to develop a country clientele that ranged from plantation owners and small farmers to free Blacks and slaves.

*　　*　　*

For three years, Leon traveled the mud-caked tracks between the various plantations, step by step, day in and day out, upriver and along its tributaries, living hand to mouth and at night spreading his bedding in barns and sheds. In those years, while he peddled his goods in the countryside, memories of a dangerous, disadvantaged, difficult life in Herbéviller would have been sharp and painful in Leon's youthful mind. He identified with the poor, the abused, and the enslaved in his adopted land. He was at ease in their company. As a lonely teenager out in the villages of rural Louisiana, along his path he became friendly with young men and women he met of all skin colors—the people with whom he felt an affinity.

During these early days, Leon's older brother, Mayer, and perhaps younger brother, Lazard, came across the ocean from Herbéviller, possibly with their mother, Michelette, and possibly with other siblings, landing in New Orleans in late 1839. Mayer's passport dated September 14, 1839, identifies him as twenty-one years old. The members of the Godchot family who might have visited New Orleans in 1839–1840 returned to their home village. Steamship records document Lazard arriving in New Orleans from France on his own at the age of seventeen in 1843 to join his brother.

Lazard, two years younger than Leon, was made of the same adventurous mettle as his brother. He left New Orleans in 1849 to join the legendary get-rich-quick rush to the California gold fields. Upon arrival in California, rather than prospect in the hills, he opened a butcher shop (his late father's trade) in partnership with Meyer Brandenstein, located in Watsonville, a small town near Santa Cruz. Content with catering to the appetites of the throng of hopeful adventurers, Lazard ended up a titan too—in control of cattle stock-farming properties in California in addition to his wholesale butcher business. (Lazard's great-great-grandson, Keith Richard Godchaux, would achieve fame as the keyboardist for the Grateful Dead and, alas, die untimely—in a car crash in 1980, at the age of thirty-two).

3

Joachim And Thérèse

From his earliest days peddling in the Louisiana countryside, Lion concentrated his territory in St. John the Baptist and St. James parishes, strung along the Mississippi beginning some thirty miles north of New Orleans.

That land had been seized from its original indigenous inhabitants by German and French immigrant farmers intent upon a new life. By the time Leon knew the territory, nonindigenous settlement had been continual for over a century. A patchwork of larger plantation properties was aligned side by side in parcels stretching back from the river. The larger spreads were dependent upon slave labor and were surrounded by smaller hardscrabble farms populated by Whites, a few surviving Native families, and parcels owned by free people of color.

* * *

As was his habit at each plantation, after displaying his new wares and delivering the goods he had promised, Leon would ask permission to visit "the quarters." There were always slaves in need of modest but essential supplies such as yarn and needles.

One of Leon's regular stops was at the plantation property owned by Jean-Baptiste Tassin and his wife, Clarisse. In time, it would seem Leon made a routine stop at one particular cabin at their place because its occupant, Thérèse, was always there. Most of the other cabins were empty during the day, their occupants working in the fields.

When Thérèse and Leon met, Leon was in his midteens; the attractive, slim, convivial Black woman was in her late twenties. Leon soon learned that Thérèse was spared field labor and remained at home unoccupied because she was Jean-Baptiste's slave *placée*. Her job was to be clean, rested, and available whenever the master, exercising his *droit de seigneur*, sent for her.

Thérèse had one other job: taking good care of her son, Joachim, eight years younger than Leon, a six-year-old when they first met. The child, light skinned and lean, with penetrating hazel eyes, had a quick smile and keen imagination. He wove rambling stories nonstop. Thérèse had high expectations for her son, and most likely shared her hopes with the young peddler. In naming him, she covered all the bases. "Joachim" derives from the Hebrew *Yehoyaqim*, meaning "raised by Yahweh"; in the Roman Catholic and Eastern Orthodox traditions, Joachim was the husband of Saint Anne, therefore the father of Mary and the grandfather of Jesus.

Joachim was surely the unacknowledged bastard son of Jean-Baptiste. Jean-Baptiste must have felt sufficiently responsible for his illegitimate slave son to arrange for his education. The child was probably tutored by his legitimate children's tutor. By the time Leon met Joachim, he had mastered the rudiments of reading, writing, basic math, and had learned to speak English properly and French fluently.

Leon would have looked forward to his stops at the cabin where he was always invited by Thérèse to sit on the porch and talk about his life as a boy in Lorraine and his adventures on the road. He listened to Joachim's wildly imaginative stories. He might have brought a set of marbles and taught the lad how to play. They could have enjoyed kneeling in the bare earth below the cabin steps, Thérèse happily watching from the porch. Joachim could have read aloud to Leon. Leon likely would talk to the boy about his adventures on the road, at sea, in France. Without either of them realizing it, they were becoming friends, and Joachim was becoming familiar with Leon's work. Through three years of visiting the Tassin place, Leon also developed a special affection for Thérèse. Having no family of his own within thousands of miles and living across the sea from them, in time, Leon probably began to think of himself as an older brother and something like a ward of the lively, agreeable boy.

*   *   *

In everything except his extreme youth, Leon would have seemed little different from the other immigrant peddlers, many of them Jewish, also offering door-to-door service in the countryside. Before and after Leon, all through the South, enterprising, needy Jewish youngsters had taken to the road to survive and to seek their eventual fortunes. These were in effect, spirit, and aspiration Jewish pioneers in America. In the rural South, especially before the Civil War, peddling created fertile opportunity because the population (White, Black, and everyone in between) was spread far apart and because transportation options were severely limited.

These nascent merchants were self-taught. They had on-the-job training. They learned the rudiments of merchandise control, profit margin calculations, customer relations, insights about seasonal demand for product, debt management, and all the rest. No capital was required to speak of, only an initial loan of goods or funds. Overhead was minimal. Rent was avoided by living on the road. In southwest Louisiana, rudimentary English and command of spoken French was enough to get along, at least in the beginning. Peddling provided a physically demanding entry apprenticeship toward shopkeeping. Peddlers thrived in south Louisiana because they performed an essential service fulfilling a specialized need—goods delivered by door-to-door service, the era's equivalent of Amazon and UPS combined.

* * *

Leon's connection to agriculture had been nearly continual, but superficial. It began with tramping through the fields of Lorraine in the farming and grazing countryside around his village. Now he was peddling in sugarcane country in Louisiana. While selling goods on foot and from his cart during the late 1830s and early 1840s, as he painstakingly worked the plantation terrain along the Mississippi and its bayou tributaries, he gained initial exposure to rural life in Louisiana. His so-called territory was lined with productive agricultural enterprises, for the most part growing sugarcane. He was surrounded by the buzz in the fields and in the sugarhouses during harvest seasons; he knew the sweet, sticky smell of boiling sugar syrup; he found his way among wagonload after wagonload of cut cane as it was pulled by mules to the sugar mill.

In time, he became acquainted with storekeepers and the local laborers—both free and enslaved and some of them plantation overseers and their bosses to whom he sold goods. What Leon learned about the business of agriculture was slowly ingested and assimilated.

4

Convent Country

By the time he was sixteen, in 1840, after three years of lonely toil on the road, Leon had saved enough capital to stock a modest general store. He set up business forty miles northwest of New Orleans on the east bank of the Mississippi in the middle of his selling territory in a small town called Convent, Louisiana.

Convent was situated within what was then called Lafourche County, one of the twelve original counties into which the territory of Louisiana had been subdivided around 1805. (By 1869, Convent would become the seat of St. James Parish.) The village was anchored on a bulge of land formed by an abrupt turn in the river as its north-south course shifts to east-west. The land formed a barrier to the predominant north-south river flow that provided a place where riverboat traffic could be sheltered in the lee of the current. Because of its advantageous purchase along the Mississippi, Convent had evolved into a small-scale home port for businesses engaged in river-related commerce.

Leon was not only attracted to the location as a port, but also for its additional customer base that he knew well—the substantial population of Black and White plantation workers and managers in the region.

There were other possibilities for customers. Convent, as suggested by its name, was the site of nearby St. Michael's Convent. In addition, the town harbored the faculty and staff of a successful boy's school, Jefferson College, originally called College of Jefferson, founded only a decade before Leon opened his store. Congenial to Leon, the college, whose student body was both high school and college boys, had been founded by a group of French Louisianans who wanted to sustain their native traditions and thus saw to it that the college had two faculties, one French and one English. Graduation was bilingual, as were school activities.

(Incidental note: After the college suffered fire, storms, and finally sinking enrollment, in 1931, its elegant neoclassical buildings were acquired by the Jesuit fathers of New Orleans for use as a retreat center. Today, its imposing renovated principal buildings and grounds, perched in the arc of the river, constitutes Manresa House of Retreats, an inviting retreat center not only for Catholic adherents, but also open to others who want to experience the tranquil reverential spaces and routine of meditation practice offered. The gracious ensemble of principal building, chapel, and several historic houses are protected by inclusion on the National Register of Historic Places.)

Having a fixed base from which he operated solved any number of practical problems for Leon. Demand for his goods kept growing. Until he opened for business in

Convent, there was no feasible way for him to haul by wagon the large quantities to which his trade had grown. The store served as a warehouse for items he took on peddling forays.

Though now a proprietor, Leon continued part time as a traveling country peddler. He likely hired a local helper to mind the store when he was on the road. On his peddling rounds, Leon continued to make sales calls to his customers in St. James and St. John the Baptist parishes. He continued to visit the Tassin plantation. The owners were good customers. He continued to enjoy his time with Joachim as the young boy matured from childhood into early adolescence. He felt at home with Thérèse—her warmth and her hospitality were a comfort to him. It is also possible that Leon began a clandestine intimate relationship with his attractive friend.

*   *   *

Step by step, in the way of other ambitious Jewish immigrants in crossroad towns all over the South, Leon was evolving into a small-time merchant. He had obtained the personal confidence and earned the operating capital required to venture from a hand-to-mouth peddler into a retail merchant with a roof overhead and an inventory of goods to sell from a fixed space.

For the first time since leaving home, Leon began to experience a life of anchored permanence. At Convent, his presence as a storekeeper exposed him to a broad assortment of people, including students and faculty, the clerical establishment, and working riverboat crews, far beyond those who inhabited rural enterprises he knew as a peddler.

In Convent, Leon taught himself new skills crucial to his later career. As a storekeeper, he was expected to maintain a diverse and appropriate inventory of goods that mirrored local needs. He learned to be a tenant, to meet monthly rent bills, to maintain a store. He began to establish his own dedication to continual service. He learned how to anticipate, and to order in advance a wide range of merchandise that would be expected as the seasons changed. He had to keep accounts of inventory, goods on order, sales completed. He had to manage seasonal loans and budget for debt repayment. In becoming a merchant managing a retail business, he must have devised simple charts of account where the numbers told the story. Being illiterate, he must have relied upon his prodigious memory. Surely, he also depended upon a literate assistant for written correspondence.

Leon expanded his personal contacts far beyond the small Convent community. He continued to travel throughout the region, bringing merchandise to customers. As he traveled in his wagon from settlement to settlement, he made friends with young people who were coming up in the building trades, in retail sales, the children of plantation owners and successful merchants, staff assisting in local government offices, and junior employees of minor bureaucrats such as tax collectors, notaries, and sheriffs.

Though he could not have known it, when the time came three and four decades later, some of his assortment of young friends who grew into positions of importance would have matured into rural contacts who came to call on Leon for help.

5

1844: Leon Makes His Move

Within a couple years in Convent, as he accumulated both modest capital and enhanced competence, Leon boldly planned to move into New Orleans. He was self-confident enough to bet his future on succeeding in a tough, competitive market, more demanding and financially dangerous than anything he'd ever faced.

In 1844, Leon made his move, strategically timed. The general depression was winding down, confidence was rising, and business conditions were improving. In the immediate aftermath of the long recession, there was appealing real estate to rent in New Orleans at attractive prices. New Orleans had dropped from the third to the fifth largest city in the nation. Its riverside location was being challenged by the vast infrastructure networks of canals and railroads financed by investment capital in the northeast. Nevertheless, New Orleans was still a competitive growth juggernaut, throbbing with commerce. It was the most cosmopolitan city in the South, replete with both legitimate businessmen and scalawags from the East, from Europe, and from the West Indies, marketing their schemes. In those halcyon pre–Civil War days, New Orleans was a place where fortunes could be made and lost—in a twinkling.

Within the city, competition in the clothing business was fierce. New Orleans was teeming with retail and wholesale merchants, many of them first-generation Jews. Of the 250 established Jewish businesses operating in town, half were selling general merchandise, clothing, or dry goods. There were over 100 stores selling just clothing—finished goods supplied principally from the East. Many of these were also in the business of transshipping garments to the interior of the country.

Enabled by the invention of the steamboat, New Orleans had become a clothing distribution hub for reshipment throughout the four thousand miles of inland waterways of the Mississippi watershed; the trip upstream from New Orleans to a port such as St. Louis had been reduced from three months to ten days.

*   *   *

At twenty years old, Leon leased a narrow two-story red brick building at 107-108 Old Levee (now Decatur) Street, across the docks from the river, near the spot where he first set foot in New Orleans. His strategy was to situate his store at the seam between the vibrant port and the densely populated French Quarter, the city's combined retail and residential hub; it was the town's commercial center. Leon had decided to take on the competitive challenge of a lifetime. His establishment, Leon Godchaux, French and American Store, was grandly named to indicate that both languages were routine therein.

Fig. 5. Leon Godchaux, French and American Clothing Store, ca. 1840s, strategically located near the French meat market and across Old Levee Street (Decatur) from the docks. Oil and watercolor painting courtesy of the Leon Godchaux Collection, Record Group 496, the Louisiana Historical Center 2003.108.75.

To gain a competitive edge, Leon decided to distinguish his new store by offering exclusively men's and boys' clothing, in effect to become a specialty clothier.

The building at 107-108 Old Levee Street was made for his needs. At street level, a pair of large plate-glass commercial display windows were separated by a slightly recessed entrance door that opened to the sidewalk. The windowed façade, essential to the display of merchandise, faced one of the busiest streets in New Orleans, with the French meat market across the street and the port beyond. In European fashion, Leon moved into the apartment above the store; its narrow second-floor balcony above the sidewalk could catch the river breeze.

The French Quarter neighborhood Leon moved into was entirely unlike the drab northern European village he had left. He was surrounded by brightly painted brick-and-stucco one- and two-story buildings with tile roofs. Beneath them, shallow foundations tenuously anchored houses into the unstable alluvial soil—not a cellar feasible anywhere.

Most of the wooden-frame Creole buildings from the original French settlement had been destroyed by devastating fires in 1788 and in 1794. Over 1,000 buildings had been incinerated: 80 percent of the original town was gone; 70 percent of the population had been rendered homeless. The French Quarter that Leon moved into (and that still today remains the postcard image of the city of New Orleans) was based on a Spanish-mandated building code that discouraged wooden framing and wooden roofs in favor of brick and stucco structures with tile roofs.

Leon's choice of location reveals his sharp commercial instinct. He had trudged through the river parishes long enough to recognize that the Mississippi River was the interstate highway of his era. Three hundred steamboats docked at New Orleans every month, and more than a hundred oceangoing vessels regularly put in at the port.

"Nowhere," *Harper's Weekly* informed its readers, "is so great an amount of commercial activity presented at a single view as on the levee of the Crescent City."

Fig. 6. Mississippi River steamboats docked at New Orleans, ca. 1867. Leon lived alone above the store on Old Levee Street for seven years. Other than the year and a half the couple spent in New York at the beginning of the Civil War, Leon and Justine lived in the apartment near the docks for fourteen more years, 1851–1865. Photograph by Theodore Lilienthal. Courtesy of Tulane University Special Collections and the Napoleon III Museum, Arenenberg, Switzerland.

As a first and essential commercial step, Leon sought and obtained financing to stock his enlarged inventory. He formed a partnership with Jean Hahn, a local Jewish merchant and financier who had confidence in the young man. Hahn might have known Leon from his earlier buying trips to New Orleans, or perhaps the two were introduced by Leopold Jonas. Hahn lent Godchaux $3,000 for a period of eighteen months that, by the terms of their agreement, had to be matched by Leon's $1,500, all the funds used exclusively to open a clothing store ("Magasin d'Habillement") situated on Old Levee Street, between Madison and Dumaine, with management exclusively Leon's responsibility. Hahn remained a silent partner in the firm through the 1840s. In those early years, Leon was paid $20 a month to run the store; he and Hahn divided any net profits.

In 1845, as his business quickly thrived, Leon leased two nearby buildings, 213-215 Old Levee Street, and was soon adding the adjacent property at 217. The lower floors of those buildings also had generous street-facing windows ideal for display of merchandise.

Leon began to take on staff: Carl Wedderin, Charles Steidinger, and Rosemond Champagne—a clerk, a salesman, an accountant, all educated men who could fill in where Leon's lack of literacy would have been a fundamental impediment.

Like other merchants in New Orleans at the time, Leon sourced his goods primarily from the East, particularly New York, though at times from Boston and Philadelphia. A selection of his premier textiles came from abroad, produced in France and England. The port was easily accessible so that his imports could be put into inventory without additional overland transportation expense.

In the process of expanding his commercial life and broadening his sources, Leon began to form long-distance relationships with bankers, factors, commission merchants, wholesalers, and manufacturers from France and England, from the Eastern Seaboard, and, of particular future importance, from New York.

As his trade continued to grow, a broad spectrum of male customers were attracted to Leon Godchaux, French and American Store because of its diverse array of goods. Godchaux's clients came to include traders, farmers, visitors to the city, ship captains, seamen, Whites, free Blacks, Creoles, and increasingly country merchants shopping for wholesale lots.

With business thriving, Leon decided to bring his elder brother over from France. In 1845, five years after his first journey to New Orleans, Mayer promptly emigrated from Herbéviller and joined his successful brother. Leon proudly renamed the business, maintaining its dual national identity, Godchaux Frères, French and American Store.

Leon's transformative step, from country store proprietor to city merchant, was the risky, ambitious giant step that most retail entrepreneurs, many of them Jewish, scattered at crossroads all over the rural South, were never able to make.

*   *   *

As years went by and Leon became a heralded city merchant, he maintained contact with his original customers in the countryside, most particularly in St. James and St. John the Baptist parishes. He continued to make sales calls there. He probably stayed in contact with Thérèse and Joachim. Some plantation owners became loyal clients of his store in the city; some became friends who would visit with Leon when they came to New Orleans. Some, as time and fate will have it, became needy supplicants.

6

Slave Purchase And Conspiracy

In the early morning of November 3, 1849, twelve years after he arrived in America, twenty-five-year-old Leon Godchaux and his older brother, Mayer, set out by carriage on a thirty-mile trek upriver.

Notices had been posted exactly a month earlier, in both French and English in St. John the Baptist Parish, announcing that on November 3, 1849, to settle their estate, the property and effects of the late Jean-Baptiste and Marie Clarisse "Roussel" Tassin would be sold at auction. Marie Clarisse had died the year before, in April of 1848; her husband lived just over a year longer, dying in July of 1849. None of their nine surviving children wanted to continue to own the Tassin plantation.

Leon and Mayer's sole purpose on that day was to claim the mixed-race eighteen-year-old slave known in the list of family assets simply as "Joachim."

On that November morning, Leon Godchaux was unmarried. He owned no property. His workplace at street level and living quarters above his store in New Orleans were rented. The goods for sale in his shop were encumbered by loans and lines of credit. Meager profits were split with his silent partner and his brother. Nevertheless, his mind was set on what must have seemed an extravagant purchase, his youthful determination in full flare.

*   *   *

At midday, the Godchaux brothers arrived at their destination. They did not stop at the Tassin plantation. Rather, they tied their carriage in front of the St. John the Baptist Parish office of notary Charles Boudousquié, walked quietly through the door, and met the notary by prearrangement. Godchaux would have raised his hat to Boudousquié in tacit gratitude for the tip-off about the sale. In that room, witnessed by the long-serving parish sheriff, Anacharsis Luminais, Leon and Mayer presented proof of their ability to pay the $1,700 previously agreed for the purchase of "the Creole mulatto aged about eighteen named Joachim," the legitimate property of the Tassins. Neither Leon nor Mayer would have had much to say. They were meeting with local authorities in camera, outside of regular channels. They were surely nervous, beset by the feeling of being small-time city Jewish merchants on a mission that could go wrong, terribly wrong, if they made a false move.

Sitting in notary Boudousquié's office, the boys' uneasiness was well founded. Neither brother had prior experience with this sort of transaction or the funds to carry it out, not a penny of it. Leon had, with some difficulty, negotiated a loan in advance from his sophisticated commercial lender and silent partner in the clothing business, John Hahn, to finance 100 percent of the deal.

Boudousquié's scrutiny of the transaction details probably seemed interminable to the boys; the bored sheriff would have been eager to get over to the auction site. The notary examined every line of the previously executed three-year loan document, memorialized by three legally binding notes at 8 percent interest. The brothers' debt to Hahn was guaranteed by a mortgage on Joachim himself, the deal's collateral. Sitting there, Leon surely worried: if his business in town did not continue to prosper, his mortgage would be foreclosed and Joachim lost.

As soon as Boudousquié approved, notarized, and signed the back page of the sale documents, Sheriff Luminais would have walked to the back room, unlocked the door, and released Joachim into the custody of his new owners.

* * *

While the boys were fidgeting in the front office, Joachim had been waiting—waiting locked up in a jail-like airless back room to be taken away forever from his home, from his hometown, from his mother, waiting, his mind surely racing. What would become of his mother? How would he be treated, and where would he be taken? Would he be abused because he had achieved literacy, a forbidden skill? At that moment, Joachim did know one thing: his life was about to change forever. He knew that he had been released to the notary's custody rather than kept pent up in the plantation shed, there to be auctioned off along with the other slaves and other plantation property.

*   *   *

All those years on the Tassin place, though somewhat privileged, Joachim had been a slave. Like every other slave on the plantation, during the labor-intensive cane harvest season, Joachim would have been routinely forced into the fields. He would have known the sharp cut of his skin inflicted by cut stubble; he'd chopped cane under a beating sun and under a pelting rain; he'd felt the glare of a mounted overseer towering above, pistol gleaming from his scuffed leather holster. He had lived with his mother, Thérèse, in a tight, airless cabin in "the quarters" like every other slave on the property.

*   *   *

Leon knew more than notary Boudousquié realized. He knew that the thin *café au lait* young Black slave, about an inch taller than himself, waiting in the back room was no ordinary field hand. As evidenced by his aquiline features, hazel eyes, and very light skin, Joachim had surely been conceived by none other than his master.

Leon knew that Joachim had been made an exception— purposefully educated, taught to read, to write, and to speak several languages. And he knew that Joachim's mother had been the master's *placée* before she was no longer, suddenly freed of that obligation once Jean-Baptiste Tassin died.

*   *   *

When brought out of the back room and unshackled, Joachim would have recognized Leon, but not said so in the presence of the others. Joachim's relief at not being auctioned to a planter, or to an overseer in the middle of cane country, and sent to work as a field slave, would have been extreme. Godchaux probably said nothing. He might have smiled at the boy. In his relief, Joachim likely wondered if his mother might be joining them.

With his few belongings in hand, Joachim followed the Godchaux brothers outside, climbed the carriage step, and sat down on the bare floor at the back of the Godchaux *frères'* wagon. He probably hoped that Boudousquié or the sheriff would get word to his mother that he'd been bought by the peddler.

* * *

Once in the street and in his wagon with no one around, Godchaux, never one to be talkative and always one to remain focused, likely turned around to face Joachim and presumably explained that he had no money to rescue the boy's mother, but that he would make every effort to help Joachim find a way to visit her.

In a low voice that was closer to a whisper, Leon likely said something like "You are safe. I know from your mother who your father was. From now on, you have a last name. You are Joachim Tassin. I have a plan for a new life and a career for you. I cannot know what will happen in the future in the South. But this I know: never reveal where you were born, who your father was, that you began life as a slave."

There in the wagon, before that brief conversation was over, I believe Godchaux made a proposition to Joachim and Joachim agreed. Thereafter, Leon would conceal Joachim's slave status, and so would Joachim. In return, Joachim would never expose what he knew of the relationship, whatever it might have been, between his mother and his new owner.

*   *   *

Joachim's original status as an ordinary slave was itself the consequence of laws in Louisiana that governed the progeny of mixed-race unions when the sire was White. Jean-Baptiste Tassin had nine recognized White children (seven sons, two daughters) with his wife Marie Clarisse. He had taken advantage of Louisiana laws in effect since the 1820s that protected White men who had fathered mixed-race children. After statehood, during periods when Black and White extramarital unions were illegal in Louisiana, there had long been a side-bar legal framework, established by the White legislature. The White father had an option. If he chose to legally adopt, the child would be recognized and become entitled to assume the surname of the father. But if formal adoption was not sought by the father, the children were not entitled to the father's name or any claim on the father. In 1849, when Joachim, with Leon Godchaux's encouragement, co-opted the Tassin family surname, he did so illegally.

The most thoroughly documented account to date about the life of Leon Godchaux written by Bennett H. Wall was published in the 1976 *American Jewish Historical Quarterly*'s special bicentennial issue. Wall wrote, "What he (Leon) thought of the institution of slavery and of the human beings so degraded is not recorded; however, he never purchased a slave."

7

Weaving The Shroud

When the young Godchaux men pulled away from the notary's office, Leon's intention to obtain Joachim entirely out of public view had been achieved. He bought the boy in a private transaction in a private room, one recorded by a notary so that it was legally documented, but nevertheless kept private.

Leon's intention was to permanently obscure Joachim's past, to immediately transform Joachim's identity, to obliterate the slave stain on his new acquisition. As part of the deal, he wanted to, likewise, permanently obscure any evidence of whatever his relationship with Thérèse might have been. At this time of rampant White racism and deeply embedded laws that enslaved Blacks were indentured property, with no rights, Leon Godchaux was crossing a line, becoming craftily, purposefully, and intentionally subversive.

There was another practical reason why Leon wanted to protect Joachim and to permanently transform his identity.

He wanted Joachim to become a new staff member at the store. He believed well-spoken, literate Joachim would attract the affluent free Black and mixed-race customer base in New Orleans, a base that was still significant at around 10,000 residents, down from some 20,000 a decade earlier. (During the decade between 1840 and 1850, many free people of color had found the prejudice and stratification in New Orleans stifling and elected to move to Mexico, the Caribbean, and up north.)

Leon's first gifted young hires in the Old Levee Street stores, Wedderin, Steidinger, and Champagne, had been immigrants and White. Diversification of his staff was essential to attract the more racially diversified clientele Leon wanted to reach. The unusually entwined relationship that evolved between Leon and Joachim also suggests that Leon was determined to serve as a mentor, or perhaps had promised Joachim's mother that he would do so.

* * *

Home territory in New Orleans for most Creoles and free people of color was in the older well-established often-beautiful parts of the city that included the French Quarter and neighboring faubourgs Marigny and Treme, all readily accessible to Leon's store. Here was a conveniently located, desirable clientele with discretionary spending power that Leon wanted to tap. Joachim—young, handsome, light-skinned, more than rudimentarily educated, English and French speaking and affable, and necessarily loyal—would be Leon's key into that community.

Joachim began working for Leon immediately, late in 1849. Leon's instinct that Joachim would be a competitive draw and attract a very substantial *gens de couleur libres* clientele proved prescient. Joachim became a popular salesman with the *gens* almost instantly. Omitting reference to his status as a slave enhanced Joachim's appeal to this proud race-stratified clientele. As a purported freeman of color, he was one of them.

Of great importance to Tassin, as he worked in the store cloaked in his covert identity was protection against mandatory obedience to any number of ignominious legal strictures and a lifetime of personal humiliation.

*   *   *

The way Leon went about acquiring Joachim reveals traces of his character as a young man that would be apparent for the rest of his life. With limited resources, he proved able to plan effectively, to think strategically, and to execute his plan seamlessly. He was willing to prearrange to pay three times field slave market price for a teenager with whom he felt a palpable bond, to craftily and very deliberately protect him from bid at auction, to insulate him from being sold as a slave and put to labor as a piece of indentured property. His purchase of Joachim, under it all, reveals bold confidence, willingness to take risks, and a determination to get what he wanted within a competitive market environment, even when it required him to become both legally subversive and legally responsible for the behavior and health of another human being, as was required of owners of slaves.

8

Selecting A Lady

Coming into his own in the 1850s, Leon was engaged in a linked celebration of escape from his lowly past and traveling into the dawn of his own self-confidence, gained through his success.

He began to assign more responsibility to his staff, a step toward executive management. He engaged in more sophisticated advertising. He liberated time to personally focus on his customers. I can imagine him escorting patrons to the door saying something like "Come see me or anyone of us whenever you need something." He knew intuitively that a successful executive of a family enterprise must embrace both a visionary imagination and a solid hands-on ordinary work-a-day earthiness. He worked hard, always. Leon never forgot the lessons he learned from the provincial everyday hardscrabble life from which he came.

*   *   *

Godchaux's expanding self-confidence was a help in courting. By the time he was twenty-six, Leon would have deplored his status as a perpetual bachelor and would have been more eager than ever to find a suitable woman to marry. He owned his own business, and it was thriving. He had money in the bank, a modest rental apartment of his own, and his English had improved to the point where he could participate in a conversation that no longer masked his own innate intelligence. He was handsome and most likely charming and personable. He felt steady enough financially and knowledgeable enough about himself and his adopted city to consider finding a companion. He'd been alone in America for fifteen years. It was time to stop being lonely. By this time, he no longer thought of himself as a marginal person, unable to create and care for a family of his own.

Thinking was easier than miraculously transforming, but he nevertheless began to work on his goal of finding a mate. At the French Market coffee shop near his store, where he walked most afternoons for a large café au lait, Leon would have asked married merchants gathered there if they knew of any eligible young ladies. Leon probably began to court young women whose families he'd come to know through business. His shy, hesitant manner and embarrassing state of relative illiteracy probably doused potential sparks before they might ignite. Yet he soldiered on feeling financially capable and lonely, telling himself that it was time, that a positive change in his life was possible and up to him.

I like to imagine, one fine early spring day, perhaps on his way to a coffee at the French Market, as Leon walked a few blocks down Old Levee Street from his little store that he turned into picturesque St. Anne Street. There in a shop window he saw attractive handmade knitwear. He entered the store. A young girl was seated in the back of the room, peacefully at her task. He was attracted to her youthful complexion and long abundant brown hair that framed an appealing nearly round face. Justine Lamm was sixteen years old, already a deft hand at crocheting, knitting, and sewing. The young girl was working as an apprentice to the dressmaker.

Leon likely approached her chair, his hat removed, and asked politely about her knitting. He did not particularly want to know; he liked the way she looked. To both of their surprises, when she demurely responded in French, her accent was his Lorraine accent. When she talked about her work, she was talking the language to which he had committed his life—fabrics and clothing. Their blue eyes met in a dazzle. To Leon, Justine must have seemed born, like Shakespeare's Beatrice, under a star that danced.

* * *

With her parents, Anne Sarah Alexandre and Isaac Lamm, Justine had immigrated as a child from Aie, a town in Lorraine not far from Herbéviller. Anne and Isaac were Orthodox Jews, like Leon's parents and like most first-generation Jewish immigrants from Alsace-Lorraine. Justine's grandfather, her mother's father, was given the unusual name of Alexandre Alexandre, and her grandmother was named Anne David, so the very sonorous name of Justine's mother, Anne Sarah Alexandre, was a tribute to her own parents and suggests a possible non-Jewish heritage. (The "Justine" came without patrimony, but was to carry forward all through the Godchaux family for generations upon generations.)

Because her father and mother were schoolteachers, Justine was uncommonly well educated, especially for a girl of her time: she was steeped in classical music, versed in traditional Jewish law, and, most important of all where Leon need be concerned, she was as fluent in spoken and written English as she was in French. Justine was also appealingly petite—just under five feet tall, and winsome, with "serious blue eyes" that belied what several of her grandchildren later called "an impish sense of humor." Months after he met Justine, the relationship bloomed into something permanent. Long a bachelor, Leon was now engaged.

*   *   *

Three months before their wedding, Leon sought an experienced housekeeper. In those days, there were no employment agencies or help-wanted columns in the newspaper. As a routine part of everyday life in the South, anyone who could afford it and needed help bought it.

Leon purchased a housekeep slave, again outside of the city, this time in St. James Parish. The act of sale, dated February 19, 1851, was recorded in the General

Index of Conveyances of St. James Parish. Leon was present at the transaction. In legal proceedings before a notary, recorded in French, he purchased from Lucien and Augustine Arceneaux *"une négress nomineé Francoise ageé d'environ cinquante"* (a Negress about fifty years old called Francoise). Though by now Leon could probably sign his name, his purported signature is in the precise hand of the document's author. Leon preferred to have the notary sign for him.

*   *   *

Godchaux's few authentic signatures have the uncertain, oversized, slightly wobbly appearance of a child's first efforts. Even these, over the years, are not consistent one with another, not consistent enough by a long shot to be used for evidentiary identification. Most of Leon Godchaux's so-called signatures on commercial transactions were written in the same sturdy, meticulous, practiced professional hand of whoever drafted the document itself. Time and again, as acknowledged in each document, Godchaux was present. But someone else, with his permission, did the signing for him.

*   *   *

Leon and Justine were married on May 24, 1851. Though usually reticent throughout his life, on their wedding day, Leon would have been suffused with an overwhelming sense of joy. He'd found a young attractive well-educated

Jewish woman at a time and place where the number of Jewish men far outnumbered the eligible Jewish girls.

Leon had crossed Europe, sailed for months at sea, walked the solitary rough roads and silent fields along the Mississippi, sold goods from a pack on his back to survive, set up shop, and lived alone as a small-town merchant in a remote rural town in the Louisiana countryside, all as he slowly and deliberately saved enough money to risk opening a store in the city and to marry. He'd been a stranger, an immigrant, alone in a foreign country, unable to competently read or write for years. Now twenty-seven years old, his days of interminable loneliness were over. He'd attracted a bright, talented, educated, healthy young woman—and just the right size; he was five inches taller than his bride! Their marriage inaugurated what would prove to be an enduring domestic happiness, the central satisfaction of Leon's life, apart from his work.

*   *   *

In marrying Justine, Leon Godchaux was able to dilute the impact of his illiteracy. He must have been ashamed of that yawning chasm in his ability. He might have concealed it from Justine in their early courtship. For such a bright and ambitious man to remain illiterate all his life indicates that he might have been dyslexic or had some other learning disability. To compensate, his memory must have been prodigious, his alertness to what was said around him acute, his selection of confidants and employees whom he could trust to be loyal and honest would have been fine-tuned, and his ability with numbers of exceedingly high caliber.

*   *   *

Always frugal, Leon moved his bride into his modest second-floor apartment above the store. His bachelor quarters were less than ideal to the young girl; she probably did not complain. Merely a child who had lived only with her parents, Justine would have had no furniture and few things of her own.

Nor did she complain about the neighborhood. Just beyond their front door, the docks thronged with libertine sailors from all parts of the world; horse-drawn lorries pounded the cobbled street day and night, sending up a raucous racket. Conditions in town were hazardous—at times, cholera and yellow fever struck concurrently. The year before they married had been the worst for yellow fever fatalities in the city's history. But they were young, in love, and felt invincible.

As soon as they married, with her mother's assistance, Justine set up housekeeping. Leon continued to work diligently at the store, and Justine probably continued her own work as a seamstress, at least for a while. In the morning and after work, Justine would have read the papers to Leon to satisfy his innate curiosity about business trends, competitors, affairs of state, and the broiling uncertainties in the nation. They would have closely monitored the ideological national debate over slavery that consumed the local press. Would the Kansas territory join the Union as a slave state or as a free state? The resolution of that question, which provoked years of violence in the Kansas territory, would affect the balance of power in the U.S. Senate, itself intractably divided over the issue of slavery.

In the evening, Justine probably helped her ambitious husband try to achieve a basic level of literacy. The teenage child bride was not particularly successful. According to Leon's granddaughter, the celebrated author Elma Godchaux, who knew him, "he never did learn to read or write." Another grandchild, Walter Godchaux Jr., said, "Grandpère never learned to read nor to write other than his name which he only did later in life; the early documents we have are signed 'x'—his mark. . . . I have some of the letters that grandpère dictated to my father and some of my uncles when they were in college. They wrote to him, and someone had to read the letters to him."

To keep current with his extensive engagement with business contracts and eventually with deeds and mortgages, Leon probably depended upon confidants at work, where he had specific trusted employees who oversaw the daily tasks of checking bills of lading, preparing invoices, and the like. This in-house help must have been supplemented by a team, as needed, of lawyers and accountants, at least until his children were educated and working with him. At home, Justine would have made sure that Leon knew everything essential in sensitive commercial letters, loan documents, and private business correspondence that he preferred to not share with his staff.

9

Crossing The Mason-Dixon Line

In 1854, six years before the onset of the Civil War, at the age of thirty, with his business humming in Louisiana, Leon Godchaux boarded the steamer *Asia* (railroad service between New Orleans and New York would not open until the 1870s), headed for New York. Justine was not with him. This trip was all business. In contrast to his first voyage on *Indus*, when he had been too young and too obscure to be included on the passenger list, Leon was described in the *Asia*'s manifest as a full-fledged merchant.

Descending from his steamer on the West Side of Manhattan, the not-long-married, still-childless youthful, slight, newly minted Southerner would have felt dazzled and intimidated by what was, even then, the Big City. He knew nothing of the geography of the city, still less of the habits of its inhabitants—a genuine rube. Leon's European home had been a rural village. His American base of flatlands, wet marshes, and one- and two-story houses looked and felt nothing like the sturdy wall-to-wall four- and five-story—and many even taller—masonry structures looming above him in New York.

Leon's timing was probably prompted by his prescient apprehension of a potential war between the states. He suspected that the South was set upon a perilous trajectory given its addiction to slavery, together with its economy dependent upon it.

Leon was almost certainly motivated by other interests as well, those connected directly to his work. He wanted to meet the people in the garment industry who supplied many of the goods he sold and was otherwise connected to routinely in the conduct of his retail trade. In addition, this inquisitive advanced thinker wanted to learn more about the emerging trade in the manufacture of clothing, a facet of his industry that had not yet reached New Orleans.

By this time, by letter and telegraph, Leon would have established a variety of long-distance business relationships in New York. His connections now extended beyond wholesale merchants to original manufacturers, bankers, factors, and shippers. In addition, he had developed business relationships in other important Eastern Seaboard cities such as Baltimore and Philadelphia, as well as with certain mercantile houses in the great hubs of the continent. To the established big city businessmen whom Leon came to meet, he would have seemed a small-time shopkeeper from a place that was commercially dependent on slave labor—an abomination in the minds of many of them.

To learn more about the vaunted garment industry, Leon wanted to see firsthand how the Singer sewing machine had transformed—indeed disrupted—the ancient art of making clothing by hand. This early in his career, Leon very likely had in mind learning the ins and outs of setting up a manufacturing operation. He would have politely, and a bit shyly, asked one of his suppliers' permission to visit their production plant in the garment district.

It was a propitious moment for the young merchant to find out firsthand what was happening at the leading edge of his industry. In New York, when Leon arrived, clothing manufacturing had become one of the largest industries in the nation and was the single largest manufacturing sector in the New York economy. There was also extensive clothing manufacturing going in other American cities such as Boston, Philadelphia, and Cincinnati, but nothing close to the scale of New York, where in the 1850s, close to sixty thousand people were at work in the industry.

In New York, Brooks Brothers was at the forefront of the craft of standardizing sizes, which made it possible to sell a man's ready-made suit for as little as ten dollars—a customer no longer had to be wealthy to afford well-made clothing. Leon had come to investigate the transformation of an entire global industry that had, since the beginning of time, been dependent entirely upon handcraft. Doing so was a goal that spoke to the alert innovator in Leon Godchaux.

* * *

On this visit, Leon probably also made his first resolute preparations for war. He likely had in mind, as a cautionary initiative, to establish above the Mason-Dixon Line, at the

American center of international commerce, a system of personal bank deposits and safekeeping accounts for his company, for himself, and for his family. To do so, he would have met with bank executives with whom he'd had commercial connections by wire. Leon would have been intent upon evaluating which firm or firms he might entrust his assets to. He was determined to move some of his financial relationships beyond the Southern network of banks. He would have been concerned that throughout the South, the credit agents and the banks were engaged in transactions dependent upon an agricultural economy that he judged to be unstable due to its dependency upon a slave economy.

*   *   *

We know from later accounts that upon his return home, Leon transferred some of his liquid assets to New York banking houses. He did not stop there. Over the next few years, fearing countrywide instability due to the impending outbreak of the Civil War, and deeply uncertain as to its outcome, he had his funds on deposit in New York exchanged for silver and gold, the internationally accepted financial assets that had proven over the centuries to hold or even to increase in value during the time of war and domestic turbulence. Leon did what thoughtful, wise managers have done forever: he diversified.

He also probably had in mind, at this turbulent time, a backstop in the event he wanted to leave the country. New York was the American center of international commerce, many of its banks connected to European houses. It would be easy to transfer funds to Europe if the family decided to flee America in the event of an impending national debacle. Leon was, after all, a French citizen. His gold and silver accounts could be seamlessly converted with the click of a telegraph key to any currency.

10

From Nowhere To Every Wear

For all its commercial hegemony, New Orleans in the middle years of the nineteenth century was still an unsavory backwater. In 1853, the city's worst yellow fever epidemic claimed somewhere between 8,000 and 12,000 lives, one tenth of the population. In the following decade, the toll kept rising to more than 22,500, with 1858 the city's second worse year—4,800 people perished from the disease. At the time, Henry Ashworth, a British traveler, described the city's flawed infrastructure: "[The] only means of drainage is an outlet at Lake Pontchartrain, six miles distant, and as the surface is nearly on the level, there is a great difficulty in providing an adequate means of sewerage. They have not any covered sewers, but wide-open drains are formed alongside the parapets of every street . . . poisoning the atmosphere, and creating epidemics and fevers, which carry off the inhabitants by the thousands."

Leon's retail enterprise grew more complex and more profitable despite these hazards. His competent staff was more crucial than ever to the success of his growing business. Joachim Tassin became a star fitter and tailor. Joachim probably developed a system of notated reference cards to remind him of the measurements of each customer. Once a client had been fitted by Tassin, a reliable record would have been on file at the store and so the ordeal of being remeasured was eliminated. Everyone who came to him the first time wanted to return and be fitted by Joachim Tassin.

Leon's other early hires were also exceptional, keystone successes in their own departments. Carl Wedderin, Leon's accomplished chief accountant, was both Austrian and a full-fledged graduate of the University of Berlin. Before long, he oversaw all matters financial and dealt with banks, insurance companies, and other financial intermediaries. A student of philosophy, psychology, metaphysics, economics, and sociology, Wedderin was exceptionally bright. He spoke German, English, French, and Spanish and read Latin and Greek. Like all of Godchaux's early employees, Wedderin remained with the company all the years of Leon Godchaux's working life. (Upon Godchaux's retirement, Wedderin opened his own accounting office and quickly became the leader in his profession in the city.) Because of Carl Wedderin's enduring presence at Godchaux's side, there can be no question about whom Leon relied upon to decipher written business documents and to review financial agreements.

Charles Steidinger had been Leon's first clerk. Born in Freudenstadt, Germany, Steidinger came to America when he was ten years old. He began work for Godchaux in the Old Levee store at age twelve. When the Civil War broke out, Steidinger took a leave, was inducted, and joined the Twenty-first Louisiana Infantry. He was taken prisoner at Vicksburg, escaped, negotiated his way through the lines, and came back home to resume work at Godchaux's. In an interview late in life after being retired for many years, and a decade after Leon Godchaux died, Steidinger told a reporter, "Like Mr. Godchaux I think a man should do good while he lives and not wait until he is dead. . . . I think I am like my old employer in many things. I have always done my best by those who have befriended me." By the time he retired, Steidinger was recognized not only as Godchaux's oldest living clerk but was also described by journalists as "the oldest clothing clerk in Louisiana." When his health weakened around 1908, in appreciation of his years of service, the Godchaux firm treated Mr. Steidinger to a long tour of the best resorts in Europe.

Rosemond Champagne was Godchaux's first full-time salesman, employed at the store on Old Levee Street. He was tall, dignified, and handsome—so handsome he was thought by new customers to be the proprietor. After the Civil War, Champagne became the head floor man in Godchaux's new Canal Street establishment. Leon respected Champagne's marketing ideas. He convinced Leon Godchaux to offer linen clothes at a price that permitted persons of moderate means to obtain them. Rosemond Champagne worked for Godchaux through his entire career. He retired comfortably, lacking nothing. His son, Rosamond Champagne Jr., also became a Godchaux employee.

*   *   *

By the late 1850s, with an expert staff now a well-coordinated team, even as war was looming, trade in the Godchaux retail enterprise continued to thrive. Customers from every walk of life sought out Godchaux retail merchandise for boys and men. In addition, orders for bulk merchandise from out-of-town storekeepers began to pour in. Country merchants were cautiously stockpiling against anticipated supply shortages if war did erupt.

Given the growing demand, Leon decided to launch a dedicated wholesale operation alongside his retail services. He engaged agents to search for a well-positioned property specifically on Canal Street, suitable to his purpose. Leon recognized that clothing commerce was moving away from the evermore congested old narrow streets of the riverfront and the French Quarter. The blocks near the river were in transition from a residential neighborhood into a commercial hub, a trend Godchaux's rival, D. H. Holmes, had anticipated years before. (Homes was founded in 1842 and sold in the 1980s to Dillard's.)

* * *

Long and wide, Canal Street had been built in stages. It began to take shape in the early nineteenth century when a large open drainage canal was filled in. The failed canal had been grandiosely envisioned, in the early days of statehood, as part of a waterway expected to link the Mississippi River to Lake Pontchartrain and to become a boundary of the Old French Quarter, separating it from the emerging American section of town. It ended up as something entirely different—a broad thoroughfare 171 feet wide, the widest street in the country, 30 feet wider than New York's Park Avenue, and the tacit boundary between the Vieux Carré French and Creole settlement and the newer Anglo-American emerging section of town.

Canal Street became a showcase. For its more than four-mile length, the center of Canal Street was dedicated as a broad swath of landscaped public space that came to be called the Neutral Ground. In local lore, this was the space in the middle of this wide street where delegates from the old established French Quarter and the newly arrived Anglos, building on the other side of the divide, could meet to amicably settle their differences. (Substantial street medians all over New Orleans are still called neutral grounds.) By 1866, the *Daily Picayune* described Canal Street as "the heart of New Orleans. . . . The broad foot-walks, the double, wide and well-paved carriage ways, the green 'neutral ground,' with its refreshing vistas of trees, the brilliantly colored tram cars, which are constantly moving in the midst of them, the lofty stores . . . all that is elegant and beautiful . . . seeks 'the grand Boulevard' for its display."

* * *

New Orleans, in the decade before the war, was prosperous. The general population expanded by 17 percent and the White population ballooned to over 50 percent. It was in this time period that Leon considered opening a clothing manufacturing plant. New Orleans merchants continued to source bolts of raw goods as well as ready-made inventory from out of town as they had for generations. No one had begun to manufacture clothing in New Orleans yet, even though the invention of the sewing machine had modernized the trade.

If he became a manufacturer, Leon recognized he would be able to eliminate dependence upon some of his out-of-town sources, and simultaneously he would be able to fill demand from merchants in and around New Orleans. For his own customers, he would be able to assure a high level of quality control. For the first time he could tailor and rapidly deliver at reduced cost an entire outfit to accommodate the specific taste of each individual client.

*　　*　　*

Leon had been inspired when he visited New York by Isaac Merritt Singer's sewing machine, introduced in the early 1850s. There had been earlier versions, the first patented in France by Barthélemy Thimonnier in 1830. That inaugural version, a new and as yet imperfect contrivance of the Industrial Revolution, was invented to mass-produce French army uniforms. The first sewing machines, understandably, terrified the substantial community of tailors in Paris. A mob of two hundred formed and succeeded in destroying all new sewing machines within the next year. Other patents and mechanical improvement followed on both sides of the Atlantic.

Isaac Singer (1811–1875), living in Boston, who characterized himself as an inventor, was engaged in

1850 by a local machinist to improve another inventor's model of the sewing machine. Rather than tinker with it, Singer proceeded to redesign the Lerow and Blodgett Company version. When Singer's work was completed, his machine could sew at the rate of 900 stitches per minute. An accomplished professional seamstress working on a straightforward project could be expected to sew at a rate of 40 stiches a minute. In 1851, Singer proceeded with his partner, Edward C. Clark, a lawyer from New York, to obtain his first patent and to incorporate I. M. Singer & Company. When the factory relocated from Boston to New York in 1853, a Singer sewing machine sold for around $100. In 1856, Clark had the idea to enable sales that could be paid for in installments. The Singer company became the first in the world to offer sale on credit. Their advertisements announced that "persons who cannot afford to purchase a sewing machine, can have a machine, too."

By the 1860s, the sewing machine had transformed the making of clothing. A man's shirt that formerly required over 1,400 hours to sew by hand could be finished in an hour. A shop outfitted with 400 Singer machines, the company promised, would be "able to do any piece of work that may be done by two thousand workers." By 1863, while the Civil War was in full fury, Singer had amassed 22 patents, and the company was selling over 20,000 machines annually.

Singer's key to success was both his transformative machine and Clark's mastery of marketing and distribution. The partners opened classy showrooms, instituted a repair service, produced sewing instructions for home use, and planned for nationwide sales of new machines, parts distribution, and a service network. Through the benefits of volume trade, the cost of a machine dropped to ten dollars, making it affordable to a wide array of households, where most clothing all over the world was made. Their customers' ability to buy on the novel installment basis vastly expanded the market. When the company began to accept trade-in machines so that customers could continually update, sales soared beyond expectations. The partners—industrial and commercial visionaries—proceeded to create the first multinational American company, the Singer Sewing Machine Company. Before the Civil War was over, Singer sewing machines had become the most popular in America, the first global brand ever produced in America, and eventually what amounted to a worldwide monopoly.

* * *

Leon had been aware since his visit to New York that this one industrial invention had the capacity to transform the time-worn labor-intensive by-hand method of making clothing. He also probably recognized that one machine, so recently invented, had the capacity either to seriously challenge his business or be the engine of his inventive expansion. On fire with a plan to go into manufacturing, he was thwarted. War got in his way.

* * *

At nineteen, now a long-married woman of three years, Justine became pregnant. Contemplating the expansion of their household, Leon sought additional help to assist with child care. What to do, other than the logical and inevitable? On February 20, 1854, Leon and Mayer appeared before the New Orleans notary Jean Baptiste Adolphe Boudousquié, generally called Adolphe. Their purpose was to conclude, in a private transaction, the acquisition from Jean Sauvage, of Eliza, twenty years of age, "house maid, laundress, ironer, very clever and of good will, with her twenty-month-old son Frank."

In going this route, the brothers again refused to participate in the slave auction market, but rather patronized a trusted responsible professional intermediary. The seller, who was present at the sale, had provided positive character references. The transaction cost was 888 piastres, each equivalent to about a dollar at the time. (*Piastre* was the French term for Spanish pieces of eight, used commonly in French-denominated transactions in Louisiana and served as legal tender in the United States until the Coinage Act of 1857.) The brothers' business had improved considerably. No loan was needed; no debt was incurred. They paid cash.

*　　*　　*

Though Eliza was obtained in a private transaction, until the Civil War there were as many as fifty professionally run busy slave markets in New Orleans. Whereas in most Southern slave-market towns the commerce in human beings was confined to one or two locations, in New Orleans, slave "pens" and auction sites were widespread; auctions took place all over the city. The slave mart action was located at venues as simple as a ship's deck, a vacant storefront, or an empty lot. The most elegant took place under the chandeliered rotunda of the French Quarter's St. Louis Hotel, one of the two elaborate palace-like hotels in the city.

There were three particularly prominent locations where the most intense slave trading occurred, each in or near the French Quarter. These relentlessly busy sites of slave commerce were at the corner of Esplanade Avenue and Moreau (now Chartres), St. Louis Street between Royal and the levee, and the third in the Anglo area bound by Common, Carondelet, Union, and Philippa (now O'Keefe) streets, the emerging financial district of the city. The slave market at Esplanade and Moreau, according to Erin Greenwald, an authority on New Orleans slave markets, was "a slave pen, with a showroom, like an auto dealership, and a yard where enslaved people would sleep, exercise and cook. These pens were basically jails. And the eating-well and physical activity was all so that the traders could sell their property—humans—at the highest possible profit."

The slave market business in New Orleans had swelled as the century matured, beginning, as I have said, after the federal government in 1808 prohibited American participation in the international slave trade. Once legal importation to the states of enslaved people from abroad was shut down, demand did not abate. Just the opposite. The Louisiana Purchase opened hundreds of thousands of new fertile acres in large contiguous tracts, especially in the Deep South, for cultivation in cotton, sugar, and many other crops. So nearly simultaneously with abolition in America of the international slave trade, there emerged in the Deep

South enormous new demand for agricultural labor. With supply restricted, prices rose. In response, the many owners of slaves in the east, the upper South, northern, and central states forcibly exported to the Deep South some of their human property. Enslaved Blacks were transported by boat, by rail, by wagon, by stagecoach, and the most unfortunate by foot—close to a million indentured people—to the lower South to be sold at favorable escalating prices where demand had ballooned. Before the end of the antebellum period, booming New Orleans became the largest slave market in America.

*　　*　　*

Leon and Justine's eagerly awaited child, called August, was born sometime in 1854, probably in August, in the apartment. But the baby died within a matter of days. This tragedy cast a pall of sadness over the young couple, who, for the rest of their lives, memorialized August by including him whenever listing their children.

Two years later, in December of 1856, Eliza, now twenty-two years old, and her children, were sold. Eliza's family now included two children: there was Frank, now four years old, and a second child, Edgard, "aged about ten months." Eliza had become pregnant, and baby Edgard was born while Eliza was in Leon and Justine Godchaux's service. As city slaves were routinely granted one day a week off duty, or at the very least a part of a day, traditionally Sunday, Eliza had found time to become involved with a lover. According to notarized sale documents, Mayer and

Leon were paid $1,200 for the three slaves, $400 in cash and a note for the $800 balance at 8 percent interest due in six months. Security for the note, as was common in such transactions, was Eliza, Frank, and Edgard.

The timing of this transaction is curious as Justine was again pregnant. Eliza might have been sold because of unacceptable performance in her work, or perhaps because she could not work and care for her own two young children at the same time. It is also possible that by this time, Justine and Leon had decided they were uncomfortable owning a young slave with children for both humane and economic reasons. At this point, one housekeeper and general all-around helper was enough.

*　　*　　*

Four months after Eliza was sold, on April 17, 1857, Justine gave birth again, this time to a healthy boy, the first of the couple's ten children to survive. The baby (my great grandfather) was named Paul Leon, after his father and his deceased grandfather. In perpetuating both names, the young Godchaux couple began a tradition of repeating family names that would play out down through the generations and in time cause identity havoc among the myriad cousins and uncles and aunts and parents at increasingly large family gatherings.

Francoise, their one remaining slave, cared for Paul Leon and made sure he was safely through his early months. This must have been an emotionally fraught interval for the young parents, considering what they had been through with their firstborn. A joyous mood prevailed between Leon and Justine, to say nothing of Justine's proud parents, who were now first-time grandparents. The parents and grandparents were immigrants. Now they had a native son, a real American. The young Godchaux family was becoming established in one of the fastest-growing premier cities of America. At least it was, for the time being.

With the birth of Paul Leon, Francoise, who had been with the family since 1851, became more essential than ever. Given space limitations in their small apartment, Francoise had probably always lived apart and worked as day help. Leon likely followed his compassionate instinct, paying Francoise a fair salary, as he did Joachim.

But the couple sought additional help as the infant became more rambunctious. In September of 1858, Leon purchased Pauline, a twenty-eight-year-old female slave for $1,030, in a private notarized transaction, presumably to help out with child care and household tasks.

*   *   *

As his family began to expand, Leon remained cautious about the future of a region dedicated to and economically based on a slave economy. Even though their small apartment above his store was in the middle of the raucous, noisy neighborhood that surrounded one of the largest commercial ports in the world with over three thousand steamboats calling annually at America's second busiest port, he was hesitant to move. Though talk of war was rampant, ships were still loading and unloading in

New Orleans at all hours, wagons and horses still clanged on cobblestone streets, stevedores shouted, and overseers cursed. Though he could now afford to upgrade from the Old Levee Street apartment, Leon refrained from either renting a bigger place and certainly from buying a house.

On noisy evenings, Justine would probably plead, "Let's move to a neighborhood, *cher* Léon, where the family will have a quiet yard, a place to grow flowers, and a place for baby Paul Leon to play outdoors."

But Leon, now thirty-three years old, remained ever wary and cautious and prescient. He would likely have answered her quietly, a tinge of fear in his tone, "We must see how these dangerous disagreements between the Southern states and the North work out. You know from everything you read to me, trouble is rising in the country. Remember what happened in France. Real estate prices are high, much higher than I think they should be given what could happen here. We should wait. I'll continue to expand the business to meet the big demand at the store, but I don't want to risk anything more here now."

*   *   *

By the end of 1857, Leon had leased a string of five stores on Old Levee Street to contain his thriving business while he was steadfast about not buying commercial property or a new house. He would have warned his staff at the store to be careful, that there was the real possibility of a terrible war. The stores might be destroyed. The business, as good as it is now, might collapse.

At this juncture in his career, Leon had taken on a fulsome payroll of productive employees who were earning good wages; he had paid off the debt incurred by the purchase of Joachim, who had proved to be an enormous success at the store, and his staff had settled in as an efficient and resourceful coterie essential to the business. In the years leading up to the Civil War, Godchaux Frères had achieved the largest retail trade in New Orleans and was distinctly profitable.

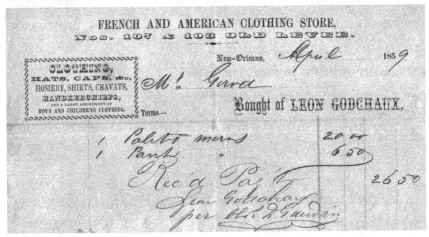

Fig. 7. French and American Clothing Store sales receipt of April 1859. Leon shortened the name of his establishment at 107-108 Old Levee Street but kept the French and American description. Courtesy of Tulane University Special Collections.

As he came to experience Joachim's levelheaded clarity about fashion trends and management, Leon slowly came to depend more on Tassin and his good judgment. When the staff gathered at their monthly meetings, if there was a crosscurrent of opinion about what merchandise would sell best in the next season, Godchaux began to defer not just to

Rosemond Champagne, but also to Tassin. When Leon was not present, the employees developed the habit of seeking Tassin's decision if one was needed on the spot.

In time, Joachim Tassin rose to become a master tailor, a star salesman, and a surrogate manager. His loyal customers returned again and again to have their clothes and their sons' clothing fitted. He knew every customer by name who sought his help; he would have made a point of speaking to them about their families, womenfolk included. When appropriate, I imagine, his greeting always included, "And how is your miss doing at school?" or "How is your mississ feeling after her bad fall last week?" His deft skill with measuring and tailoring was always backed, I imagine, by saying, as he walked his customer to the door, "If anything isn't right, I'll fix it for you, right away, no charge."

*   *   *

As a successful freeman of color holding a respected position in a thriving retail firm, Joachim was welcomed into the privileged pre–Civil War coterie of Creoles in New Orleans. His status in the *gens* community, as Leon had anticipated, enhanced his appeal to a wide spectrum of customers. His engaging personality, his literacy, and multilingual skills all helped him pave his way into the circle of talented and successful people in the upper reaches of the free Black community in New Orleans.

At the same time, Joachim was surely restless. He was now twenty-five years old. He had a secure job and an acknowledged talent for his work. The danger inherent in his secret life as a rogue slave would have been fading from top of mind. He had been living as a freeman for almost a decade, an attractive man accepted as a Creole, living among a mixed-race community of talented and capable people. Joachim was likely lonely for a companion. He would have been trying to find out for the past years where his mother might be. That's not all he was likely thinking about.

11

Tassin's Middle Passage

Starting in his mid-twenties, Joachim probably became dissatisfied with his status as a covert slave. At some point, perhaps in early 1857, Joachim approached Leon to begin a momentous conversation about his freedom. He probably entered the office late one afternoon, just before closing time. "Mister Leon, I'd like to close the door and talk to you privately. Is this time all right?"

Awkwardly unable to think up a preamble, Tassin might have looked at his benefactor and said something like, "I've been thinking it was time to know so I can plan: When were you thinking about setting me free?"

Leon knew that with Joachim's help, he'd be able to expand his mercantile operation continually. He had married. He had visited New York and learned firsthand what life was like in America for Blacks and Whites outside the slave economy. Though perhaps caught unprepared, Leon must have agreed that it was now time to come to terms with the future he had promised his loyal helper, the man he might secretly have thought of as his ward and the son of a woman with whom he might have had his first sexual experience.

* * *

Eight years after he bought Joachim and brought him to New Orleans, a new legal chapter in the secretive link between Leon Godchaux and Joachim Tassin as a sub-rosa slave was recorded, quietly and privately.

A meeting was held on June 8, 1857, in the notarial office of Adolphe Boudousquié, the New Orleans–based cousin of Charles. As I imagine the proceedings, Leon and Mayer arrived together. A few minutes later, Joachim came into the office, now voluntarily, a full participant, dressed like the Godchaux men in a dark suit, starched white shirt, and black cravat. Tassin took a seat at the table with the others. At that moment, he had worked effectively and exclusively for Godchaux Frères for the past eight years; he had established a fine reputation as an astute salesman and skilled tailor.

At the big conference table, there would have been no need to have a conversation or even to review the papers on the table. The participants' mutual purpose, previously discussed in detail with one another and with the notary, was to finalize documents that memorialized a complex and legally sophisticated way to quietly and yet decisively emancipate the slave, Joachim.

The document the men had met to sign would have appeared convoluted and punitive to any uninitiated observer—to the point of being nonsensical. Adolphe Boudousquié wrote the agreement in French, using florid sepia ink using looping and slanted script. It stated (in translation), "Proof of their [the Godchaux brothers'] satisfaction and . . . at the same time (to) reward him (Joachim) for the good and faithful service he never ceased giving to them . . . they agree hereby to give him freedom, in four years . . . during those four years, said Joachim will remain employed as a worker in the business of Godchaux Frères." At the end of the four years, Joachim "cannot be given away, assigned, mortgaged to any third parties under any pretext except for that of his freedom." In conformance with the restrictive conventions of the time, the contract repeated standard language about liberated slave compensation. The owners were required to declare, in effect, that their slave had been "allocated" the sum of fifty dollars each quarter of the year for the past two years and would continue to receive such a credit for his work for the next four years, which amounted to a total of "twelve hundred piasters." Nevertheless, as was the punitive law at the time, he would not be paid the money due and earned until his freedom was granted four years hence. At that time, he would be entitled to "said sum of twelve hundred piasters and such other amounts that his employers may give him at the time, a reward for the cares he will have demonstrated in favor of their interests and of the industriousness that he will have exercised as an employee." The document went on to declare that Joachim was present and in agreement with these terms. It was signed by Joachim Tassin as "J. Tassin," Mayer as "M. Godchaux," and by Leon in his own wobbly hand as "Leon Godchaux," as well as by Boudousquié and two witnesses.

When Boudousquié read out the terms of the contract agreement, the men around the table each knew that four more years of Joachim's required indentured service, earning no direct payment but only a credit, on top of the sums presumably credited to him over eight years of prior service, was a fiction and not the goal of the deal or the substance of the deal and not an accurate description of what was taking place. They knew that the legally stated restrictive harsh procedure mandated by current law as terms governing the promised future liberation of their friend and faithful colleague would not be dutifully followed.

The Godchaux men and Tassin recognized that executing this document of future liberation was the most feasible way to work around current repressive law. At the time, under the prevailing American Poor Laws, taxpayers in each jurisdiction were responsible to care for any needy individual among the free population. This stipulation terrified Whites when they thought of slaves' being liberated and then becoming, they assumed, legitimate charges of the public. Slave owners, on the other hand, were responsible for the care of their slaves for their lifetimes.

To assuage these predominantly White taxpayers' fears, laws had been enacted to force slave owners who might want to liberate someone to take on mandatory continuing financial responsibility for their slaves for at least the next four years before they could be liberated. Thus, to qualify a slave for future emancipation, the owner was obliged to certify, as the Godchaux men had, that the slave in question was of good character and would not become a public responsibility and expense over the four-year probationary period.

The focus on this issue was so obsessive in Louisiana that through most of the 1850s, laws existed to make sure a liberated slave would not become a public responsibility at the end of the four years. A slave once freed was required not just to leave the state within one year, but to leave the country entirely. To guarantee departure, the slave's owner was required to deposit $150 to pay for the freed person's voyage to Africa.

Given the world in which they lived, none of the parties to the transaction wanted it ever known that Joachim Tassin was a slave. Yet to clear his status forever, no matter what the future may bring, the brothers and Tassin sought a path to legally free Joachim under the prevailing law.

Leon, Mayer, and Joachim were working together to comply with a set of highly restrictive regulations and at the same time assure Joachim Tassin's ability to continue living in New Orleans as a paid employee. Whether or not notary Boudousquié had any idea of their ruse is unclear. A tightrope act, indeed, with all three collaborating in the center ring.

The Godchaux brothers and Joachim Tassin conducted this legal transaction out of fear of what was coming. Given the increasing hostility toward Blacks and free people of color in the late 1850s, Tassin might someday need proof of liberation in case his slave identity ever became known to the authorities. They recognized the evermore rabid antislave atmosphere boiling over in Louisiana as reaction to the feared interference by Northern abolitionists. The legal maneuver at the time it took place reveals the brothers' and Tassin's fear that slavery, as a way of life, might continue for many years.

Their timing was indeed prescient. Manumission in Louisiana under any conditions became illegal at the end of 1857.

* * *

Life got worse for all Blacks in Louisiana, not just for slaves, shortly after Joachim's manumission agreement was signed. Beginning in 1857, every Black person and every free person of color was required to carry an identity pass, observe curfews, and have their racial status designated in all public records. Ironically, even though Joachim had been at liberty for years in the guise of a free person of color, now he was suddenly subject to most of the same regulations as a slave. The other irony was timing: Joachim's planned future emancipation four years hence was set for 1861, the year the Civil War broke out.

12

Preparing For War

On Christmas Eve of 1859, Leon Godchaux arrived again in New York, this time aboard the steamer *Baltic*. He must have felt a great sense of urgency to be traveling at the Christmas season into the cold climate. The situation between the slave states and the North was fast deteriorating. Fearful of the future, with no way to judge what might occur between the states, Leon was no longer hopeful about the fate of the city in which he and his family lived. Like many recent immigrants, and as still a citizen of France, he was not an advocate of the institution of slavery, even though he participated in the system for his household help. At this moment in his life, Leon had probably not abandoned the idea of returning to France if necessary.

Once settled in a hotel in New York, Leon got down to serious business even though it was the holiday season. He likely met with the banking connections with whom he had been in correspondence by letter and telegraph since his prior trip. He confirmed that most of his liquid funds had been securely transferred out of New Orleans and converted to gold.

He also began an urgent search for shelter for his family and a place from which he could work. After perusing several neighborhoods, he found a well-constructed building that allowed him to replicate the work/living spaces arrangement in one building that he was accustomed to in New Orleans and that he had known in Europe. Within its ample five stories, 171 Duane Street combined generous family quarters above a well-lit, expansive workspace at street level.

Fig. 8. 171 Duane Street, New York City. Leon's headquarters in New York where he and Justine lived with young Paul Leon for a year and a half prior to and during the first year of the Civil War. It is here in a mixed thriving industrial-residential neighborhood (now trendy Tribeca) that Leon set up his first manufacturing operation. A small park across the street was a welcomed change from sooty Old Levee Street for Justine and Paul Leon. Courtesy of the author.

Now that he was at the epicenter of world commerce, Leon was at the cusp of finally realizing his dream. In New York he could expand into manufacturing while continuing in New Orleans as a retail and possibly wholesale merchant. Within a few months of intense effort, Leon got his New York affairs in order, his workspace outfitted, his first set of employees identified.

*   *   *

Leon's competitive instinct to enter the manufacturing side of his trade as rapidly as possible likely had been intensified by a New Orleans–based retail shirt competitor, a man called Samuel Nadin Moody, who manufactured in New York. English born, Moody had established a manufacturing operation in the garment district by the time Godchaux got to New York the first time, operating a sprawling shirt factory at 315 Broadway and employing five hundred people. In the mid-1850s, Moody expanded into New Orleans, where he became a successful Canal Street retail merchant specializing in shirts.

Moody developed a robust trade in his store at the corner of Canal and Royal, devoted exclusively as a shirt retailer. By 1857, propelled by being an early advanced technology adapter, buttressed by his marketing and retailing skills, Moody had earned the sobriquet "the shirt king of Canal Street" and a reputation as "the biggest shirt tailor in the Southern States."

Fig. 9. Moody's Shirts, at the corner of Canal and Royal, ca. 1866. English-born Samuel Nadin Moody, "the shirt king of Canal Street," an immigrant to New Orleans, began manufacturing in New York before the Civil War and might have inspired Leon. His outlet in New Orleans is seen behind the fourteen-foot-high Henry Clay statue in Canal Street, erected in 1860 and moved to Lafayette Square across from Gallier Hall in 1900. Photograph by Theodore Lilienthal. Courtesy of Tulane University Special Collections and the Napoleon III Museum, Arenenberg, Switzerland.

*   *   *

After several months in New York, Godchaux returned to New Orleans as quietly as he had left. Back at home, with the prospect of war thick in the air and in the news, he and Justine would have discussed what to do. She had been frightened and wary and wondered if she should gather up her parents and sail immediately back to France. He, in turn, suggested going as far as New York to await what would happen in the states before they decided to leave. This approach suited Justine. The couple would have told no one except Leon's brother and Justine's family what they had in mind.

With deliberate stealth, Leon and Justine planned for their entourage to leave town—for however long they knew not. Mayer was willing to stay behind to manage the business along with Tassin and the other employees for as long as necessary. Neither brother knew what to expect if war broke out.

After Leon departed, on June 6, 1860, Mayer released to the public the notice the brothers had prepared to reveal their business plan. By a paid announcement published in the New Orleans *Daily Picayune*, they detailed the reorganization of the firm, including the presence of a new partner, Mr. Joseph Simon, based in New York. The business, they assured their New Orleans clientele, would continue in New Orleans "in the wholesale and retail clothing business . . . under the name and style of M. GODCHAUX, FRERE & CO. In New York, the firm would be known as 'L. GODCHAUX, FRERE & CO.' The New York firm would be devoted to 'the manufacturing and wholesale clothing business.'"

The Godchaux brothers were the primary principals in these partnerships, but Joseph Simon probably made a meaningful contribution to the New York branch. Leon had likely arranged to operate in New York within Simon's preexisting business charter and licenses and with the leased use of his equipment and some of his expert manufacturing personnel.

A week after the firm's expansion to New York was announced publicly in New Orleans, on June 13, 1860, ten months to the day before the outbreak of the Civil War, Leon, Justine, a servant, and two small children unnamed on the passenger list arrived at New York Harbor on the *Moses Taylor*. The steamship had sailed from Havana and made a stop at New Orleans en route to New York. One of the unnamed children was the couple's four-year-old son, Paul Leon, the other most likely their servant Pauline and her child.

The housekeeper nanny and her child were probably Pauline, though the child is not documented in the original act of sale. It is likely that by this time, wary of impending war and hostile to slavery in the first place, Leon and Justine had arranged in New Orleans for the emancipation of aging Francoise. They needed a younger person to work in their household, to help with childcare, and someone willing to travel to New York with them where slavery had been outlawed since 1827.

*   *   *

When the Godchaux entourage arrived in New York, Justine was, yet again, pregnant, though not noticeably. Seven months later, on January 18, 1861, eight days before Louisiana voted to secede from the Union, she gave birth to a boy. The New York City birth register, which recorded the newborn's death, disclosed neither the place of birth nor the name of the unfortunate child. The baby seemed to have died immediately after birth. No other record of the death was recorded. Nor is the child listed as a deceased descendant in any Godchaux family records. By way of contrast, as I have said, the couple's first child, August Godchaux, who was born in New Orleans in 1854, three years after their marriage, and died in infancy, was inscribed in the couple's records.

Many years later, the comprehensive obituary of Leon that was published on May 19, 1899, in the *Daily Picayune*, the New Orleans paper of record, states, "She [Justine] survives with ten children, seven boys and three girls" and that "these are all of the children that were born to the couple, not a child having died." As Justine was not visibly pregnant when she left New Orleans, friends and family members back home probably had no idea that she had lost a child while in New York.

* * *

Leon took prompt formal action to establish his business presence in New York while he expanded into wholesale in New Orleans. The New York City residential and business directories for 1861 and 1862 list Leon as a clothier living at 171 Duane Street. The firm's letterhead used in New Orleans and New York directs customers to both locations, as do printed receipts for clothing.

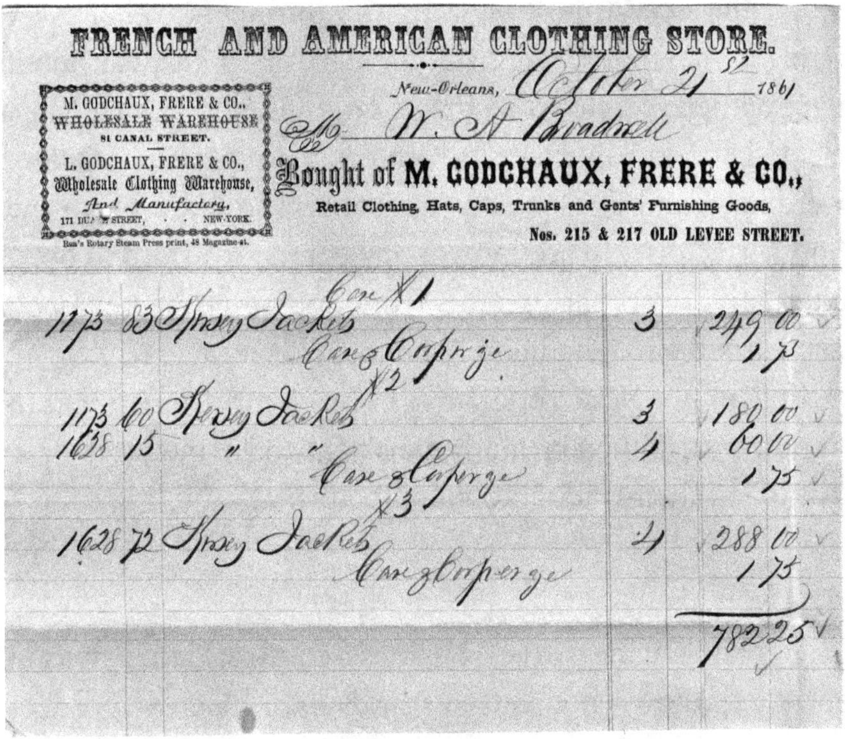
FRENCH AND AMERICAN CLOTHING STORE.

New-Orleans, October 21st 1861

Mr W. A. Broadnell

M. GODCHAUX, FRERE & CO.,
WHOLESALE WAREHOUSE
81 CANAL STREET.
L. GODCHAUX, FRERE & CO.,
Wholesale Clothing Warehouse,
And Manufactory,
171 DUANE STREET, NEW-YORK.
Rea's Rotary Steam Press print, 48 Magazine st.

Bought of M. GODCHAUX, FRERE & CO.,
Retail Clothing, Hats, Caps, Trunks and Gents' Furnishing Goods,
Nos. 215 & 217 OLD LEVEE STREET.

Case #1		
1173 83 Kersey Jackets	3	249 00
Case & Cartage		1 75
#2		
1173 60 Kersey Jackets	3	180 00
1628 15 " "	4	60 00
Case & Cartage		1 75
#3		
1628 72 Kersey Jackets	4	288 00
Case & Cartage		1 75
		782 25

Fig. 10. French and American Clothing Store receipt, October 21, 1861. It is wartime. Leon and family have moved to the safety of New York. This receipt shows how much Leon has expanded. His retail operation in New Orleans is at 215 and 217 Old Levee Street. He has in addition moved on to 81 Canal Street, where he has inaugurated a wholesale warehouse. The New Orleans business, run by Mayer, is operating as M. Godchaux, Frere & Co. In New York, Leon has set up his wholesale clothing warehouse and manufactory at 171 Duane Street, operating as L. Godchaux, Frere & Co. Photograph courtesy of Roger Joslyn.

By October of 1861, the firm had been well established and was operating from its new address in New Orleans at 81 Canal Street, as well as in the place and format of L. Godchaux, Frère & Co., Wholesale Clothing Warehouse, And Manufactory, 171 Duane Street, New York.

At the very time that war was imminent, other New Orleans merchants were not as alert or as suspect about the Southern economy as the immigrant Frenchman. Most elected to stay in place to protect their property. Many were hard-and-fast Southern patriots who believed in the Southern cause. In addition, many could not afford to open alternative workplaces out of the Southern sphere. Leon had earned enough and saved enough to be able to expand his reach into New York. Most of his competitors failed to move a part of their firms to the North and at the same time to expand their trade into manufacturing.

* * *

Leon's Duane Street business-cum-residence was a substantial town house five stories high, twenty-five feet wide by ninety feet deep at the corner of Staple Street—a distinct upgrade from the cramped Old Levee Street apartment. Leon devoted the street level to office and workspace to take commercial advantage of the mixed residential and industrial neighborhood,

He began manufacturing clothing. The principal floor came equipped with desks and cutting tables and sewing machines. A hoist fitted into the street accessed ample storage and utility vaults below grade, where raw goods and inventory were likely stored. The premises had abundant natural light, so important and suitable in Leon's trade. As a professional seamstress, Justine likely felt right at home with the work that took place on the ground floor.

Within a year, Leon built up a sizable operation, expanding beyond Duane Street. Reports that I have been unable to verify state that Leon had as many as two hundred people at work in a New York factory.

The upper floors of 171 Duane Street were equally suitable to the family's needs. The leased corner row house was unusually bright for New York City, an appeal to this couple accustomed to bright interiors. The building featured large windows facing Duane Street. Its location assured ample daylight from the Staple Street side, five windows per floor. The building's domestic attraction was further enhanced by its location on a relatively quiet street facing an irregularly shaped neighborhood pocket park (as it would be termed today where it is in active use). Duane Park, where Justine or the family servant took Paul Leon to play, was for Justine a welcomed step up from her apartment on Old Levee Street. Duane Street was busy, but not nearly as busy or noisy as facing the bustle and racket and steamboat cinders that coated everything near the port of New Orleans. That pocket park, situated just outside of her front door, would have been a joy to the mother of a four-year-old.

Moreover, New York was a thriving entertainment center with plays and opera on offer, appealing to both Leon and Justine. Being far away from omnipresent and irate discussions of race and war, laced with the pervasive tinged slant of Southern pride, must have been appealing to the young French immigrant Jewish couple. They surely felt comfortable residing in a cosmopolitan city where so many

Jewish people lived. In his trade, Leon was surrounded by more Jewish merchants than ever before.

* * *

Down in New Orleans, people were uneasy, and business slackened. Even before war broke out, wary businesspeople across the country and in Europe suspended trade into the port of New Orleans, though it remained open through 1861. It was not shut down by the advancing Union fleet until April 25, 1862. Nevertheless, European and many New York manufacturers did not want to risk exporting to the South. Who knew when goods might be seized, who knew when buyers would be unable to pay, and who wanted Confederate currency in exchange for valuable goods? Whatever Leon could produce in New York was in demand at the New Orleans store or could be sold to other merchants in town. The supply chain was tight. Unlike independent manufacturers who might decline to furnish clothing to the South, Leon had a guaranteed outlet for goods that he manufactured—his own store. And unlike independent manufacturers, he knew the precise taste and the exact proclivities of his customers. His risk, shared by other New York and European manufacturers, was that demand might falter, that sales might collapse in New Orleans, that Confederate currency might not be valuable as a means of exchange. Nevertheless, now that he was able to produce clothing in New York, he had the option of selling to the eastern market, to the export market in

Europe—overseas trade originating from the Eastern Seaboard was not threatened—or to his own enterprise in New Orleans.

* * *

Meanwhile, the situation back home had been fast changing. Leon and Justine left New Orleans on June 6, 1860. Exactly five months later, on November 6, Abraham Lincoln was elected the sixteenth president of the United States. Lincoln's election had caused Louisiana's ardent secessionist governor, Thomas Overton Moore, to squash an effort to declare New Orleans a neutral "free city." A rabid Southern Democrat, Moore went on to spearhead a legislative movement that on January 26, 1861, over a month before Lincoln's inauguration, voted Louisiana out of the Union to join the Confederacy. Four months later, on April 12–13, Pierre Gustave Toutant-Beauregard (aka P.G.T. Beauregard), the first general in the newly formed Confederate States Army, fired upon Fort Sumter, South Carolina. The Civil War was on.

Shipping and communications between New York and New Orleans became a grave problem. Trade in New Orleans slowed decisively, even though the port of New Orleans remained open for private business until mid-April of 1862. Lines of communication between New York and New Orleans were uncertain, at least for a while, abruptly curtailing merchant supply lines. The two branches of the Godchaux operation were forced to function independently for a time.

While still in New York during 1861, the Civil War now under way, Leon, with Mayer's oversight in New Orleans, purchased a building at 81 Canal Street, a few blocks away from his Old Levee Street location. Property values in the center of New Orleans had plunged to giveaway levels. Leon had in mind a place to house his robust wholesale operation—what is called today a fulfillment center. This was Leon's first purchase of property ever, courageously and opportunistically acquired amid a national calamity.

Leon chose the location carefully. Though a potentially disastrous war had just begun, the battles were far away. Godchaux's vision jumped past the present terrifying difficulties. He recognized that once life resumed to some form of normalcy, however unpredictable, that prime retail commerce in New Orleans would as well, and probably on Canal Street. He also would have appreciated the bargain real property prices on offer.

* * *

However sanguine they were at first, by late 1861, some six months after the onset of the Civil War, Leon and Justine probably began to question their plan to live out the war years away from New Orleans. As communications between the North and South broke down, surely, Leon worried, *Who knows how long I will be unable to oversee what is going on in the business down there!* Justine would have missed her parents and been concerned about them.

By late 1861, Leon had been out of direct contact with his principal business for a year and a half. For the couple, being away for so long—cut off from their life in New Orleans—began to take its toll. Paul Leon would soon be old enough to begin school. The port of New Orleans was still open to passenger vessels. In anguished discussions fringed with uncertainty, they would have debated what to do. Justine likely pleaded, "We should go back while we can. Our roots are in New Orleans now. My parents are there. I long to go back."

Leon's concurrence likely came with a quiet, "Yes, dear, I agree. Let me figure out what we can do." He was concerned about his store, his brother, and his staff.

In late 1861, through his sources down South, Leon probably obtained reliable intelligence that when the time came, New Orleans would surrender peacefully. He then felt assured that the city's population and his business would be spared from ruin, that their lives would not be in danger. The couple's deliberate weighing of their precise plan and risk of a journey back South during wartime continued probably for weeks. Could they obtain passage, could they be certain that no one would be harmed along the way, and once home, would the port remain open long enough?

Leon and Justine were eager to return to New Orleans for another reason—Justine was pregnant yet again. The expectant mother surely wanted to give birth in familiar surroundings where she felt safe, especially after the death of her child in New York.

The couple at last decided to return home. What Leon did not take back South were his liquid assets, primarily gold and silver on deposit in a New York vault, there to remain safely until the war was over. Through his prudence and prescience, his savings—accumulated over the eighteen years since his childhood began in America— were protected precisely when it counted most.

Nor did Leon leave absolutely everything connected to his work. He carried home one very precious item: a Singer sewing machine, possibly the first ever brought to New Orleans.

As it turned out, Leon and Justine's decision to return to New Orleans was made at almost the last feasible moment. The family arrived by steamship the first week of January 1862. Less than two weeks later, beginning January 15, 1862, Union gunboats stationed at the mouth of the Mississippi blockaded the river and shut civilian access to the port of New Orleans.

13

Peace During War

For a time, New Orleans was untouched by the war. When it came, the Battle of New Orleans was brief and, as these things go, relatively bloodless. On April 18, 1862, Union naval flag officer David G. Farragut's fleet, forty-three-ships strong, entered the mouth of the Mississippi and steamed upriver to Fort Jackson and Fort St. Philip. These two forts, built in 1822–1832, situated facing each other on the east and west banks forty miles upriver from the mouth of the Mississippi, had been erected to safeguard New Orleans. (Fort Jackson is now a National Historic Landmark.) Farragut's armada pounded both forts for six straight days until they hoisted the white flag of surrender.

New Orleans was soon captured without a fight, let alone a battle. Wisely unwilling to be needlessly destroyed to defend a principle, the city submitted to federal forces at first provocation, as Leon had been informed it would. On May 1, 1862, to escape destruction, the city sensibly acceded to occupation without military engagement. Apart from a momentary flare-up of arson, the city remained unscorched.

It was spared the destructive material consequences attendant on a siege, such as those that decimated parts of other Southern cities that resisted, such as Jackson and Vicksburg and Atlanta.

*   *   *

The onset of the Civil War brought about a rousing new initiative for Joachim Tassin. In the first months after Leon left town, Tassin was more crucial than ever, helping Mayer with both management and sales. But once war was declared, in an act of Southern patriotic fervor, in the spring of 1861, along with hundreds of other men of color in and around New Orleans, Tassin enlisted in the First Louisiana Native Guard. This Confederate militia regiment was composed primarily of free persons of color. Although Governor Thomas Overton Moore appointed three White officers as commanders of the entire regiment, individual company commanders were chosen from among the volunteer free Blacks. Consequently, this militia unit became (famously) the first ever of any in North America to be led by Afro-American officers.

However, Tassin's defend-the-Confederacy service was short-lived. As federal ships arrived opposite the city on April 25, 1862, the Native Guards were ordered by General John L. Lewis of the Louisiana Militia to disband. He cautioned the men to hide their arms and uniforms before returning home. Tassin returned to work at the store.

Given what Tassin and many of these other young men of color had been through over their lifetimes as natives of Louisiana, it sparked my curiosity to think about why they would have enlisted—indeed, potentially risked their lives—to defend the very society that had so profoundly and for so long mistreated so many people of color. In Tassin's case, there was certainly no patriotic obligation: his boss was very dubious about the South's prospects and its dominant proslavery ideology. But might Tassin and other free Blacks have been convinced by local boosterish and populist braggadocio that the South would prevail, and that military service to defend their region would redound to their personal reputations and social acceptance and futures in the continuation of a slave society? Once his unit disbanded, both Joachim Tassin and Leon Godchaux were back to work in occupied New Orleans.

There was a long-standing Louisiana tradition going back to colonial times for slaves and free Blacks to participate in White-led military excursions in order to enhance their prospects. Slaves were conscripted in the French and Indian wars 1754–1763 with the promise of emancipation. Celeron de Bienville's 1735 six-hundred-man militia assembled to fight the Choctaw Indians included forty-five Black soldiers who fought not so much to protect the White population as to raise their perceived status nearer to the respected position of White soldiers. During the Spanish colonial period in the late 1770s and 1780s, freemen of color—generally organized in separate "colored militia"—were engaged in routine military service in conflicts against the British (Baton Rouge, Natchez) and against Native Americans (Mobile, Pensacola) in exchange for promises of generous compensation and enhanced status, promises that were not always honorably fulfilled. Free Blacks enlisted to confront the British in the War of 1812's decisive Battle of New Orleans and served with distinction.

*　　*　　*

Unlike many Southern cities both along the Mississippi and inland, the war years for New Orleans were difficult, but not devastating. Counterintuitively, Union occupation of New Orleans occurring as it did early in the war brought an unusual degree of normalcy to the city. Once New Orleans was peacefully occupied, river traffic and general commerce resumed at about 50 percent of antebellum levels.

The blockade of the port of New Orleans lasted only a year. It was lifted once troops arrived and the city peacefully occupied. Beginning in April of 1862, control of New Orleans was first under the command of General Benjamin F. Butler, followed by General Nathaniel P. Banks. By July of 1863, the port was again open for sanctioned trade. From that point on, business resumed in a more characteristic manner, but not nearly as vibrantly as it had before the war.

During the war, the occupation government did not forbid trade and commerce through and in New Orleans; nevertheless, every form of business suffered. Leon Godchaux's enterprises suffered a decline along with the others' but was active enough and profitable enough to sustain its locations and to support its employees.

Indeed, there were aspects of the situation that helped the Godchaux store do more than survive. During peaceful occupation, New Orleans provided a relatively safe haven compared with more belligerent communities. The city attracted newcomers: residents from the nearby countryside seeking safety, slaves who abandoned their indentured surroundings, and refugees from other Southern cities who sought the shelter and prospect of opportunity in safe New Orleans.

Forever a proponent of deliberate evolutionary change, even after becoming a stakeholder on Canal Street, during the Civil War, Leon kept the main branch of his retail business operating on Old Levee Street. Aside from his innate caution, he would have reasoned that wartime is not a propitious interval for drastic change.

*   *   *

During the first half of 1862, while national turbulence prevailed, the Leon Godchaux family got reestablished in New Orleans and Leon severed his New York operation. As early as February of 1862, Leon was advertising in New York newspapers the availability of the "corner store No. 171 Duane Street, 25 x 90, well lighted, with hoistway on a side street and large vaults. The lofts are fitted for the manufacture of clothing with water closets and every convenience—cutting tables, desks, stove, etc."

Two months after the beginning of the Union occupation of the city, on July 19, 1862, the couple's first daughter, Anna, was born without a trace of a problem. Leon resumed his daily routine of managing the store on Old Levee Street and began to expand his Canal Street wholesale clothing operation.

Leon was not only back, he was back in New Orleans with all his energy focused, again in full control of his business. With real estate prices in New Orleans collapsed, Leon, both optimistic and opportunistic, seized the moment. He acquired two more buildings on Canal Street, numbers 83 and 85, adjacent to his Canal Street store.

He also made it publicly clear that he was solely committed to New Orleans and that he was entirely in charge. Godchaux posted a notice that ran in the *Daily Picayune* on June 16 and 17, 1863, to the effect that the copartnership with Joseph Simon "heretofore existing in this city under the name and style of M. GODCHAUX FRERES & Co., and in New York under the name and style of L. GODCHAUX FRERES & Co. was dissolved by limitation on the 12th day of May . . . and that THE SAME BUSINESS will be conducted as heretofore, at the old stands, 81 Canal Street and 215 and 217 Old Levee under the name and style of LEON GODCHAUX." No more partners. No more *frères*.

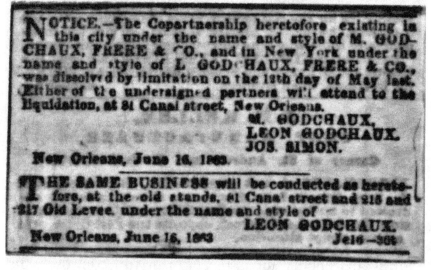

Fig. 11. Notice in the Daily Picayune *posted by Leon Godchaux on June 16, 1863. Leon announces dissolution of his partnerships with his brother Mayer in New Orleans and with Joseph Simon in New York. Leon, back from residency in New York, is taking over the business. Courtesy of the Louisiana Historical Center, the Leon Godchaux Collection, Record Group 496.*

In early 1865, with business humming, Leon got in trouble by selling clothing to an occupying union soldier. Whether or not he understood that doing so would constitute a violation of military orders is uncertain, and it is even uncertain if he knew his customer was in the military. Nevertheless, he was cited by U.S. Union Provost Marshals for a violation of two Military Orders. The first charge was: "L. Godchaux, civilian of New Orleans, La….did sell, or cause to be sold to soldiers in the service of the United States, citizens clothing; the sale of such clothing to soldiers being a violation of military orders." His second cited infraction, connected to the first, was "By such sale (he) was aiding and assisting soldiers to desert the service of the United States." Rather than stand trial, Godchaux elected to pay the large fine of five hundred dollars. A few months after this incident, the Civil War was over.

Fig. 12. Clothing manufactory receipt of December 2, 1867. Leon has expanded further with branch stores at 213, 215, and 217 Old Levee opposite the French meat market. His principal stores are now at 81 and 83 Canal Street. Merchandise is bought from Leon Godchaux only, no longer reference to Mayer or Simon. Courtesy of the Louisiana Historical Center, the Leon Godchaux Collection, Record Group 496.

*   *   *

Having watched over the business while Leon was in New York, in 1866, Mayer retired from the firm but remained in New Orleans. Even before leaving the firm, Mayer had become an astute investor in French Quarter property. He acquired several income-producing buildings between 1857 and 1859 in the vicinity of Levee, Dumaine, Chartres, Madison, St. Ann, Royal, Conti, and Bourbon streets. In a much less prescient acquisition, in April of 1860, two months before Leon and his family arrived in

New York, Mayer also purchased a second slave. Célestine, described in notarial sale documents as "a dark griff woman about twenty-two years old," was acquired by Mayer in a transaction before and recorded by Adolphe Boudousquié, the notary public well known to Mayer and to Leon. (During slavery in the United States, the term *griff* was used to describe a Black slave of mixed heritage, whose skin was lighter than a pure African, but not so light as a mulatto, implying less than 50 percent White ancestry, but more than 0 percent White ancestry.)

Mayer had married on June 29, 1853, and enjoyed a long, successful marriage to Rosine or Rosina Kahn (1834–1894), a native of Paris. They had two children, Paul Mayer (1854–1922) and Mathilde (1855–1935). Mayer's first slave purchase had been three years after their marriage and two years after their first child was born, probably to acquire household and child-care help. "Nancy" was a nineteen-year-old sold by Jules Armant for $1,000, as recorded by Adolphe Boudousquié. Mayer died in New Orleans in March of 1873. To his heirs, he left the bounty of his rental property investments in prime locations in the French Quarter.

*   *   *

The war years were more difficult for the region's agricultural enterprises, the economic backbone of New Orleans, dependent as they were upon slavery and relying as they did on national and international shipping. The sugar industry collapsed. The cotton trade was forbidden, though some runners and speculators managed to sell into Mexican ports. After the Union Army occupied New Orleans, commodity prices fluctuated wildly. The price of bulk cotton and sugar fell drastically. Though the infrastructure of New Orleans remained virtually intact, and commerce continued in the city at a slower pace, business outside of town in the agricultural domains of sugar and cotton came to a screeching halt.

*　　*　　*

With agricultural markets in free fall during the war, Leon decided to take one of the few financial speculations of his life. At the rock-bottom price of ten cents per pound, with his brother Mayer as a partner, he bought over a hundred bales of cotton stored in warehouses in Woodville and Summit, Mississippi. The brothers' speculation in over 46,000 pounds of raw cotton was dangerous—the baled cotton could have been requisitioned or even destroyed during the war. Their bet was that cotton would be scarce and in demand once the war was over, a combination that would drive prices back up or beyond prewar levels. Cotton was a world they knew something about, being in the business of selling products that were made predominantly of it. They had faith that demand would be robust again.

They were right. At the end of the war, cotton rose to the more normal prewar price of forty-five cents per pound and soon higher. This large, outright risky speculation in which they could have lost their entire investment was out of character for the conservative, frugal likes of Leon and Mayer.

They also had a hedge, a plan B, which emboldened the brothers to take their wartime speculative plunge. Plan B depended upon Leon's and Mayer's properly classified residential status as French nationals living in New Orleans, in good standing with the administration in France, and protected as unaligned neutrals by the authority of the French consulate. By operation of law, their unaligned neutral status entitled Leon and Mayer to be compensated for personal property destroyed during the war. Any number of well-off New Orleans residents who maintained foreign citizenship used this potential backstop to embolden wartime speculation in both sugar and cotton.

* * *

Once Joachim was forcibly decommissioned and thereby denied his wish to defend the segregated city of New Orleans from the Union onslaught, Tassin returned to his post, tending to his customers, even to numerous new ones from out of town. He had his old job back. But things were changing.

As the Civil War approached its third year, Tassin found himself amid new legal circumstances. On January 1, 1863, President Lincoln issued the Emancipation Proclamation. This executive order that applied only to the rebellious states declared "all persons held as slaves are, and henceforward shall be free." Tassin, once an undisclosed slave now holding undisclosed emancipation papers, must have felt optimistic even if he could not celebrate overtly.

With prospects for his future bright, and now his social status potentially less tenuous, Joachim concluded a two-year courtship with a free woman of color, Marie-Madeleine-Elene Coustaut (or Cousteaut or Coustant). On August 12, 1863, eight months after Lincoln's proclamation, they married in St. Augustine Church, in the Treme neighborhood, the most hallowed church in the Catholic Creole community.

St. Augustine's had been the locus of a social, political, and religious milestone of its own. A few months before its dedication in 1842, free people of color had rushed to rent the most desirable pews, which incited Whites in the area. The free people of color succeeded not only in acquiring more of the premier pews than the White congregants but gained control as well of most of the less desirable side-aisle pews. To what purpose soon became apparent: those pews were turned over to slaves who were permitted to worship on Sundays. When services got under way, nearly half of the congregations were either free Blacks or slaves. St. Augustine's became the most integrated congregation in the nation as well as the oldest African American church in the Archdiocese of New Orleans. (In 2008, when the Louisiana African American Heritage Trail was created, St. Augustine's became one of the first sites designated.)

Comfortable in his protected work environment offered by Godchaux, more settled in his personal life, and feeling optimistic and energized by Lincoln's Emancipation Proclamation, Tassin spoke out publicly for the first time as an independent, aggrieved Black man. Along with more than eight hundred freemen of color, in 1864, he signed the "Petition of the Union Radical Association Presented to Abraham Lincoln." The large format petition, delivered to Congress and to the president, demanded the right to vote as "natives of Louisiana and citizens of the United States." The Emancipation Proclamation had been silent about voting rights.

Even though Tassin signed this impassioned plea to Washington, his name did not appear on the official New Orleans Register of Free People of Color Entitled to Remain in the State 1840–1864. His name did not appear on the register because he could not have legally qualified as an f.p.c. (a commonly used abbreviation for free person of color) before a parish judge, who would have required him under oath to state and prove his age, place of birth, and place of previous residence.

*   *   *

Though the city was not materially assaulted, the toll of the Civil War on New Orleans was significant. The port of New Orleans never regained its preeminence, nor did the city ever again grow at its dynamic pre–Civil War rate. Just before the Civil War, in 1860, New Orleans had slipped from the third largest city in America to the sixth. In the aftermath of the Civil War, by 1870, its rank had fallen to the ninth largest city. By that time, because of robust emancipated slave emigration off the fields and into the city, the population of New Orleans grew to 26 percent Black, as compared just prior to the war with 15 percent, a figure that included all slaves and free people of color combined, a near doubling.

Postwar population growth rates never recovered, either. With the basic economic drivers of cotton and sugar upon which New Orleans had previously depended all but decimated, between the outset of the Civil War up until 1910, all of fifty years, the total population of the city of New Orleans merely doubled. During the same interval, formerly relatively latent regional cities of what is today called the New South such as Atlanta, Houston, Nashville, and Memphis experienced population growth of some 500 to 1,500 percent. These newly growing cities had not as deeply depended upon slave-supported cotton and sugar for their underlying vitality as had New Orleans. Nor had they been as thoroughly anchored to a river port that was confronted after the Civil War by competition throughout its service basin by rail and canal expansion.

The sad decay of postwar New Orleans was broadly recognized. Charles Dickens had visited New Orleans on his American tour before the war. He had been a guest at the magnificent St. Charles Hotel. Dickens kept up with conditions in post–Civil War New Orleans, a town that interested him. After the war, he was moved to write, "What with the disastrous results of the American Civil War . . . the once proud and prosperous Crescent City is at a deplorable discount. . . . The [once] opulent and prodigal cotton and sugar-planters, whose business and expenditure constituted two-thirds of the prosperity of the place, are ruined, or struggling ineffectually to accommodate themselves to an entirely new and half-chaotic state of things: the brokers and merchants are impoverished; the people generally discouraged, and all but despairing. . . . They have paid, and are paying, a terrible price for the folly of secession."

14

Prudence To Prosperity

When the war was over, Leon Godchaux had preserved his wealth. He did not own a thimbleful of the two-feet-deep premier agricultural soil that stretched far up the Mississippi's alluvial plain on which cotton and sugar fortunes had been based. He had made no meaningful investment in slaves and held de minimis Confederate currency. His retail and wholesale clothing businesses had remained viable through intensely adroit management. Leon did not yet own a house. His Canal Street properties had been purchased at knockdown wartime prices. At war's end, the price of land, cotton, and sugar had plummeted. The value of a slave had been obliterated. The value of Confederate currency was zero.

In addition to his other precautions, in one masterstroke, Leon had protected his liquid wealth by maneuvering outside of the Southern banking network and indeed out of the nation's banking system. The value of gold before and after the Civil War remained $18.93 per troy ounce.

Once a peasant immigrant, he was now a rich man in the profoundly devalued world around him.

Any of the vast crowd of formerly wealthy planters, shipowners, bankers, traders, cotton factors, sugar-export merchants, real estate brokers, and property owners—the whole comfortable commercial New Orleans and Southern regional community—could have done the same thing. Currency exchange was open across the Mason-Dixon Line until the outbreak of war. Capital could have been transferred in the click of a telegraph key. But most holders of major assets in the South had been enveloped by a reason-clouded chauvinism or saddled with holdings of magnificently productive but nevertheless illiquid vast stretches of land and captive slaves.

Leon sailed clear of ruin because of his own wit, his good judgment, his conservative nature, and his aversion to slavery. In the few instances when he acquired a slave for household duties, he surely paid fair wages and treated his household help fairly and humanely. By preserving capital and not being decimated by a vast and terrible national strife, Godchaux created the solid financial underpinning that enabled him to enlarge his clothing business after the war and at the same time to enter an entirely new career, all while providing more than adequately for his family.

As the *New Orleans Item* wrote in a posthumous tribute to Leon, "When the Civil War broke out the Godchaux stores had the largest and most profitable trade in New Orleans. Leon Godchaux began to trade in almost everything salable, except slaves. . . . He had his troubles of course, because of the conflict, but his shrewd foresight saved him from heavy losses that crippled many of his competitors. Even when the armies of the Confederacy were invading the manufacturing districts of Pennsylvania and the agents of the rebel government were selling bonds in Europe with only the ability and daring of their generals to give them the security that bond buyers demand, Leon Godchaux was saving gold and silver and getting rid of paper money as fast as he could. Those were four hard years, but they were harder on his rivals. When the war was over, Leon Godchaux's fortune was intact and many a formerly richer man was pondering how to get rid of bales of paper money. Godchaux, having owned no slaves, lost no money in them."

*   *   *

As the denouement of the war became obvious but was not yet over, and real estate prices in New Orleans—as in the surrounding countryside—collapsed, Leon and Justine began house hunting. The city had remained intact. The couple had resources to buy anywhere in town. "It is time," Justine probably pleaded. "Let's move out of the cramped apartment above the store facing the wharves and away from the congested racket and heavy industry of the port. We're a family of five now, and who's to say that's the end?"

Leon knew it was time; he would have complied, agreeably, with "Yes, dear, but not too far, not too expensive. I need to be near the store." They began looking.

Late in 1865, months after Robert E. Lee surrendered at Appomattox courthouse, Leon purchased for $11,000—to Justine's delight—a twenty-eight-foot-wide fifty-three-foot-deep   two-story   plaster-over-brick architecturally conservative house facing Esplanade Avenue, designed in 1854 by Alexander Hypolite Sampson. The house sat on a generous lot 126 feet deep along Treme. In a town where most of the houses were made of wood, brick was the preferred building material for those who could afford it. A structure made of brick complied with the current building code, and, even more important, provided a measure of safety against fire and fierce winds that accompanied hurricanes.

Leon and Justine selected a house and a site that spoke volumes about who they were and where they placed themselves in the New Orleans social mélange. The corner of Esplanade Avenue at North Liberty (now Treme Street) sat at the seam between the old French Quarter and the long-established Creole Faubourg Marigny. Together, these locales occupied home-base for much of the French and Creole population. Leon and Justine chose to live right in the middle of it.

The house Leon and Justine purchased from its first owner, Claude Tiblier, was devoid of external ornament—a reflection of the couple's modest temperament.

Fig. 13. 1240 Esplanade Avenue, corner of Treme, formerly North Liberty Street. In 1865, months after the end of the Civil War, with real estate prices severely depressed, Leon purchased this house, where he and Justine lived until his death in 1899. At the time, the couple already had three of their ten children. Esplanade was one of the most beautiful streets in the city, located at the epicenter of French and Creole New Orleans. Photograph by Betsy Swanson, ca. 1973–1977. Courtesy of the Historic New Orleans Collection, acc. no. 1978.2.77 i-iv Negative 24.

Facing the street, there was a simple recessed off-center entrance door and two traditional short double-hung windows flanked by louvered cypress shutters. These shutters, then and still today traditional throughout the city, served to assure internal privacy, to dampen street noise, to protect from hot direct sun, and still allow filtered light and prevailing breeze to flutter in from across the broad boulevard. A traditional second-floor balcony with cast-iron railing was just wide enough to serve as a modest terrace for the front bedrooms, accessed by stepping through any one of the three well-spaced floor-to-ceiling double-hung windows. The house's vernacular façade is so like many of its neighbors as to be nearly indistinguishable from them. Yet its refined interior detailing and fine proportions made their house pulse with dignity.

Behind the main house, there were originally three detached small buildings, one the kitchen, one a laundry, and one to shelter servant slaves. The rest of the lot was an open courtyard. Leon and Justine updated the back part of the property to accommodate their fast-growing family. Along one side of the courtyard opposite North Liberty Street, they constructed and attached to the main house an elongated two-story service wing to accommodate staff and additional bedrooms that would eventually house what would become a family of ten children.

Fig. 14. 1240 Esplanade Avenue, garden service wing. The spacious wing parallel to Liberty Street accommodated the couple's ten children and servants. Between the wing and Liberty Street, Justine finally had her large garden courtyard. Photograph by Betsy Swanson, ca. 1973–1977. Courtesy of the Historic New Orleans Collection, acc. no. 1978.2.81.i-iii Negative 27.

To enhance the plain façade of the brick wing facing the courtyard, which is larger than the original house, they included a cast-iron gallery decorated with grape motifs to match the ornament on the rear gallery of the main house.

The remaining portion of the original courtyard was transformed into an appealing shaded garden patio. It was secluded from North Liberty Street by a handsome stucco brick wall, topped by fine, decorative, heavy cast-iron work that foreshadowed the intricate designs that Louis Sullivan created a few years later. At last Justine had her safe garden and a shady, beautiful, quiet place for the children to play right in their own large courtyard, surrounded by her own house and away from the noisy coal-exhaust-filled air of the waterfront

*　　*　　*

Though the house they selected did not call attention to itself, Esplanade was not an ordinary street—far from it. The *Daily Picayune* in 1852 proclaimed it "the handsomest street in the city . . . with a broad space in the center planted with a double row of forest trees, now forming a long arch of bright, thick verdure to shade the grass below." Developed out of an abandoned water-portage route that linked Bayou St. John to Lake Pontchartrain and to the Mississippi, by post–Civil War, Esplanade was the New Orleans residential thoroughfare second to none. Peppered with cafés, parks, and pleasure gardens, the avenue teemed with strolling pedestrians and was served by a mule-drawn rail omnibus. The residential boulevard they chose to live on was conceived as both a transportation corridor and "garden suburb" for the city's francophone elite.

Esplanade Avenue continued to gain in reputation for the Creole set, as St. Charles Avenue emerged for the Anglos.

The Picayune's Guide to New Orleans admiringly noted in its 1904 edition, "Esplanade Avenue . . . is one of the most beautiful streets in New Orleans and is to the Creoles what St. Charles Avenue is to the Americans, the aristocratic residence street. . . . The avenue, through its entire length from river to the Bayou St. John, is lined on either side of the car tracks (streetcar or omnibus) with a continuous row of shade trees, which makes the street very pretty and attractive. The homes in the avenue are the center of Creole culture and refinement."

For all his street's postwar elegance and beauty, Leon would have been aware that his new house was situated only a few blocks from the edge of the river where he first landed as a penniless youth, and that, at the time, its terminus with the river had been the site of a seething slave market.

A formal photograph of the time presents Justine conservatively dressed in a tightly buttoned high-necked blouse, hair wrapped up demurely at the back of her head (the way her granddaughter—my grandmother—styled hers). She appears a resolved and cultivated woman. Her lambent gaze conveys a serene humility and kindheartedness. In her prim dress and steady gaze, Justine is every bit the caring mother, the wife of a successful merchant, and the mistress of a busy household that she is pleased to inhabit.

Fig. 15. Justine Lamm Godchaux, ca. 1880. Justine, only five feet tall, was now the wife of a successful merchant and the mistress of a child-filled throbbing household. Alas, the black-and-white photograph deprives us of Justine's alluring blue eyes. Photograph courtesy of Gail Wolf Lewis.

*   *   *

Leon and Justine lived at 1240 Esplanade for thirty-four years, to the end of Leon's life. She would have said to Leon whenever they heard of friends moving uptown, "But, Léon (she probably always pronounced his name with her French intonation), let's never do that. We are so happy here, so settled here, why ever think of leaving?" Leon's answer would have been, "Chère, I'd never considered moving. After New York, once is enough. This neighborhood is where I want to be."

They were both content to remain among the downtown Creole community. It was where they felt comfortable; it was where they belonged. They did not yearn to join the socially ambitious French and the economically and professionally successful Anglo families migrating to the larger suburban-style properties with large lawns being developed in uptown New Orleans. As a way to particularize the man, Leon's obituary in the *Daily Picayune* recalled the couple's resolve to remain in place when so many others did not: "Mr. Godchaux was never willing to move away from his house on Esplanade Street . . . where he and his family had been so happy, and, while his friends were erecting magnificent residences on St. Charles Avenue, he insisted on remaining in the old home, which is modest-looking outside but elegant within."

15

Reserve Finds Leon

Unintended, inexperienced, untrained, and unrelated to his known trade, soon after the war was over, Leon Godchaux became involved in agriculture. He gingerly stepped upon the path that led him to become the Sugar King. He began alone, without the collaboration of Joachim Tassin or any of his other carefully honed staff at the store.

* * *

The Civil War had laid waste to the sugar industry in south Louisiana, a keystone enterprise that had supported the region for over a century. In the autumn of 1861, the cane crop was successfully harvested and run through the processing houses. The sugar crop reports for the region show that through 1861, sugar production levels were near all-time highs in the river parishes upriver from New Orleans.

Then war made marketing and distribution of refined sugar practically impossible. A subsequent Union blockade at the mouth of the Mississippi succeeded in bringing global export to a standstill: foreign buyers had no recourse but to cancel orders; Northern and Western domestic customers withdrew in droves for a toxic combination of political, moral, and ideological reasons, as well as practical ones.

Sugar production, like all agricultural enterprises, depended upon credit. In normal times, loans were made at the beginning of the planting season, to be repaid when the crop was sold. Before (and after) the Civil War, in the rural South, it was commonplace for banks and factors, also for retail merchants, to lend money to landowners to finance crops, taking back mortgages and notes as collateral backed by the land on which the crops were growing or, as an alternative, backed by rights to a percentage of the crop yield.

Post-1861 in Louisiana, the depleted banks were extremely cautious or not lending at all; factors and other professional lenders charged exorbitant rates to desperate and destitute landowners in dire straits; even most rural merchants were reluctant to risk an agricultural loan. Plantation owners were compelled to sell sugar production at depressed prices, which in turn constricted their ability to make good on outstanding loans and to plant the next year's crop. As sources of credit dried up once war was declared, the consequences were immediate and dire. In addition, much of the collateral pledged to the banks by planters was denominated in now virtually worthless Confederate currency or land that was plummeting in value monthly as the war wore on. Many once well-off plantation families became needy, some became penniless.

During the war, as the agricultural economy faltered, friends, small farmers, and some formerly wealthy landowners sought out Leon as a possible source of financial aid. Some were supplicants to whom, twenty years earlier, he had hawked fabrics and notions from the tattered pack on his hard-pressed back. Leon found himself in the unexpected position of being asked to provide loans and mortgages. Unlike many city and especially rural storekeepers, Leon Godchaux had never been in the money-lending business. But these were not ordinary times.

As the war continued, it is likely that Leon responded affirmatively, only to people he knew well. Those loans were made on terms favorable to the borrower. In some cases, Godchaux did not require collateral; in others, he might have offered a job.

*   *   *

The first loan that Leon made to a needy plantation owner who was not a close friend had consequences that changed his life. He had known Marguerite Sophie Andry Boudousquié—generally called Sophie—for years, but only casually. Sophie (1808–1894), together with her husband Antoine Anatole Boudousquié (1803–1855 and cousin of Charles Boudousquié) and her brother Michel Thomassin Andry (1811–1869), had bought a small working sugar plantation at auction in early 1833. Later, sometime in the 1850s, for reasons still disputed, they named the place Reserve plantation. The property had been one of Leon's regular stops along his St. John the Baptist Parish peddling route. The Boudousquié-Andry property was located not far from the Tassin place.

When Sophie married Antoine in October of 1827 at the town of Edgard in St. John the Baptist Parish, the young couple had promising prospects. On each side, their parents and grandparents had been successful entrepreneurs and extensive owners of both New Orleans real estate and plantation properties. The place the young couple bought in partnership with Michel comprised 480 acres of fine agricultural soil, with 2,800 feet of frontage along the Mississippi River.

The site had changed hands multiple times. They purchased Reserve plantation from a Creole woman, the widow of Francois Rillieux, member of a distinguished New Orleans–based *gens de couleur libres* family.

Once in possession, the wealthy new owners promptly expanded their landholding, buying up contiguous parcels: an additional 19½ arpents along the riverfront, 40 arpent to the north, and several hundred acres of swamp timberland. (In Boudousquié's and still in Leon's day in south Louisiana, rural property descriptions were often signified by the French units arpents rather than acres. One square arpent was equivalent to 0.85 acres.) By the end of their buying spree, the owners had accumulated over 1,900 contiguous acres. In doing so, the youthful farmers incurred debt, enough that they depended upon good crop years and stable or higher sugar prices to satisfy their creditors.

As they expanded their land footprint, they also developed their plantation, which grew to become an assemblage of multiple utilitarian buildings related to the production of sugar. Reserve included a modest family residence; a separate kitchen structure (as was common for fire protection); a storehouse; a hospital; a carriage house; a stone mill; a sugarhouse; a *purgerie* (the building where vats of sugar were drained of molasses, the final step in sugar processing); and a row of cabins to house their forty-nine slaves.

* * *

Antoine Boudousquié's ambition extended beyond farming sugarcane. His political skill had propelled him into the Louisiana House of Representatives representing St. John the Baptist Parish. In 1845, he was appointed Speaker, the presiding officer of the lower house of the state legislature. It was during his term as a member of the Louisiana House of Representatives that Antoine managed to significantly expand the acreage at Reserve, a reflection perhaps of his being able to leverage his esteemed and insider political position—the old story in Louisiana politics.

On Antoine Boudousquié's frequent downriver trips to the city for legislative sessions—New Orleans was then the state capital—he would have been often accompanied by Sophie, who probably liked to shop for her sons and husband at Godchaux's. She and Antoine would have likely become casual friends with the congenial young merchant on Old Levee Street who almost certainly developed the habit of waiting on them personally. After all, Mr. Boudousquié was one of the most influential political men in the state.

On entering the store, Sophie would probably ask, "Could Mr. Leon spare a few minutes?" He would have always made time available for Sophie. He had another reason to be so attentive.

Sophie and Leon had known each other under very different circumstances in her early years at Reserve. Back in the days when urchin peddler Lion Godchot came by to sell his wares, Sophie would have been rarely available to him. When she was at home and interested in seeing his meager merchandise, he would have been asked to wait in the basement entrance room. There she would pick out ribbon or fabric or needles. "Thank you, Miss. Sophie," he would have said on his way out, with a polite tip of his straggly cap. "Do I have permission to see if anyone in the quarters needs anything?"

It is said in local and family lore passed down through the years that on one of his peddling sales calls, as Lion opened his pack of goods to present notions to Sophie, he fainted from dehydration or exhaustion. Sophie did not call the sheriff to have the impaired young peddler removed. She did not command a house slave to take Lion to the sugarhouse, give him water, and send him on his way. Instead, she directed a house slave, "Install this boy in one of the bedrooms upstairs. I'll tend to him."

The *Daily Picayune* published one of the many accounts of this episode, based on a family retelling. Elma Godchaux wrote about a conversation she had with her *grandpère*: "When he stood upon his legs again, he told [Sophie] he would never forget her. She had saved his life. If he could ever do her a good turn, he promised he would do whatever good he could for her. He promised solemnly. The words seemed absurd, coming from the mouth of a child, the immigrant who could not read or write, the peddler owning no more than the few clothes that kept him clean and the bagful of odds and ends he liked to think of as a store. Perhaps the lady did not even know the blue-eyed peddler's name. But he promised earnestly and with some poise. He remembered her and the promise, too, for something over 20 years."

(Note: There has been long been a story circulating that Lion as a peddler was mistreated at Reserve and forced to leave when very ill. Treated badly, he vowed to return some day and buy the plantation. The incident, if true, should be ascribed to an experience at Souvenir Plantation, which he did indeed purchase and consolidate into the Elm Hall group.)

* * *

Within a few years after the Boudousquiés and Andry bought Reserve, a series of unfortunate changes occurred. Michel sold out his interest to his sister and brother-in-law in order to liberate time to tend to his other plantation properties, one located next door. The couple had to come up with the money to pay out Michel. Michel might have continued to live at Reserve for some time and to help Sophie. Reserve is listed as Michel's residence as late as the 1860 census.

Sole ownership of the plantation passed to Sophie when, in 1855, after a dynamic career as both a planter and member of the Louisiana House of Representatives for nearly ten years, Antoine died. Suddenly, Sophie was a widow plantation owner, a forty-seven-year-old mother of four, who knew next to nothing about managing an agricultural enterprise complete with more than four dozen slaves. Michel, living next door, pitched in to help his inexperienced sister. But Michel had his hands full, being the owner of a substantial plantation in St. Charles Parish and another in St. John the Baptist Parish. As the economic situation in the South's agricultural complex deteriorated, Michel, who was himself in debt, was forced to sell his properties at diminishing prices, incurring losses. He could no longer be helpful to Sophie.

As war loomed, Sophie resorted to last-ditch efforts. In 1860, she mortgaged the plantation to a wealthy local landowner named Louis Generes in exchange for a loan of $35,000. Two years later, during the Civil War, having fallen on even harder times, she was forced to refinance with Generes, adding another $9,270 to her debt. She pledged as collateral the "sugar plantation and 104 slaves." At the time, Sophie had two minor sons, Charles and Henry, and two married daughters, Anais and Appoline, who renounced their rights of inheritance. It is possible that Sophie appealed to Leon at this time, having heard from other property owners that he might be a source of financing and hoping that their mutual familiarity would be helpful in her quest. If she did make the trip to New Orleans to appeal to him, most likely Leon would have turned her down because Reserve was run on slave labor. "My dear Mrs. Boudousquié," he might have said, "I want to help you and I will whenever I can. But I am not able at this time, under the circumstances. I think you understand." At this time, it seems she still did not recognize him, or remember their encounter of years ago.

When the war ended, Sophie's finances were in shambles. She was unable to keep up payments on the Generes loan. She had no more slave labor. Nothing had been planted. Sugar prices were severely depressed. Her fields were idle, her buildings deteriorating.

Sophie approached Leon. "It's been a terrible time for me," she would have said to him. "I have no help now. I'm not even able to plant a crop."

This time, Leon was willing, her slave labor emancipated. "Yes, I know. And yes, now I can," he likely answered. They discussed a plan, and Sophie was grateful. "I'll do whatever I can," Leon probably said. "I will arrange for you to have enough time and enough money to make Reserve again prosper."

"Léon," she likely whispered, "*merci, merci, mon cher Léon.*"

* * *

Leon spared Sophie Boudousquié the ignominy of foreclosure and bankruptcy. On May 28, 1866, along with a fifty-fifty partner, Francois Valcour Labarre, a member of a distinguished Creole family, Leon bought the Generes mortgage plus twelve other smaller mortgages and notes that Sophie Boudousquié had outstanding. This refinancing amounted to consolidation of notes owed to Godchaux and Labarre and others. Within the year, Leon went on to purchase Labarre's interest in the Boudousquié debt.

After his purchase of Sophie's extensive debt, Godchaux might have invited Mrs. Boudousquié to call at the store. When she arrived at his office, Sophie would have been nervous. She could not know what to expect. After a short sociable chat, Leon might have calmly handed Sophie a large envelope and said gently, "Here are the canceled existing notes and mortgages on Reserve."

Then he outlined a plan to permit Sophie to resume. Out of long-held gratitude toward Sophie, Leon had drafted new documents that granted Sophie a generous reduction of interest on the mortgages and notes from 8 to 6 percent retroactive to the beginning; and they provided an extended payment schedule with the final installment not due until January of 1872 rather than the original January of 1867. These terms were fashioned to decrease Sophie's immediate expenses and to enhance her prospect for success in the postwar economy. Sophie would have left the office with renewed hope.

As it turned out, three years later, caught amid the still-failing postwar sugar economy, Sophie was unable to meet even the below-market mortgage interest rate and stretched payment schedule. She came back to see Leon, resigned. "I cannot go on any longer," she must have said. "I cannot. I must default and give up. Someone will take Reserve. My secret hope is that it will be you."

*   *   *

By an act of sale dated June 1, 1869, Leon purchased Reserve on terms generous to Sophie Boudousquié: in addition to tearing up the twelve notes plus five separate judgments and sundry other debt instruments that she had incurred and that he had bought up, Godchaux settled various lawsuits against Sophie. In addition, Leon paid to Sophie in cash a charitable $20,000 premium—the equivalent today of some $600,000. Deeply gratifying to the widow, Leon added a further beneficent provision: Sophie Boudousquié could live for the rest of her life rent and cost free in her house at Reserve. By bailing out Sophie Boudousquié, Leon entered the south Louisiana sugar business in the late 1860s without intending to do so. The industry in a shambles, he was taking an enormous risk. He was also displaying fine judgment and a taste for risk by entering a new business he knew nothing about and purchasing a large landholding at the bottom of the market.

Sophie remained for only a short time at Reserve. In 1870, she moved into her son Charles's impressive house on Kerlerec Street in New Orleans. That household, only a couple of blocks from Godchaux's house on Esplanade, consisted of her two sons, their wives, and children; four servants; and a children's nurse. After living with her sons and grandchildren for fourteen years, Sophie died of cancer at Charles's house in 1894 at the age of eighty-six.

*   *   *

Sophie was but one of the thousands of large landowners who failed in the outwash of the Civil War. Before the war was over, with but a token labor force left on the plantations, and with capital rapidly dwindling and markets tumbling, planters faced certain ruin. By the end of the Civil War, Louisiana's thousand sugar plantations had dwindled to fewer than two hundred.

Through the 1870s and into the 1880s, the scale of the economic debacle that reigned upon proprietors enmeshed in the agricultural economy of the region is all but unimaginable. In the Mississippi Delta, home of some of the most productive soil in the world, nearly half of the land in the area—almost 2.4 million acres, most of it formerly developed cropland—was forfeited to the state of Mississippi by owners unable to pay accumulated taxes. It would take thirty arduous years for the postwar regional economy to achieve its prewar level of sugar production.

16

Postwar Promise

At the end of the war, Leon expanded his clothing business again, this time into manufacturing at scale, realizing his long-held ambition. That division would augment his retail and wholesale business. The impact of the Civil War on most established businesses operating in the city had been severe, though not as drastic as on commerce in cities that had been devastated or harshly occupied. Ten percent of Leon's Jewish clothing merchant competitors had abandoned their trade; some 30 percent of all businesses in New Orleans had ended in bankruptcy. Leon leased, outfitted, hired staff, and opened a clothing-manufacturing plant on Elysian Fields Avenue, not far from his stores.

Leon had recognized, as early as his first trip to New York in the mid-1850s, that opening his own manufacturing operation made eminent sense. He was already dealing in the supply and sale of dry goods in the form of cloth. He was already engaged in the enterprise of tailoring by hand those goods into finished clothing—the department entrusted to Joachim Tassin. He was already dealing with the public in sales and on a wholesale basis with merchants near and far in the countryside around New Orleans. These were the basic ingredients that the New York firms had brought together to turn clothing manufacturing into a prominent and profitable modern trade. Furthermore, American clothing manufacturing—from its beginning and then onward for several decades—focused exclusively on the male consumer, again Leon's niche.

Clothing manufacturing also incorporated a strain of social egalitarianism that appealed to Leon Godchaux. Savings that ordinary people could realize by buying ready-made had been celebrated as early as the 1853 Exhibition of the Works of Industry of All Nations at New York's Crystal Palace. One exhibitor, Alfred Monroe & Co., boldly proclaimed that the time had passed "when every man or boy in want of a new coat . . . must resort to his tailor and pay exorbitant prices in order to be satisfactorily suited."

The one precious Singer sewing machine that Leon brought home from New York was soon in the company of many more. Those instruments, easily available and serviced by the Singer Sewing Machine Company, allowed Leon to begin manufacturing clothing. The combined business was renamed the Leon Godchaux Clothing Company, commonly known ever since as Godchaux's. Godchaux's became the first general clothing-manufacturing enterprise based in New Orleans. The company promptly adopted its inviting new slogan: "Goods manufactured at short notice."

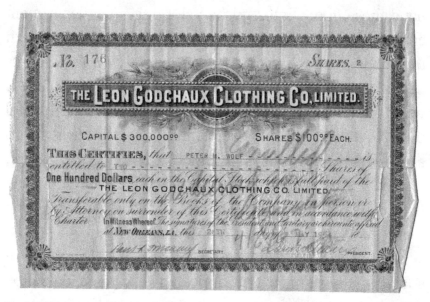

Fig. 16. The Leon Godchaux Clothing Co. Limited, stock certificate no. 176. Canceled when the company went bankrupt. Courtesy of the author.

* * *

For Joachim Tassin, the immediate consequence of peace was much more than normalization of business at the store and participation in the sale of manufactured goods. Lincoln's Emancipation Proclamation led directly to the Thirteenth Amendment to the Constitution, ratified in 1865, which abolished slavery. Had Tassin ever been recognized as a slave, he would now be legally free. Even unrecognized, possible future adverse consequences to him if discovered as a formerly covert slave were greatly diminished.

The Fourteenth Amendment, passed by Congress the next year and ratified in 1868, did have positive immediate consequences for Joachim as a Black man. It prohibited states from enacting discriminatory legislation. Specifically, its first clause resoundingly and famously proclaimed that "all persons born or naturalized in the United States, and subject to the jurisdictions thereof, are citizens of the United States and of the State wherein they reside. No State shall make or enforce any law which shall abridge the privileges or immunities of citizens of the United States; nor shall any State deprive any person of life, liberty, or property, without due process of law; nor deny to any person within its jurisdiction the equal protection of the laws."

Leon Godchaux was not yet a citizen. Joachim Tassin, born a slave in St. John the Baptist Parish, now was.

When Leon and Joachim discussed the implications of these two constitutional amendments, they would have decided to do nothing and to say nothing to clarify Joachim Tassin's past—doing so would serve no purpose that either wanted. Joachim would have said to Godchaux something like, "My situation is as good as it can be with the war over. You know what I'm saying? These federal laws are fine, but who knows what will happen here? Let's not stir up anything that will bring attention to me."

Godchaux would have been glad to keep their understanding just as it was and likely replied quickly, "Of course, of course, I agree with you, Joachim."

* * *

With New Orleans recovering, and the South no longer a belligerent factor in the nation, Lion Godchot, who had been known for years in New Orleans by his creolized name of Leon Godchaux, turned to civil matters.

The surname recorded on Leon's birth certificate had been Godchot. Paul Leon, Anna (born in 1862) and Blanche (born in 1864) had also received Godchot as their recorded last names.

Leon reckoned it was time to amend the legal standing of the family surname. Leon and Justine made an appointment at the New Orleans office of the Board of Health, Recorder of Births, Marriages and Deaths. The couple arrived as scheduled on January 3, 1866. At the office, they filed a petition to have the family name legally changed from Godchot to Godchaux. While going about it, Godchaux decided to have his first name legally changed from Lion to Léon (maintaining the *accent aigu*). The florid memorializing petition that Leon and Justine signed that day stated, "Be it Remembered That on this day . . . for the purpose of avoiding confusion hereafter and establishing that Lion Godchot and Léon Godchaux is the same and identical person he has passed (this) act." Once again, Léon's witnessed and notarized signature is unmistakably written in precisely the same hand as the drafter of the lengthy affidavit.

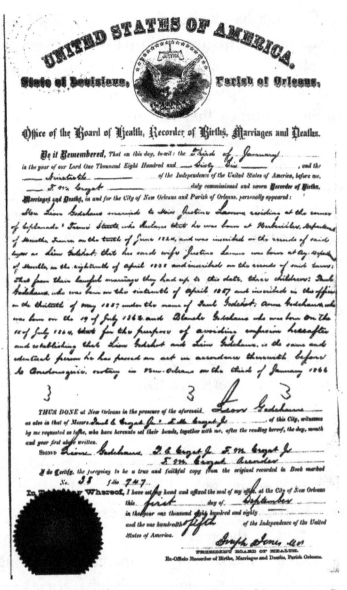

Fig. 17. The United States of America, State of Louisiana, Parish of Orleans, legal record of name change, January 3, 1866. The Lion Godchot family name was legally changed to Godchaux for Leon and children, Paul, Anna, Blanche—and presumably Justine, "for the purpose of avoiding confusion hereafter and establishing that Lion Godchot and Leon Godchaux is the same and identical person." Courtesy National Archives and Records Administration and David Spielman.

Lion Godchot had waited for his own good reason all those years to have his name formally inscribed into the local creolized vernacular. By 1866, he was convinced America was no longer going to be at war with itself. The civil rights inequities that had torn the nation asunder seemed to have subsided into a promising future of peace and national accord. The future of New Orleans was no longer threatened with oblivion. His years in New York with Justine had convinced them that they wanted to live their lifetime not just in America, but also in New Orleans. He and his family had survived the war and all the uncertainty of that turbulent era. Now safe and prosperous, Leon experienced a feeling of stability, which led him to no longer—even remotely—consider returning permanently to Europe, to being Lion Godchot. He was now all in— though not yet an American citizen.

*   *   *

The final keystone in the trifecta of postwar Republican-sponsored progressive federal legislation, the Civil Rights Act, was ratified in 1875. Its purpose was to root out discrimination in the private sector, as the purpose of the Fourteenth Amendment had intended to extinguish discrimination within the public legislative arena.

As the Godchaux retail, wholesale, and manufacturing enterprises had not participated in racially discriminatory practices since long before the Civil War, this measure did not cause any changes at the store or factory. Godchaux and Tassin would have felt reassured that business could continue undisturbed. They believed that peace would be kept, and federal laws obeyed, at least so long as they were reinforced by federal troops stationed within New Orleans, in Louisiana, and throughout the South.

17

Tassin's Declaration Of Independence

The dramatic social and legal environment in which Leon Godchaux and Joachim Tassin lived was changing at a dizzying pace, a pace that caused Joachim to reconsider his future.

By the spring of 1876, Joachim Tassin was restless and sensed new opportunity. New proclaimed freedoms for Black people were resounding throughout the land. He had worked diligently for Leon Godchaux for twenty-seven years, was happily married, and had no children. It had been eleven years since the end of the Civil War. The breathtakingly progressive and consequential Thirteenth and Fourteenth Amendments were established as the law of the land. The Civil Rights Act had just become law. In this perceived dawn of the new era of Reconstruction, the way ahead looked so much better than ever before in the South for talented, skilled—and in Tassin's case—well-established Black people.

Tassin decided, *Now is the opportune time to think over the direction of the rest of my life. My work is secure. My marriage of thirteen years is solid.* He likely said to Marie, "What do you think? The store is doing so well. We are free to travel. I could take some time off. Let's go to Europe. We never have gone anywhere. While we are there, let's think about what to do with our future."

Marie didn't want to go abroad. Sensing how restless her husband had become, Marie presumably said, "Go do it, Joachim, or you'll regret it for the rest of your life. I know you."

Europe beckoned. Joachim Tassin had never traveled beyond his birthplace in St. John the Baptist Parish and his involuntary residence in New Orleans. He had not left the city for thirty years. He had met people at the store and in New Orleans from all over the world. Tassin did what many others have before and after him at a midlife seam: at age forty-four, he decided to take time off, to see Europe. Fluent in French, German, and Spanish, Tassin had no qualms about embarking alone on this adventure.

Tassin had to speak to Leon. Tassin would have asked to meet with his boss in his private office. Leon would have been curious about the overture, but gladly complied. Tassin must have been nervous and unsure about how Godchaux would react: he had never asked for an extensive leave.

When they met, Joachim probably opened with a halting preamble about how he had loyally performed during a long period of exemplary service, without having taken an extended vacation. Finally, coming to the point, he would have said quietly, "I'd like to take a leave of absence to go to Europe, perhaps for as long as six months."

In the silence that would have immediately followed, Leon would probably have been relieved that Tassin was not resigning or complaining about the store's operation. After a few quiet moments of thought, Godchaux surely knew he had no choice but to approve. He would have said, "Well, Joachim, you are entitled to a rest. I wish you safe travels, tell me how soon you want to leave and *bon voyage*."

Tassin would not have confided that he was thinking about how and where he wanted to conduct the next stage of his career now that the opportunities for Black men had so thoroughly expanded in the South.

With Godchaux's blessing, Tassin spent six months abroad. While he traveled around Europe, Joachim would have experienced another way of life and most particularly a distinctly alternate and freer way of living for people of color. For the first time in his life, the former slave became independent, not attached to a set of daily obligations at work and freed from the racial stratifications of New Orleans. When in Paris, Joachim would have been welcomed into both grand restaurants and quaint bistros, shown to any available table. He would have seen mixed Black and White couples strolling hand in hand along the Seine and through the Luxembourg Gardens. In his visits to the best clothing shops in Rome, where he decided to find out what was fashionable for men, he would have been welcomed as a colleague by owners curious to discuss what was going on in the American clothing business.

* * *

Upon his return to New Orleans during Reconstruction, Tassin reentered a Southern culture in which his legal rights appeared to be more protected than he had ever known, though his social standing as a Black man remained distinctly second class.

On Tassin's first day back at the store, Godchaux almost certainly welcomed him back with a hearty handshake and a distinct smile. His stalwart mainstay was home, his status as an employee resumed. Leon Godchaux would have been relieved and reassured. But in Tassin's mind, a new point of view had taken hold. He aspired to become an owner, a founder of a business of his own, his own man. He now thought of himself as a successful merchant with a loyal, long-established following. Once a slave, now free, he imagined the late 1870s as a golden moment for him in America.

Tassin would have talked with Marie about what he'd experienced in Europe. He might have said, "Marie, it is my time, it is our time, for the first time ever. My age, my skills, my experience, my reputation are all aligned. I want to be my own boss, my own man. What I've seen in Europe makes me hopeful about our future here in New Orleans. Or maybe we should think of moving to France. Blacks are openly welcomed there."

Joachim Tassin, at that moment in time, embraced the American dream, an aspiration he could never have imagined while growing up a slave in the Louisiana plantation economy and repressive social order of St. John the Baptist Parish.

*   *   *

Soon after returning home, with his aspirations and convictions supported by his optimistic state of mind and his wife's approval, Tassin decided to launch an independent career. He acted swiftly. With a mixture of trepidation and guilt, overcome by ambition and hopefulness, he went in to see Leon once again at his office upstairs in the store.

Upon hearing Joachim Tassin lay out his ambitious plan to open his own store, Leon would have likely been stunned into silence. His immediate reaction was surely confusion, as if punched in the belly, suddenly, by a friend out of nowhere for no reason. He probably got up from his chair and paced back and forth for a few minutes while Joachim sat quietly. Leon likely gazed out the window down on to busy Canal Street. He would have stood there, bewilderment welling up, then subsiding. Godchaux would have quickly calculated the impact of this loss to the company and to himself personally before making any reply. All these years sharing business decisions, all these years of sharing a sense of mentoring someone like a ward, all these years of a direct connection to his own hardscrabble life out in the countryside—all that would now be but a memory and gone away. Mixed with those resentful fleeting feelings, the nurturing part of Godchaux probably thought, *Can he make it as an independent merchant with no experience in finance or overall management? Will I have to pick up the pieces? But I have no choice. He is free to go.*

Rather than share his own swirling thoughts, Godchaux probably remained silent. He decided within moments to say nothing to discourage this man whom he had known since he was a child, a man he relied upon, with whom he shared long-established personal secrets, with whom he had shared precious long-won trade secrets that were the foundation of his business—the network of suppliers, customer names and addresses, marketing, and advertising strategies and all the rest, this man he had rescued from an indentured life.

Once he recovered his equilibrium, and even before responding to Tassin, Godchaux would have quickly tried to assess the impact on the business of Tassin's breakaway. *Will any of my staff follow Tassin if he tries to recruit them?* He would have been confident that his employees would not leave, given the vibrancy of the business and the more-than-fair wages he paid. None would take the risk, no matter what Tassin offered. He probably quickly reassured himself that his loyal and diverse clientele would not leave even though Tassin's skill as a tailor was legion. All in all, he likely felt confident that the firm would continue to prosper with or without Joachim. They had done very well without him for the past six months.

During Godchaux's prolonged silence, Joachim probably experienced fleeting moments of fear that he'd made a mistake. *Is this risk worth it? Should I leave a secure position and a firm in which I have gained respect among Blacks and Whites? And a lifetime of economic security? How can I leave this man who has done so much for me?*

In his office that morning, while his friend and employee sat quietly and patiently, Leon must have decided there was no point in delaying his response by saying, "Let me think about this, Joachim." I imagine Leon Godchaux walked across his office to Joachim's chair. Joachim stood up instinctively. Godchaux, though flustered and upset, extended his hand. Joachim's reached for it involuntarily. "Good luck, my boy," he probably said.

Joachim's emotion-filled response was likely no more than "Thank you, thank you for everything, Mr. Leon." He would have been relieved that the meeting went so well and terrified that it had. Now he was on his own.

*　　*　　*

In October 1876, Joachim Tassin opened J. Tassin Co. at 241 Old Levee Street (currently 933 Decatur), just a few doors from Leon's original New Orleans store. Leon had recently relocated his merchandising operation from 213, 215, and 217 Old Levee Street to 81 and 83 Canal Street.

Fig. 18. J. Tassin Clothing entrance at 241 Old Levee Street (now Decatur Street). Tassin conducted his retail clothing business independent of Godchaux for nine years, 1876–1885, during the end of Reconstruction and into the onset of Jim Crow. Tassin's shop is seen behind a milk wagon. Photograph by Stephen Duplantier, ca. 1880–1885. Courtesy of the Historic New Orleans Collection, acc. No. 1992.65.3.

Tassin's new business, from the start, mirrored the precise lines of merchandise his former boss was known for. Tassin was not embarrassed about competing with his former employer. Quite the contrary. He trumpeted his past employment with Godchaux as a hallowed credential.

Within the text of J. Tassin Co.'s inaugural advertisement in the *Picayune*, the new founder and proprietor of his own retail clothing company declared, "Mr. J. Tassin, who for the last thirty years has been connected with the well-known clothing house of LEON GODCHAUX, at Nos. 213, 215 and 217 Old Levee street, will open a house for his own account at No. 241 Old Levee street . . . where he hopes, by his strict attention to the wants of his friends and customers to meet the same patronage which they have so liberally extended him in the past. J. TASSIN."

Fig. 19. J. Tassin and Leon Godchaux advertisements in the Daily Picayune, *October 6, 1876. Similar merchandise at a location near Godchaux's original store indicates Tassin's intention, right from the beginning of his independent career, to be directly competitive with Godchaux. Courtesy of the* Daily Picayune.

Tassin, specifically imitating Godchaux, specialized only in men, boys, and youth apparel. In his first commercial advertising, his bold print specialties were declared as "HATS, CAPS AND FURNISHING GOODS." Whereas in the same newspaper on the same day, as was his usual emphasis, Godchaux headlined in his ad "CLOTHING, HATS AND FURNISHING GOODS."

Godchaux's advertising copy, released on the same day as Tassin's first print ad, is an obvious response to Tassin's challenge. Leon Godchaux informs his established clientele and reaches out to new customers in the same issue, on the same page, and just above Tassin's copy, "Having transferred the business of my stores (on Old Levee street) to 81 and 83 Canal street, I would respectfully announce to the public in general that I now have on hand and am duly receiving the largest stock of Men's, Boys' and Youths' CLOTHING, FURNISHING GOODS, HATS ever had in the city, in order to meet the increased trade at my present location, and I invite my friends and customers to call and examine prices. In the future, as in the past, I shall allow nothing to remain undone to meet the demands of the trade, and will always be prepared to fill any orders, large or small, for every style of Clothing, Hats and Furnishing Goods, from the common plantation to the finest dress suit, all at the very lowest prices. Country orders filled with dispatch."

Tassin not only directly mimicked and imitated Godchaux in terms of merchandise and style of advertising. He purposefully misrepresented facts by stating in a public announcement that he had worked for Godchaux for the "last thirty years" rather than the actual twenty-seven years—Tassin pushed his employment back in time prior to his purchase as a slave.

The similar merchandise offerings between Godchaux's and Tassin's stores reveals Tassin continuing to do what he'd learned to do best, but it also exposes his lack of a plan to create a distinctive trade of his own. As a consequence, Tassin put himself in a position to compete head-on with his former employer. Tassin's ads in the local newspapers made it clear to everyone in town that the former colleagues were now arm-wrestling competitors.

With more robust capital than Tassin and a much larger clientele, Leon was also eager to attract buyers large and small from outside the city. In his outreach by this time, Godchaux was announcing "country orders filled with dispatch" and routinely solicited orders from "country buyers."

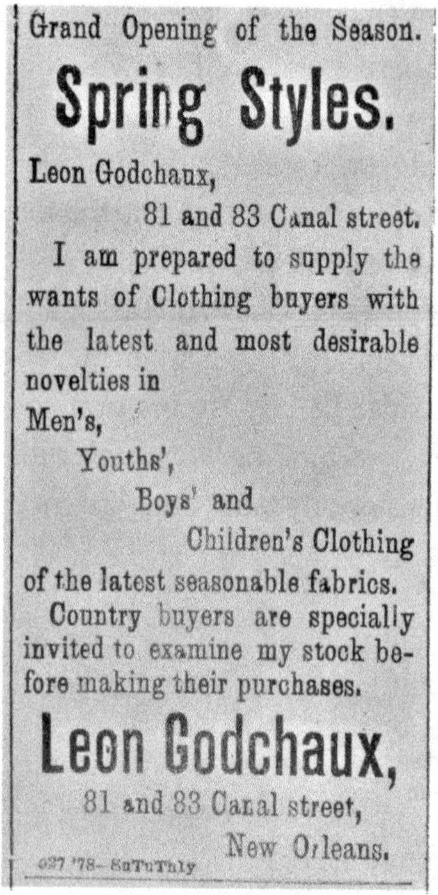
Grand Opening of the Season.

Spring Styles.

Leon Godchaux,
81 and 83 Canal street.

I am prepared to supply the wants of Clothing buyers with the latest and most desirable novelties in
Men's,
Youths',
Boys' and
Children's Clothing
of the latest seasonable fabrics.

Country buyers are specially invited to examine my stock before making their purchases.

Leon Godchaux,
81 and 83 Canal street,
New Orleans.

o27 '78–SaTuThly

Fig. 20. Godchaux's spring opening from 81 and 83 Canal Street, 1870s. Leon would continue to engage in well-targeted, effectively seductive advertising through press, personal letters to favored clients, and charming company brochures throughout his lifetime as a retailer and wholesaler of clothing. Here he offers the "latest and most desirable novelties in Men's, Youths', Boys' and Children's Clothing. . . . Country buyers are specially invited." Courtesy of the Louisiana Historical Center, the Leon Godchaux Collection, Record Group 496.

New Orleans, October 1879

Mr.

Having just made up an entire stock of New and Fashionable Goods suitable to my customers both in the city and country, I take pleasure in informing my many patrons that they will find in visiting my establishment a most carefully selected stock, consisting of Foreign and Domestic Goods, exactly suited to our climate for Fall or Winter Wear, all of which are not only of the most Fashionable Styles, but also at prices, the lowest for which Clothing and Gent's Furnishing Goods can be honestly and justly sold. I am employing but the best cutters and workmen, and my stock is consequently such as cannot fail to give every satisfaction to those of the most fastidious taste. With forty years experience, during which period I have made my business a constant study, and my material being bought for cash, I am enabled to offer my customers inducements, that will in every instance, insure their satisfaction and continued patronage.

As ever, Yours Respectfully,

Leon Godchaux,

81 and 83 Canal Street, New Orleans.

P. S.—Full instructions sent upon application, as to self measurement, and C. O. D. orders promptly filled.

Youth's suits a specialty, both as regards durability and economical figures.

Fig. 21. Leon Godchaux's 1879 letter to clients. Godchaux, throughout his career always price conscious, announced, "Fall and Winter Wear . . . of the most Fashionable Styles, but also at prices, the lowest for which Clothing and Gent's Furnishing Goods can be honestly and justly sold." Courtesy of Tulane University Special Collections.

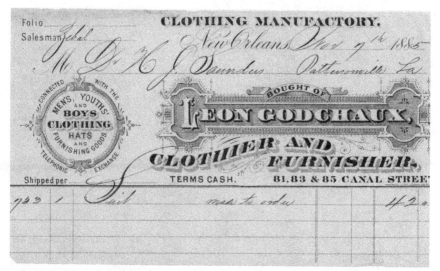

Fig. 22. Leon Godchaux manufactory receipt November 7, 1885. This receipt, for a suit made to order, shows that the business is now exclusively housed at 81, 83, and 85 Canal Street. Godchaux prominently advertised that the always up-to-date firm is "connected with the telephonic exchange." Courtesy of the Louisiana State Museum Historical Center, Leon Godchaux Collection, Record Group 496.

Despite his overwhelming advantages in reputation for service and quality, capital available, brand recognition, and depth of staff, Leon almost surely felt betrayed once it became obvious that Tassin was selling merchandise so very much like the inventory sold at Godchaux's and was doing so in the precise location where Godchaux customers had long been accustomed to shop. At home, he would have complained to Justine, "I taught him everything. No gratitude. Why didn't he decide to sell something else instead of mimicking what we do?"

Justine, ever coolheaded, likely answered, "Léon, he'll never be able to compete with you. Once he finds that out, he'll change to other lines."

Godchaux, with enough capital available to do so, intensified his public relations campaign, enlarged the size of his ads, and posted them more frequently. Large Godchaux's ads became ubiquitous in the local papers, English and French alike. He was able to vastly outspend Tassin on public outreach. The scale of his stores, the much-larger array of inventory, and its position on Canal Street assured that Godchaux's lost no meaningful trade, at least within the White community, to J. Tassin Co. At the same time, Tassin would have likely attracted a portion of Godchaux's previous customer base among mixed-race and Black people.

Despite Tassin's absence and his direct competition, Leon Godchaux's clothing enterprise continued to succeed masterfully. Manufacture of clothing gained prominence while custom tailoring became a minor part of the trade. Able to rely more than ever on his coterie of trusted, experienced employees, Leon's principal focus shifted to the challenge of salvaging, upgrading, and turning a profit on his country property at Reserve.

18

Raising Cane

Now let us return to Leon, the neophyte in the sugar industry, suddenly owner of Reserve plantation in 1869.

When Godchaux took charge of the run-down, failing Reserve plantation, none of the backbreaking operation had been mechanized, and much of it was dangerous work. The standard method of turning the harvested cane stalk into consumable and marketable sugar mirrored practices derived from the eighteenth-century European sugar colonies in the Caribbean. Cane was cut by hand with a cane knife (a cane knife is like a machete but has a sharp hook). It was then loaded by hand into carts and pulled by mules to the sugarhouse.

Fig. 23. Cutting sugarcane in the fields. Harvest season, which took place from October to first frost, was the busiest time of the year in the sugar-production industry. Before mechanization, cane was cut by hand with a special machete-like knife fashioned with a hook on its end. Courtesy of Tulane University Special Collections.

Fig. 24. Loading cane into mule carts. Leon adopted modern industrial machinery in the form of a miniature rail system to supplant this time-consuming, labor-intensive means of moving cane from field to factory. Courtesy of Tulane University Special Collections.

Once in the sheds, the fibrous full-length stalks were chopped by workers wielding machetes sturdy enough to break down the tough outer shell and sharp enough to do the requisite shredding. The outer shell residue, known as bagasse, was a waste product. Once the outer sheath was cut away and discarded, the pulp was transported in buckets to the crushing area. There, to extract the sweet juice captive in the stalk pulp, its fibers were squeezed and crushed by a three-roller mill, one roller on top, two underneath. (The sugar industry is credited with originating the roller-mill concept as far back as 1450, possibly in Sicily, for crushing sugarcane. The idea was subsequently reimagined, though much later, for many other industries such as flour grinding and eventually in industrial plants to crush, grind, shape, or deform all sorts of materials.)

At Reserve, as was common practice industrywide at every plantation, the extracted juice was heated, clarified by lime, and made to evaporate in a line of large open cast-iron cauldrons. The method, known by the nineteenth century as the sugar train or the Spanish train or sometimes the Jamaican train, depended upon the sequence of large iron kettles, each independently heated by wood-burning fires lined up like cars hitched on a train. Sugarcane juice, pressed from cane, was first poured into a large kettle where it was heated until most of the water evaporated. Each set of kettles, arranged in a line of decreasing size, was suspended above continually stoked fires maintained by hand at decreasing temperature. Impurities that rose to the surface were skimmed off prior to each transfer. Workers—in most locales, slaves—poured the boiling hot residue liquid by handheld ladle into sequentially smaller and smaller pots until the liquid thickened. At each transfer, some of the liquid at the bottom of the kettle was scorched, some of it lost in transfer, workers were frequently burned. Toward the end of the refining process, on each plantation, a sugar maker, stationed in the sugarhouse, would determine when, in the last stage of heating, with all impurities skimmed off, the purified liquid was ready. This moment was called a strike. This was the moment when the concentrated syrup would be scooped into shallow wooden tanks and left to cool and crystallize through evaporation. It required ten gallons of the initially starchy cane juice to yield one gallon of syrup and even less sugar.

This by-hand purification of sugar was a cumbersome labor- and fuel-intensive process. It was fraught with danger, especially when a worker had to ladle the molten hot liquid brewing in scorching iron containers from one cauldron to the next. Heat exposure to those working the cauldrons was intense. As an essential component of this purification process, forests near and far were chopped down to fuel the intense fires.

*   *   *

On plantations in Leon's day, and for centuries before, when a large number of workers had to be fed, the same type of cast-iron kettles used in the purification process were also used for cooking. In south Louisiana, those half-sphere robust iron kettles had long been called *teches*, a local name derived from the dense assemblage of plantations along

Bayou Teche, where Leon eventually owned property. During the Civil War, some of those kettles were melted down for arms manufacture. Years later, once the traditional sugar-refining process was mechanized, the industrial use of sugar kettles was abandoned. (Today, authentic *teches* are collectibles, fetching high prices as objets d'art. Buyer beware, many are replicas, some made of fiberglass. Sugar kettles have taken on new life as garden or patio planters or as landscape ornaments. In cane country, some serve as a base for restaurant and motel signs or as watering troughs for horses and cattle.)

*   *   *

Once Leon became the postwar owner of Reserve, filled as it was with decrepit buildings, out-of-date equipment, faltering land, and inadequate labor, the challenge of the place clearly sparked something deep within him. He was out there all alone, on his own—no Carl Wedderin, no Charles Steidinger, no Rosemond Champagne, no Joachim Tassin. He must have felt the exhilaration of a major commercial challenge absent since the day he opened shop on Old Levee Street.

Godchaux might have confided to Justine, "C*hère*, the store is doing well, the staff doesn't need me full time anymore. I'm not sure how to revive Reserve, but I will figure it out. I have a feeling the time is right. This depression in sugar can't last forever."

The feeble sugarcane-growing operation Leon Godchaux took title to was producing only half the amount of sugar it produced in 1844. The place begged for restoration: because of the war and its aftermath, and Sophie's inexperience, much of the land had been fallow for years, good planting cane had been all but unavailable, machines had to be repaired, buildings patched, land rejuvenated, and willing labor recruited.

Given that Leon's relevant experience was nominal, his business associates in New Orleans and his new neighbors up and down the east bank of the Mississippi, once they learned that Leon now owned Reserve, must have shaken their heads in disbelief, whispered doom predictions among themselves, convinced that Leon Godchaux, the boys' and men's clothing merchant from Old Levee and Canal streets, had made a colossal blunder. Some of those long-established plantation owners, recently returned from war who hoped to resume their traditional way of life, might have quietly mused: What does this citified, illiterate, stubby Jew immigrant outsider think he's doing out here in our country?

*　　*　　*

Godchaux's first order of business was to hire knowledgeable people, Black and White, and pay them well. He expunged jungle undergrowth; he purchased any viable planting cane available; he restored unplanted land, acre by plodding acre; he repaired damaged, long-idle machinery. Leon turned out to be a dab hand at fixing operating equipment himself. The little Jewish merchant from Lorraine, by way of New Orleans, was determined that

Reserve again become a successful business proposition and at the same time a place where workers were treated fairly.

The main house at Reserve fell far short of the sort of residence that the word *plantation* evokes. There were no lofty columns with ornate capitals supporting broad porches; no delicately railed galleries hanging beyond generously scaled, high-ceilinged bedrooms and reception rooms; and no sculpted plaster moldings and elaborate baseboards. Rather, the wood-frame main house was a traditional two-story raised Creole cottage, elevated off the ground and upper floor accessed by a centered external staircase. As would be expected on a property built over centuries and inhabited by hardworking agricultural families, the main house, like the other buildings on the place, was modest. The ground level, literally on the ground, functioned as a storehouse. Sturdy brick piers supported the structure; these served as an essential defense against the force of the river in flood tide. The second floor was raised nine feet above grade by those brick piers, high enough to protect the upper levels from high water. That second story, the family quarters, was four rooms wide and two rooms deep, wrapped on the outside by modest front and side galleries. At the back of the house, there was a small loggia, which Leon used as an office.

*   *   *

When he took over Reserve, though he might not have realized it, Leon became the owner of a property linked to heretofore new and scarcely exploited scientific technology that would pave the way for the modernization of the entire sugar industry.

Before the Boudousquié family owned Reserve, the land that they named Reserve plantation had been the property of Francois and Elisée Rillieux. Francois was a cousin of Vincent Rillieux, a white plantation owner (whose family was also related to the painter Edgar Degas). Vincent's *placée* had been Constance Vivant, a free woman of color. Their mixed-race son, whom Vincent adopted, was Norbert Rillieux, a French-speaking Black Creole born in New Orleans in 1806 and destined to become a famous engineer inventor.

Norbert, the eldest of seven siblings, was sent to Paris to be educated. He became a creative and inventive chemical engineer. In France, as an engineering instructor at the École Centrale in Paris, he conducted a series of imaginative and successful experiments related to the use of steam power to enhance evaporation and simultaneously greatly reduce fuel consumption and increase safety in the process of sugar refining. Norbert returned to New Orleans in 1832 as a twenty-six-year-old educated engineer. When back home, he developed a sugar-refining process that he patented in 1843 under the weighty name of "the multiple effect evaporator."

Prior to Rillieux's invention, going back as long as sugar was refined on plantations, the process had been slow, expensive, inefficient, exploitive of slave labor, and dangerous. Rillieux's multiple effect evaporation system used a vacuum chamber that lowered the boiling point of liquids. Inside the chamber, vertically stacked layers of pans contained the sugar juice. Steam from the lower pan heated the cane juice in the pans above. The released steam in the vacuum chamber allowed for much more controlled heat, and lower heat, to achieve the same result rather than depending upon a line of open fires.

Because of Rillieux's invention, huge industrial and human gains were made. The Rillieux system eliminated spillage, made the process much safer for workers, conserved fuel, and assured a more reliable way to convert sugarcane liquid to sugar. By reducing the amount of heat required, sugar mills could burn bagasse, the formerly discarded cane stalk residue, as fuel, thus reducing cost and no longer destroying nearby forests. (Note: A sugar mill is engaged in the crushing and extracting of cane syrup and works primarily through the harvest season, generally October 15 through January 15. A refinery or sugar factory does the work of a mill and in addition processes sugar to its final consumable stage, packages and distributes. Godchaux combined the processes in large industrial plants.)

Living in prewar New Orleans, amid a booming sugar economy, Rillieux was convinced that his invention had commercial promise. In the years immediately after obtaining his patent, Rillieux did manage to oversee the installation of his system in several small sugar factories in Louisiana, but his system was never implemented in those prewar years at a significant scale.

Rillieux also tried mightily to obtain a follow-on patent after his first. Docents at Le Musée de f.p.c. (Free People of Color Museum) in New Orleans believe that his application was rejected because authorities falsely believed that the applicant was a slave and thus not a citizen. Enraged, Rillieux returned to France in the late 1850s, a few years before the start of the Civil War and over a decade before Leon Godchaux entered the sugar-refining business. A victim of structural racism in the South, Rillieux found his mixed-race, partial African heritage too great a handicap to continue his life and work in America. Rillieux finally received his additional U.S. patent in 1864 upon application from Paris, five years before Godchaux came into possession of Reserve. Norbert Rillieux died in Paris in 1894. He was buried among notables such as Frédéric Chopin, Marcel Proust, and Eugène Delacroix in hallowed 110-acre Père Lachaise Cemetery in Paris.

* * *

Rillieux's invention soon revolutionized the entire sugar-refining industry. But not immediately.

By the 1850s, Rillieux's evaporator was being assessed sporadically and experimentally at a number of small sugar refineries. However, his evaporator required the outlay of significant capital. It met with slow and only sporadic acceptance in the tradition-bound, poorly capitalized, slave-enabled plantation culture of the pre–Civil War. During the war years, there was no available capital, the sugar industry collapsed, and Norbert Rillieux was back in France.

* * *

Godchaux became the first adopter of the Rillieux evaporator at a commercially significant scale. To modernize his plant at Reserve, Leon devoted large amounts of his own capital. He assembled a team of handsomely compensated chemists, scientists, and engineers. He replaced the open wood-fire kettle system, which he recognized as outmoded, wasteful, inefficient, and dangerous, with newly installed scientifically up-to-date Rillieux-type evaporation equipment. He also upgraded the crushing machines, replacing the time-worn traditional three-roller mill device with a new sequence of two nine-roller mills ganged together. He added mechanized crushers and automated knives and shredders. Nothing like a modern, scientifically sophisticated processing station for sugar had ever been built. In the late 1880s, Leon created the first one at Reserve. The factory at Reserve was so efficient that it was capable of handling more cane than grown on the place. Leon was suddenly able to process cane grown at other nearby plantations.

Fig. 25. Modernized sugarcane crushers in the Godchaux sugar mill at Reserve. Leon upgraded the crushing component of sugar manufacturing by increasing the size and technology to the sorts of crushers in his mills shown here. Courtesy of Tulane University Special Collections.

While upgrading the sugar-refining process, Godchaux began to acquire additional sugar-growing properties, initially in the vicinity of Reserve. He reasoned that added-on cane could be refined at the efficient, modernized Reserve mill.

Out of this idea, Godchaux created the centralized factory whereby one efficient mill would service the cane production of several plantations rather than, as forever previously, each individual plantation undertaking its own manufacturing. The centralized factory at Reserve had the capacity to process cane sold to Godchaux or consigned to him by neighbors. Consequently, Leon Godchaux inaugurated the first large-scale sugar-processing mechanized mill that could serve multiple properties rather than wasteful and out-of-date duplication of the refining process at each individual plantation. A successful large-scale central sugar factory had never been built and made operational. John Dymond, a planter on the lower Mississippi coast below New Orleans, had made an early effort; but he failed to proceed at scale due to absence of capital.

Eventually, the Godchaux operation transitioned to end-state packaging of the refined sugar in bags and boxes and sacks of various sizes, ready for retail and wholesale distribution.

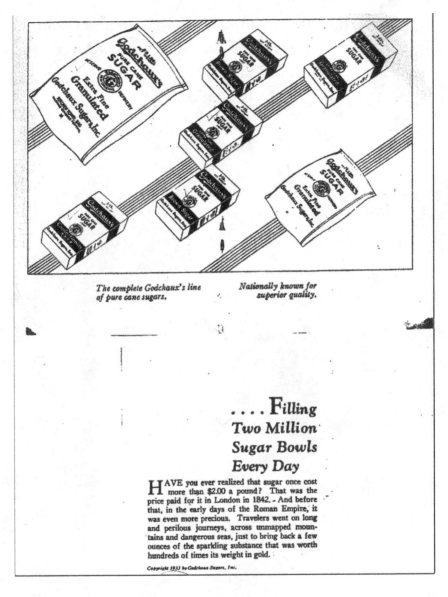

Fig. 26. The complete Godchaux's line of pure cane sugars. The large diversity of retail packaging and types of pure cane sugar available from Godchaux Sugars Inc. included "Extra Fine Granulated" delivered in a bag that could be used as a kitchen towel," as well as brown sugar, confectioner's sugar, and a variety of others. Courtesy of Godchaux Sugars Inc.

Proving the efficacy of his concept, Godchaux closed the sugar mills on his other plantations near Reserve and expanded cane-growing capacity.

But that was only the beginning.

19

The Sugar King

Once he was fully committed to Reserve and the sugar-refining business, at the age of forty-seven, five years after he legally creolized the Godchot name, and now a plantation owner, Leon Godchaux took formal steps to become an American citizen. (I assume Justine did as well, but I could not find her documents.) Perhaps he felt more American, now engrossed in work so far removed from his European heritage and from his ethnic heritage.

On the ninth of February 1871, Leon Godchaux appeared in New Orleans before United States district judge Edward H. Durrell. He was required to dutifully swear that he had "resided within the limits and under the jurisdiction of the United States of America for five years immediately preceding . . . and within the State of Louisiana for more than one year; and that he has behaved as a man of good moral character, attached to the principles of the Constitution of the United States of America, and well disposed to the good sides and happiness of the same." Suspicion lurked about his having long lived within the state of Louisiana in democratic America as a citizen of autocratic France. Before his naturalization would be granted, he was required to attest that he "has not borne a Hereditary title or been of any orders of the Nobility in the Empire of France . . . and declare on oath that he does absolutely and entirely renounce and abjure all Alleginnes [*sic*] and Fidelity to any Foreign Prince, Potentate, State or Sovereignty whatsoever and particularly to the Emperor of France of which he was a subject." It must have amused this once urchin immigrant from rural Lorraine, where his religion alone made him suspect by the state, to be asked to renounce this catalogue of possible florid affiliations.

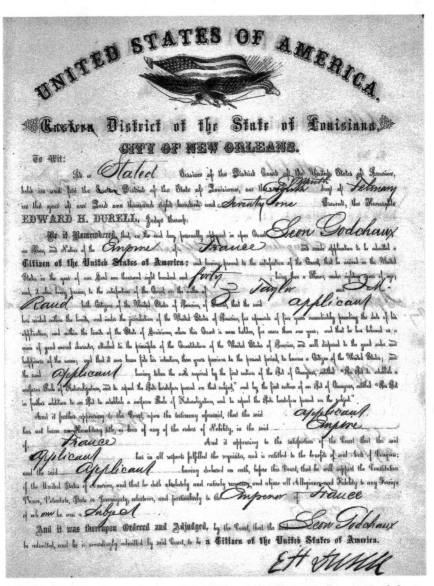

Fig. 27. U.S. citizenship order, February 9, 1871. Leon Godchaux becomes a naturalized U.S. citizen. Characterized as an "alien" at the time of application, Leon was required to swear that he "has not borne an Hereditary title, or been of any of the rulers of Nobility of said applicant's Empire of France." Courtesy of the National Archives and Records Administration.

Godchaux's citizenship application timing was deliberate and also connected to the situation in his home country. This suspicion by officials in New Orleans of the country of Leon's birthright reflects what was going on in France at the time. The year that Leon decided to cross the citizenship line, 1871, was particularly fraught for all French people. Germany defeated France in the Franco-Prussian War the month before Leon Godchaux applied for U.S. citizenship. Alsace and Lorraine, Leon's home territory, were being transferred to German control as war booty. In the same month that Godchaux sought citizenship, the National Assembly in Paris consisted of a new royalist majority, reflecting provincial interests. In Paris, the Republican minority feared that the National Assembly would restore the monarchy. A month after Leon was declared a U.S. citizen, the Commune de Paris exploded, only to eventually form a new progressive government ending Napoleon III's Second Empire. The newspapers in New Orleans, both those printed in French and in English, closely followed these fast-moving and profoundly changing events in France.

*   *   *

As the 1870s progressed, and Godchaux began to get Reserve under control, he decided to purchase other properties in and around Reserve and in two additional prime sugar-production locations, all relatively near his New Orleans headquarters to assure easy access and oversight. He contrived to cluster these acquisitions in three target areas to assure convenience of management. As he imagined the blueprint of his sugar production business, each cluster of plantations would have one manufacturing hub. Each sugar factory would be robust enough to service the refining needs of any number of other nearby plantations including those not in the Godchaux portfolio.

With his concept in mind, Godchaux turned his personal attention and capital to acquiring depleted sugar land properties. He had the wherewithal to do so not only because of his prudent asset management before and during the war, but also because his clothing retail, wholesale, and manufacturing operations in New Orleans were proving more successful than ever before. And sugar production property remained at bargain prices following the war.

Leon Godchaux knew the territory and had long-held relationships with many people in the rural areas where he bought property. In those postwar decades in Louisiana, his long-ago acquaintances, some going back to peddling days, especially from St. James, St. John the Baptist, and Lafourche parishes—now grown up and often substantial property owners themselves—turned to Leon when they needed to sell or to obtain a loan.

Godchaux acquired his properties in a variety of ways: occasionally through unavoidable loan foreclosures; most often his purchases were direct from willing sellers and at times he bid on foreclosed property at competitive sheriffs' auctions. Godchaux probably employed agents to search out opportunities. He would have also relied on his network of old friends and contacts in notarial offices, at the time the center of all legal transactional intelligence in Louisiana.

In St. James Parish alone, between 1875 and 1881, Leon bought land in nineteen separate transactions. He was just as active in St. John the Baptist Parish, where Reserve was situated. When a purchase necessarily included any section of property that did not fit his long-term vision, he would sell off that piece. Godchaux proceeded to purchase an array of productive sugar land and verdant woodlands, and many other smaller parcels, with the same sensible strategic care he had exercised as a young merchant in leasing adjacent buildings on Old Levee Street.

Between the late 1850s through to 1880, while real estate prices were depressed, Godchaux was also busy purchasing—at auction, bankruptcy sale, sheriff sales, and foreclosures—lots and buildings within the city of New Orleans. He concentrated on quality in the French Quarter, particularly on streets such as Old Levee, Dumaine, Bienville, Chartres, Madison, Bourbon, Royal, St. Philip, St. Ann, and Ursulines as well as Canal.

Within fifteen years, within fifty miles of his home base in New Orleans, Leon owned fourteen plantations clustered in three areas. He also bought numerous other parcels of country land with special attributes, as well as valuable properties in the city. His land in the countryside was composed of deep nutritious soil deposited over the ages by the river floods. He bought what later-day agronomists would call class 1 agricultural soils, the most productive and rarest cropland in America.

By the time his bold sugar lands buying spree ended, Leon Godchaux personally owned the sugar plantations known as Reserve, Star, Diamond, LaPlace, LaBranche,

Belle Pointe, New Era, Cornland, Elm Hall, Utopia, Upper Ten, Mary, Madewood, Foley, and Greater Raceland. He rejuvenated each place, raising their productivity from deplorable postwar levels. Together they covered 72,000 acres, 10,000 of which were in sugarcane fields and the balance in marsh, pine woods, and valuable cypress timberland.

Leveraging off his successful experience at Reserve, where the mill had proven to be an efficient and effective moneymaker, Leon proceeded to realize his megaplan to cluster his cropland beyond Reserve into two additional distinct networks, each served by a centralized factory. In time, all fourteen plantations were consolidated into three manufacturing districts. He built production factories at both Elm Hall and Raceland. He outfitted and staffed them with modern equipment and well-trained management. Salaries at all levels were maintained at the top of the going wage scale.

Elm Hall, located near Napoleonville, was consolidated with Foley, Madewood, properties around Napoleonville, other plantations along Bayou Lafourche, as well as several others nearby in Assumption Parish. In time, the output at Elm Hall skyrocketed to become the highest producer among Godchaux's refineries. Production at Elm Hall was eventually so robust that the Southern Pacific Railroad extended a spur track to the factory to secure its output.

The factory at Raceland plantation in Lafourche Parish connected his holdings along Bayou Lafourche and consisted of five nearby plantations, among them Utopia, Upper Ten, and Mary.

*   *   *

Leon Godchaux is universally credited with transforming what had been, worldwide, an antiquated and piecemeal industry saddled with disorganization, decentralization, and primitive refining methods. He pioneered the transformation of sugar processing into an agricultural-industrial hybrid. In doing so, he revolutionized the industry. His concept of the central refinery would in time transform the organization of the entire sugar industry all over the world. During Leon's tenure in the business, he also improved the practice and safety of labor through mechanization. The age-old way that sugar had been produced—a separate sugarhouse on every plantation, each separate and discrete in all its processes and equipment—was on the way out by the time Leon Godchaux retired.

The economic foundation of Godchaux's sugar business is also remarkable. Leon Godchaux realized his vision with his own capital. He did it without selling partnership interests or floating public stock. He was the man. As a reporter from Los Angeles on assignment in Louisiana in the 1890s explained to his hometown readers, "Far and wide, within and beyond the industry, Leon Godchaux was known as the Sugar King of Louisiana."

Two generations later, as Walter Godchaux Jr. pointed out, "The Central factory idea had progressed from Louisiana back to Cuba and to the other Caribbean countries and around the world to Java, India, Egypt and of course eventually to Hawaii."

Whether or not Leon Godchaux created the first-ever central sugar factory is debatable. It is certain that he was the first to adopt this transformative industrial approach at large scale.

Fig. 28. Godchaux sugar refinery at Reserve, ca. 1950. The large scale of the Godchaux Sugars refinery at Reserve by mid-twentieth century is captured in this panoramic photograph. The loaded rail-borne cane cars waiting to be unloaded for processing exhibit the marking of Leon's rail line, Mississippi River Sugar Belt Railroad, MRSBRR. Courtesy of Tulane University Special Collections.

*   *   *

In the process of transforming the sugar industry, Leon transformed the communities around his properties, particularly Reserve. That community's master historian, Gerald J. Keller, echoed what many others say when he wrote, "With Leon Godchaux's arrival, the fortunes of the parish dramatically changed, from being a collection of small, rural settlements to an agricultural center of regional and national significance."

Keller, who grew up in one of the company-built houses, remembers lining up each Christmas with his father, who worked as a sugar boiler in the Reserve refinery, to receive a present from the company. "And they were pretty decent too," he told me. And every Fourth of July, "the company sponsored a fair with fireworks and food booths and a Ferris wheel and all sorts of activities." The event drew as many as ten thousand people, who "came from all the river parishes, from Raceland, even from New Orleans." Other descendants of Leon's original employees who live in Reserve have attested to the humane way in which Leon Godchaux managed the sugar company, treated his employees, and enhanced their town.

Second-generation Godchaux family managers, particularly son Edward, went on to build at Reserve, circa 1917, a two-story wood-frame Reserve Community Club: downstairs, an indoor swimming pool, a concession stand, library, pool tables, ladies' lounge and men's lounge; upstairs, a three-hundred-seat theater for film and stage production; and outdoors, a dance pavilion, baseball and football fields, and tennis courts. In about 1938, an enlarged outdoor swimming pool was added, and the indoor pool area was converted to a pool hall. The lighted pool was open until 9:00 P.M. Movies were shown at a 3:00 P.M. matinee and at 6:30 and 9:00 P.M. Tuesday, Thursday, and Sundays. Dues for employees were one dollar a month for the entire family and two dollars a month per family for the general public. The building was the first air-conditioned building between New Orleans and Baton Rouge.

Employee housing was also built in volume beginning in the early 1920s. As many as eighty new single-family houses and duplex apartments were offered to employees at subsidized rents of around fifteen dollars per month with modern water, light, and gas heat. The water and electric services were free. As was inevitable and customary at the time, certain streets and areas were designated for Black employees and others for Whites. In later years, most of the housing was sold to residents at reasonable prices. Elsewhere in town, Godchaux family management donated land for the high school.

*   *   *

By the 1930s, cane growers from across the South and from the Caribbean, Cuba, Mexico, Puerto Rico, and the Philippines were sending some of their raw production for grinding, granulating, packaging, and distributing to Godchaux's facilities. In 1933, the capacity at Reserve, staffed by 650 employees (a number that would rise to over 1,000 by 1947), had climbed to a record during grinding season of 2 million pounds of refined sugar per day. Product was available for national and international export in a wide assortment of types and size bags stamped with the "Godchaux's Sugar" brand script.

20

The Railroad Baron

In his unremitting quest to modernize the sugar industry, Leon became intrigued by railroads. He, along with his son Jules, figured ways to apply this new technology to enhance his burgening empire.

The national trend in railroading reached south Louisiana late, though it did so as Godchaux was building his agricultural empire. When the Yazoo and Mississippi Valley Railroad, owned and financed by the much larger Illinois Central Railroad, barged into the region, blazed with its distinctive vibrant yellow markings in 1883, it opened the sugar trade to rail. The Yazoo and Mississippi Valley picked a commercial route that cut straight up the east bank of the Mississippi, where many of Godchaux's properties were clustered. Shipping sugar by steamboat was suddenly obsolete, as was transporting it by cart and wagon. The Yazoo and Mississippi Valley became such a familiar and beloved entity in the region that it entered the vernacular musical world as the "Yellow Dog" referred to in blues songs.

*   *   *

The advent of commercial-scale rail to the region prompted Leon and Jules, who was by then working with him, to find a way to facilitate transport not far and wide but, rather ingeniously, between and within Leon's adjacent plantation properties. Jules encouraged his father to adapt railroad technology to the interior of his plantations. While no record exists of their first use of rail on the Godchaux property, the story goes that in about 1890, Leon tested using strips of iron attached to wooden two-by-fours with heavier pieces of lumber serving as crossties. As the cane was cut, portable sections of track were moved from field to field. Mule teams dragged wheeled cars filled with cane.

Jules was the right person with the right training on hand at the right time. Educated at Philips Exeter Academy, Tulane University, and then at Massachusetts Institute of Technology (founded in 1861 and informally called "Boston Tech" originally), Jules was back home after his technical education and exposure to the East. After a brief apprenticeship at the store, Leon put Jules in charge of the mill at Raceland. Jules, informed by his experience at Raceland, then combined his knowledge of sugar processing with modern ingenuity. Why not adopt, with necessary modifications, the full potential of the railroad to his father's business?

Upon Jules's urging, Leon made the decision in 1894 to build a private narrow-gauge rail line at Reserve and to power it with steam engines. The rail line was designed as a smaller-scale replica of the full-size steel rails, transport cars, and steam locomotives spreading across the country. Its function would be to seamlessly link the cluster of nearby cane-growing land directly into the Reserve central refinery.

The project was a resounding success. It quickly met Leon's goal of replacing animals and backbreaking labor in the hauling of cut cane and delivery of other material to the factory. Once proven at Reserve, Jules and Leon built a similar rail line network at Elm Hall and another at Raceland.

Leon commissioned his first two miniature steam engines and railcars in 1895 from the world's largest producer of full-size steam locomotives, Baldwin Locomotive Works. The initial order was for a "no. 1" and "no. 2" for Reserve to travel on the new permanent roadbed. That order was soon followed by another "no. 1" for Raceland. Leon and Jules then commissioned two no. 2 engines and then two no. 3s that were delivered in 1898–1899. All the initial purchases were identical 0-4-4T steam Baldwins and emblazoned with "Godchaux's" in white letters on their respective sides written in the company's distinctive logo script.

Fig. 29. Godchaux Locomotive No. 4 hauling cane through the fields to the refinery on steel rails. Leon Godchaux not only harnessed rail technology to enhance efficiency at each mill, but also to reorganize and centralize the arrangement of sugar-producing properties. Photograph by Witbeck Studio, Hammond, Louisiana. Courtesy of Margaret Cambre Cerami.

When all the tracks were set and the equipment fully operational, the Godchaux line was extensive enough in each location to tap into the Godchaux plantation network surrounding each of the three central refineries. In time, Leon and Jules anointed their narrow-gauge tramway railroad fleet of steam locomotives, track, and cane cars rather grandly as the Mississippi River Sugar Belt Railroad (MRSBRR).

Fig. 30. Leon's rail line. The MRSBRR markings are visible on the rear-loaded cane car in the background. The engineer has moved across the cab and left his controls to pose along with his assistants for this professionally staged picture. Photograph by Witbeck Studio, Hammond, Louisiana. Courtesy of Margaret Cambre Cerami.

The MRSBRR roadbed extended for some twenty miles from the St. James Parish line on the north, across all of St. John the Baptist Parish, through the town of LaPlace and into St. Charles Parish. Godchaux's Diamond plantation was the end of the line, terrain now part of the Bonnet Carré Spillway—present-day flood-control land monitored by the U.S. Army Corps of Engineers that extends between the Mississippi River and Lake Pontchartrain.

Bonnet Carré Spillway

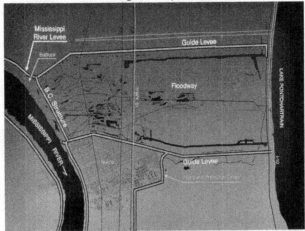

Map of Bonnet Carré Spillway (top), and aerial of the spillway in operation during the flood of 1975. The view is from the Mississippi River with Lake Ponchartain in the background.

Directions to the Bonnet Carré Spillway: West on I-10 from New Orleans to I-310. Take the Norco-Destrehan exit, head west (right) on River Road for 6 miles.

Fig. 31. Map of Bonnet Carré Spillway. The spillway's infrastructure and flood-tide area in part occupy land formerly known as Diamond Plantation, once owned by Godchaux. The aerial view shows the spillway in operation during the flood of 1975. The spillway was built north of New Orleans between the Mississippi River and Lake Pontchartrain with locks in the levee. Its purpose is to divert river flood tide through the floodway lowlands into the lake in order to protect the city. Courtesy U.S. Army Corps of Engineers, New Orleans District.

The rail system worked perfectly, thanks to stalwart devoted employees such as engineer Sidney Cambre and superintendent W. H. Jones, who oversaw the rail operations, the former for thirty-five years and Jones for forty-eight. Bulk cane was transported efficiently through fields and into factories. Repair shops were built at each factory site. Specialized mechanics were hired to keep the equipment in good order. Locomotive engineers became minor celebrities among the children who sometimes hitched a ride to school. Over time, additional equipment and locomotives were purchased and track modernized.

Much of the Godchaux narrow-gauge rail system remained operational through the 1940s. It was eventually replaced by trucks. The line at Raceland, the last to close, shut down in 1949.

*　　*　　*

Leon's narrow-gauge network was not the last stop, the end of the line, for his engagement with railroads. Fired up by the utilitarian success of his narrow-gauge adventure, Leon barreled on to become something of a regional railroad baron in the standard-gauge full-size business. He'd been impressed by the expansive railroading burgeoning across America, fueled by the capital and swagger of adventurous tycoons such as Cornelius Vanderbilt, Edward Harriman, James Hill, Jay and George Gould. Their stories and achievements filled the political and financial news and seeped into Leon's imagination.

Like the Harrimans and Vanderbilts, Leon took a plunge into endeavor financing, but unlike those storied tycoons, Leon kept the scale of his ambition local. He did not try to build or to take over a railroad company. Rather, Leon committed the Godchaux Company to provide venture capital as lead investor in building a full-scale regional rail line that in time came to be called the Sterling Sugar and Railway Company. Jules was put in charge of Sterling. The line operated across the river from the Yellow Dog in the unserved river parishes on the west bank of the Mississippi. It connected the town of Sterling near Franklin, Louisiana, in St. Mary Parish, to Milton, near Bayou Vermilion in Lafayette Parish, an intense sugar-growing and -producing region. Soon after it began operation, the successful line was extended from Franklin on one end to Abbeville on the other, forty-four miles, passing just north of Avery Island, a verdant land preserve and bird sanctuary and longtime home of the Avery family and its related McIlhenny Company. (The McIlhenny operation famously produced, and still does, its iconic Tabasco hot pepper sauce.) The rail line continued through the sugar-producing area around New Iberia (a town justly celebrated to this day for its excellent seafood, picturesque town square, and exuberant dance halls in which couples serenely parade their Cajun two-step and waltz). The name of the line was also extended, becoming a mouthful: the Sterling Central, Franklin and Abbeville Railroad. In time, the name was simplified, changed to Stirling Central, acknowledging the power of the Godchaux interest and Jules overseeing both the railroad operation and the mill at Raceland.

Leon's backing of Sterling was not propelled, as might be expected of this very deliberate man, by raw ambition or his wish to emulate Vanderbilt or Harriman or anyone of that high-flying financially savvy ilk. Leon's rationale for investing so heavily in Sterling Central was driven by a locally focused two-pronged plan. His first goal was to tap surrounding plantations situated beyond his own minirail network, to attract their cane to his Elm Hall and Raceland operations, the two Godchaux sugar refineries on the west side of the river. Once Sterling reached their property, a whole new set of customers could transport cane conveniently and cheaply to the Godchaux mills.

Leon's second objective for Sterling was to gain rail access deep into wooded areas where he owned stands of valuable red cypress timber. He had acquired these precious water-resistant woods, much sought for construction, in vast tracts over the years, accumulated within forests and wetland bayou stretches both within the boundaries of and beyond his plantations. Sterling enabled Leon to easily and inexpensively convey this precious cargo to lumber mills in the region.

*　　*　　*

Leon's fleet of miniature steam engines, after being industrial workhorses, ended up having a life of their own. Once retired from plantation life, they went on to stage their own next acts. Raceland No. 1 was sold twice before it was acquired in 1957 by Walt Disney, an aficionado of steam trains. Disney sought a showpiece for his narrow-gauge line at Disneyland in California.

Fig. 32. Godchaux Locomotive Raceland No. 1 at Disneyland. The engine is now an attraction at Disneyland after a recommissioning rumored to cost $1 million. It rolled into Disneyland on March 28, 1958, renamed the Fred G. Gurley, in honor of the Disney-friendly president of the Atchison, Topeka, and Santa Fe Railway. Photograph by Witbeck Studio, Hammond, Louisiana. Courtesy of Margaret Cambre Cerami.

Fig. 33. Godchaux Locomotive Raceland No. 1 hauling visitors at Disneyland. Photograph by Witbeck Studio, Hammond, Louisiana. Courtesy of Margaret Cambre Cerami.

Raceland No. 2, in its post-Godchaux incarnation, got off to a less-celebrated start. In fact, it didn't start at all, but rather was left nonoperational for years on the property at Reserve with its original markings fading away. When finally purchased by the Chandler Vintage Museum of Transportation and Wildlife in Oxnard, California, the original muted olive green of the cab was repainted in garish bright colors. After 2006, when that museum's collection was auctioned off, the miniature engine changed hands several times. Today, restored to functionality, it holds sway at the ninety-acre Orange Empire Railway Museum, in Perris, California (now known as the Southern California

Railway Museum), keeping fully charged company with its neighbors—more than two hundred other historic railway cars and locomotives.

For many years, Raceland No. 3, remarked as Godchaux No. 3, sat idle, decaying on a scant fragment of rusted track in a grassy field in front of what came to be called the Godchaux house at Reserve. This wood-frame building was the most prominent residential property on Reserve plantation during Leon's day. It was the place the first generations of family stayed when at Reserve, the place where Leon conducted business when he was there.

Today, Godchaux No. 3 is still resident at Reserve, but now protected as a revered relic. It has been adorned with an added cowcatcher, shiny brass bands to highlight the boiler, cleaned pistons, and steam pipe domes. It rests, crisply painted and shined, protected under its own specially built open-sided corrugated metal shed in full view of the Godchaux house.

Some of the other engines that constituted Leon's narrow-gauge rail realm—each one of them once a proud little engine that could—were scrapped. Others were sold and reused for various purposes in places as far-flung as Reno, Nevada; South Carver, Massachusetts; and Cuba. Most of the other rolling stock was scrapped in the 1950s, though some might have been traded among collectors and still survive.

21

The Duke Of Clothing

Late in life, while building his sugar empire, and continuing to modernize and expand his clothing business, Leon resumed pursuit of a long-held ambitious plan to redevelop his Canal Street properties. Leon wanted to build a magnificent new store from scratch. The new store Leon had in mind would be a grand, indeed very grand, landmark retail emporium, a store that would express the prominent, successful, French-tilted merchant he had become.

Godchaux's plan was to consolidate his two properties already in use on Canal Street with the adjacent lot he did not own at the corner of Chartres and Canal. He would demolish all three structures and, in their place, erect his dream store. For years, wish and vision were not enough. The owner of the crucial key corner had no interest in selling. He preferred to continue operating his thriving saloon.

*   *   *

In the late 1880s, Leon finally had his opportunity: he might have made the saloon owner an offer he could not refuse. After years of patient waiting, Leon bought the corner lot.

Leon quickly put his dream plan into action. He hired esteemed local architects Sully, Burton and Stone and added to the team experienced New Orleans builders Darcantel & Diasselliss, a firm familiar with erecting large-capacity steel-frame structures. The new building would be a grand men's and boys' showcase housing retail on the ground floor and offices on the five upper stories. Leon's impressive new department store would rise exactly where he wanted it, exactly where he had painstakingly planned for it over nearly twenty years. Its principal entrance would be the prime commercial corner of Canal and Chartres streets. By building permit published on May 6, 1893, Leon was green-lighted into action: "A pemit has been granted to Mr. Leon Godchaux to erect a six-story brick building at the corner of Canal and Chartres streets, to cost $25,000."

Aesthetically, the new flagship store, with its entrance address as 531 Canal, was a stunner. It had been built in the record time of approximately one year.

Fig. 34. Godchaux Store and Building, 531 Canal Street, completed ca. 1894. Leon's emporium was located at the desirable corner of Chartres and Canal streets, built after a long and patient land assembly. Its address was variously listed as 527-537 and sometimes as 525-531 Canal and sometimes 100-114 Chartres. Designed under Leon's guidance by architects Sully, Burton & Stone Company Ltd., the technologically up-to-date building was aesthetically reminiscent of the grand magasin in Paris. In 1924, the Godchaux clothing business moved again, this time three blocks farther from the river to 828 Canal Street. Leon's emporium building was demolished in November 1968, forty-four years after the Godchaux clothing business moved out. The site is now occupied by the Marriott Hotel. Engraving courtesy of the Historic New Orleans Collection, the Collins C. Diboll Vieux Carré Digital Survey Square 32, N-2414.

Leon's dream store was elegant and dignified. The Canal Street corner entrance was announced by an awning of Parisian stained glass fanning out over the sidewalk. For a mile or so in every direction could be seen the two rooftop super graphics attached to water towers that spelled out GODCHAUX BUILDING. In its sumptuousness, Godchaux's evoked *les grands magasins* of Paris—Le Bon Marché, Le Printemps du Louvre, and Galeries Lafayette.

Though the skin of the new Godchaux's looked seductively old school and reminiscent of grand European Victorian emporia, most everything about its inside was very much up to date based on the latest scientific advances. The skeleton was fireproof steel. "Sanitary, fireproof and modern," the *Daily Picayune* summed up, "every appliance relating to hygiene, lighting, heating, comfort and convenience has been attended to and installed without regard to cost."

Fig. 35. Interior of Godchaux's new store at 531 Canal Street, ca. 1894. Leon's new emporium featured the latest modern advances related to lighting, heating, hygiene, and comfort. Courtesy of the Historic New Orleans Collection, acc. no. 1984.115.59i-xi.

With the elegant expansion at Canal and Chartres, Godchaux's reputation for top quality and dedicated personal service grew ever more prominent. Godchaux's was undisputedly *the* place to shop for men's and boy's clothing. Leon's finale in the retail industry, completed only a few years before the end of his life, expressed the confidence and the prominence that he had attained. It also, in harking back to the iconic department stores of Paris, revealed Leon's never-abandoned French affiliation, even pride, in having emulated the social and commercial stature of the proprietors of *les grands magasins*, the symbolic top of the fashion world on the continent.

Following difficulties that I will talk about later, Joachim Tassin became an ever-larger presence in the new Godchaux retail store. He would have personally greeted customers as they entered the bespoke department that he had made famous. Upon entering the fitting rooms, Tassin, tape measure around his neck, a box of pins at his side, dressed immaculately in a perfectly tailored dark suit and white shirt, likely smiled, saying, "It is so good to see you again." After fitting a customer, he must have routinely stood back, appraised his work, checked his customer's expression, then said something like, "That jacket will be perfect. Let's see about the sleeves."

By the early 1890s, besides being the chief fitter at Godchaux's, Tassin participated in day-to-day management. The old man had retired from daily presence at the store. His first son, Paul Leon, was a tutored apprentice executive in waiting.

LEON GODCHAUX, Proprietor Godchaux' Clothing House.

PAUL L. GODCHAUX, Manager Godchaux' Clothing House.

Fig. 36. Leon Godchaux and Paul Leon Godchaux, ca. 1890. At age sixteen, Paul Leon was taken out of school to begin his apprenticeship at the clothing company. In the 1890s, he was elevated to manager. At his father's death in 1899, Paul Leon succeeded to the presidency of the Leon Godchaux Clothing Co. Ltd. He held that title and led the business until his death in 1924. L. Graham & Son printer. Courtesy of the Louisiana Historical Center, the Leon Godchaux Collection, Record Group 496.

Paul Leon would have depended upon Tassin and been glad to have him available. Tassin knew it all, practically from the beginning. Paul Leon would have said time and again, "What would I do without you, what with *père* so busy with his sugar factories and railroads?"

*   *   *

For the next two decades, the store operated with great success at Canal and Chartres, in spite of unprecedented labor discord within the city. In the 1880s, as reaction to the rollback of Reconstruction and onset of Jim Crow, labor walkouts and strikes were not uncommon. Toward the end of 1892, over twenty thousand White and Black participants went on strike for half a week, abruptly stopping nearly all commercial activity. The port slowed; transport in town was crippled.

Godchaux's was not affected. The company succeeded against its competitors because Leon insisted upon offering top-quality merchandise sold in an attractive setting at a fair price in an establishment where highly personal client service was routine and fair wages paid. Leon Godchaux was determined to maintain a manageable-size business that he and his son and Joachim Tassin could carefully oversee. In addition, he enjoyed the committed loyalty of his staff from top to bottom. Quietly but consistently, Leon made available, as needed, interest-free loans to all employees.

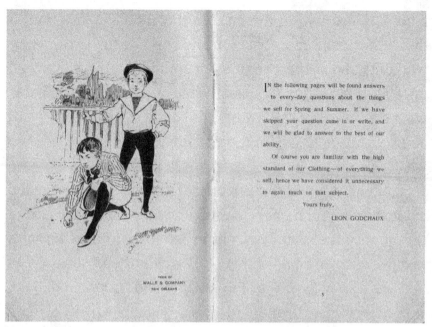

Fig. 37. Preface to Godchaux's Clothing Store 1898 spring and summer catalogue. The catalogue's letter preface, cast as a personal invitation to customers from Leon Godchaux, expressed the supreme confidence of a leading merchant: "Of course you are familiar with the high standards of our clothing—of everything we sell, hence we have considered it unnecessary to again touch on that subject." Courtesy of Tulane University Special Collections.

*   *   *

There was competition. Plenty of it. Within a decade after the war, numerous retail businesses, many of them owned by Jews, had flocked into the Canal Street corridor. Clothing stores such as Goldring's, Gus Mayer, Mayer Israel, and Marks Isaacs, along with department stores such as the Krauss Company and Maison Blanche eventually set up shop on or near Canal Street, generally four or five blocks farther from the river than the Godchaux building and nearer the previously established D. H. Holmes (they were all still in operation when I was a boy). And yet the annual *Book of the Chamber of Commerce and Industry in Louisiana* in the 1880s and 1890s consistently ranked Leon Godchaux Men and Boys Outfitter as "far and away the leading clothing house of the city." Leon Godchaux had gone the distance—from peddler to country-store proprietor to small-time merchant to merchant prince.

*　　*　　*

If expanding his merchant operation, remaking the sugar industry, and becoming an American citizen wasn't enough, Leon was also acquiring a reputation in social circles as a generous philanthropist and a leading man in the New Orleans community. He was friendly with the coterie of men who met from time to time at the St. Charles Hotel, where the idea of the Mardi Gras–focused Rex Organization first took hold. In part, this group of established businessmen was searching for ways to enhance the commercial and tourist appeal of New Orleans during the dire period of post–Civil War Reconstruction.

Leon might have been a founding member of the small group that in early 1872 created the Rex Organization. Incorporated a few years later as the whimsically named School of Design, it adopted the serious motto of *Pro Bono Publico* (for the public good). (Ever since, the Rex Organization has supported enhanced public school education in New Orleans.) When its first Mardi Gras krewe paraded in the streets of New Orleans, Louis Solomon, surely a friend of Leon's and half Jewish, was selected by members as the organization's king of Rex.

The earliest School of Design membership roster and meeting minutes were incinerated in an accidental fire years ago. Nevertheless, according to Dr. Stephen Hales, Rex's current archivist and authority on the organization's history, "Leon Godchaux's prominent profile fits with the young members at that time. He was probably part of that early group of men who created the Rex Organization, now the public face of Mardi Gras in New Orleans."

Leon was not attracted to the nostalgic longing that underpinned the pomp of New Orleans elite social organizations. He was attracted to community service and to boosting the economic viability of his city. By 1895, the Rex "Roster of Royal Hosts" of the School of Design listed Leon Godchaux as a member in good standing. The "Royal Hosts" constituted the inner circle of distinguished members of the Rex Organization. As a special high honor, each Royal Host was awarded a "letters patent," confirming his station as a duke. Each duke was entitled to proclaim his own honorific title. Godchaux, L. (as he was listed), chose to become the "Duke of Clothing," a title he might have selected for its playful humility.

22

Swift And Vicious

While Leon was expanding his commercial footprint in the city and his agricultural success in the countryside, the political situation in Louisiana and in the South was again darkening. The avalanche of progressive landmark federal legislation that became law immediately after the Civil War had managed to superficially calm the racial enmity that had characterized the South for over a century. But those same national dicta soon thrust New Orleans and the South into a social and legislative maelstrom.

The abundance and thoroughness of progressive legislation from Washington, the legal bedrock of the Reconstruction period, stuck in the craw of recalcitrant conservative forces in the South (and indeed was not embraced by many people in other parts of the country).

Social and political reaction below the Mason-Dixon Line was swift and vicious. Immediately, in response to the Thirteenth Amendment, in 1865, the Ku Klux Klan organized in Tennessee; soon afterward, other chapters metastasized across the South. By 1874, the Democratic Party, which vehemently opposed Reconstruction, regained control of the United States House of Representatives and by 1877 was dominant in Congress. Therein lay the groundwork for the erosion of the social-equity gains made by Blacks under the leadership of the Republican Party in the immediate aftermath of the Civil War.

The presidential election of 1876 became the tipping point. It was as fiercely disputed as the chad-riddled presidential election 124 years later or the disgraceful show of national disunity that blemished the presidential election of 2020. To resolve a contested impasse, the Republican nominee, Rutherford B. Hayes, was accepted by the predominantly White Democrats—but at a price, a very high one at that. In exchange for accepting Hayes as president of the country, the Democrats won a promise to have all federal troops withdrawn from the South. This informal, unwritten backroom deal hatched in Washington became known as the Compromise of 1877. This compromise, which assured Hayes the presidency, doomed all hope of civil rights enforcement in the South and thereby stifled all hope of continued progress in the cause of integration and racial justice in the region. This deal was struck one year after Joachim Tassin had boldly opened his own retail business on Old Levee Street in New Orleans.

By 1877, White Democrats were already in control of most Southern legislatures; private armed militias were common in small towns and rural areas. Once federal oversight was withdrawn, town after town and state after state rushed through various forms of pro-segregationist legislation, which came to be known as Jim Crow laws. However elaborately justified and however arcane the language employed, these laws served primarily to segregate Blacks—all and any Blacks—from Whites and to deprive people with dark skin of their legal rights. Through a malign combination of poll taxes, literacy and comprehension tests, and cumbersome residency and record-keeping requirements, the Jim Crow laws were primarily designed to disenfranchise the recently emancipated Black male population. Between 1890 and 1910, ten of the eleven former Confederate states, including Louisiana, passed new constitutions or constitutional amendments that effectively made voting all but impossible for most Black people, along with scores of impoverished Whites. Joachim suddenly had a stake in any legislation that affected every non-White.

*   *   *

Even before the onset of the Jim Crow period, Reconstruction had created cruelly ironic adverse legal and social consequence for Joachim Tassin. Reconstruction-period federal legislation that guaranteed expanded rights to Black people applied to *all* people of color. Distinction was no longer made in the legal system between the large and largely uneducated previously enslaved Black African population and all other people of color.

The loss of protective legal distinction left the influential free people of color community distraught and wary. They proved unable to maintain the legal distinction, enjoyed for so long, between themselves and formerly enslaved Blacks.

When the backlash set in and Jim Crow discriminatory legislation prevailed, local law in Louisiana became predictably color-blind to prior hallowed distinctions within the non-White population. Suddenly, you were White or you were not. Centuries of protective racial exceptionalism dissolved over the ensuing years. Many New Orleans Creoles and free people of color were eased out of their businesses and trades. Their privileged position within the formerly complex social hierarchy that had prevailed for centuries in New Orleans became less secure. Many left.

*   *   *

In response, prewar free Blacks and Creole organizations strove to maintain the prewar status quo. One, the Comité des Citoyens (a Creole name with French Revolutionary undertones), rallied in 1890 after the Louisiana State Legislature passed Act 111, a state law allegedly promoting in Section 3 "the comfort of passengers on railway trains."

Act 111, popularly known as the Separate Car Act, was a piece of unconcealed discrimination—a product of retaliatory post-Reconstruction segregationist fury imposed by the White-dominated reactionary Louisiana State Legislature. The text of the law spoke plainly: "All railway companies carrying passengers in their coaches in this State, shall provide equal but separate accommodations for the white and colored races. By providing two or more passenger coaches for each train, no person or persons shall be permitted to occupy seats in coaches, other than the ones assigned to them, on account of the race they belong to."

In direct reaction—following the suggestion of Albion Tourgée, a White lawyer and civil rights activist—appalled African American, White, former free Black, and Creole members of the Comité des Citoyens devised a piece of carefully crafted civil-disobedience theater to test the Separate Car Act. Their strategy—a civil disobedience "performance" to be staged at the rail yards at the corner of Royal and Press streets in New Orleans. The theater selected to attempt derailing the legislation was a routine commuter and holiday train that ran from a neighborhood in the center of New Orleans to the resort town of Covington, Louisiana, north of Lake Pontchartrain. The action had been greenlighted by the owners of the East Louisiana Railroad Company. The rail carrier objected to the expense of having to provide extra railcars on its line that this new legislation would require.

By prearrangement, on the morning of June 7, 1892, thirty-year-old Homer Adolph Plessy, a shoemaker born free during the Civil War, of mixed race (seven-eighths European-descent Caucasian and one-eighth black) but technically Black under then-current Jim Crow Louisiana law, purchased a first-class ticket at the Press Street Depot, so named for the abundance of cotton presses and warehouses surrounding the rail yard. (Today, those warehouses have been replaced by residential cottages and new condominiums. The station, still perched alongside the track, is now a party venue: *"Whether you're looking for a place to host a wedding, lecture, dinner, or other gathering, Press Street Station offers a range of options to suit every budget."*) As Plessy passed his fare beneath the ticket window gate, impossible-to-miss placards pasted at the ticket booth and glaring from the station walls recited the newly passed Separate Car Act. Homer Plessy slid his ticket into his pocket, walked deliberately along the crowded platform, stepped into the train, and took a seat in a "Whites only" railcar.

Homer Plessy was a free-born French-speaking extremely light-skinned Creole member of the privileged New Orleans caste into which Joachim Tassin had found his way. Plessy was vice president of the New Orleans Justice, Protective, Educational and Social Club, a group affiliated with the Citoyens. At the age of twenty-five, he had married nineteen-year-old Louise Bordenave in the Creole-dominated St. Augustine Catholic Church, the church in which Joachim Tassin had been married during the Civil War.

Plessy could easily have passed for White. The conductor, J. J. Dowling, as planned, asked Plessy, by prior arrangement, if he was colored. Plessy answered in the affirmative. When asked a second time, he repeated his assertion. He was then asked to leave, not once but twice. The Comité had Chris Cain, a private detective with arrest powers, standing by to charge Plessy with violating the Louisiana Separate Car Act.

The *Plessy v. Ferguson* case—the Honorable John Howard Ferguson, a carpetbagger scion of a Martha's Vineyard shipping family, was a judge in the Criminal District Court for Orleans Parish—seemed at first a local matter. But it was not ever intended to be just that by the directors of the Plessy theater piece. As it morphed through appeals beyond the confines of the local civil court, *Plessy* became the first legal effort to validate the "equal protection" provision of the Fourteenth Amendment and to challenge the "separate but equal" concept in the Louisiana law.

The case wound its way for four years through the nation's judicial appellate system until it reached the Supreme Court. Plessy's lawyers argued that the Separate Car Act violated both the Thirteenth and Fourteenth Amendments. The court, still mired in the national ethos of post–Reconstruction Jim Crow America, ruled 7–1 on May 18, 1896, that Louisiana's state law was indeed constitutional. The majority opinion (now to us amazing) in Washington was that the Separate Car Act indeed assured equal treatment for Blacks and Whites. In upholding state-imposed racial segregation, the high court held that segregation did not in itself constitute unlawful discrimination.

The *Plessy* ruling provided justification for public facilities of all kinds in America—including, most egregiously, schools—to be segregated for almost sixty years.

Joachim Tassin, and indeed any individual judged by law to not be White, could now be required to use spaces, places, facilities, what have you, that were separate and distinct from those available to White people. Tassin had skirted the taint of being classified a slave, but he was trapped as a Black man in the separate but equal net. For this one, Godchaux had no escape for Joachim.

(The setback to social justice delivered by the *Plessy* verdict was not reversed until 1954, a half century after Leon Godchaux's death and more than forty years after Joachim

Tassin's. In its landmark *Brown v. Board of Education* decision, the United States Supreme Court ruled that state laws denying access to education based on race violates the equal protection clause of the Fourteenth Amendment. In the wake of that still-reverberating decision, the legal wall of race-based segregation based on the separate but equal concept crumbled—though de facto segregation certainly did not.)

The lone dissenter in the *Plessy* case was Justice John Marshall Harlan, a former slave owner from Kentucky. Early in his career, Harlan had condemned the Thirteenth Amendment, which had abolished slavery, as "the overthrow of Constitutional liberty." With his appointment to the Supreme Court, however, Harlan grew more independent. As the sole dissenter in assorted civil rights cases between 1883 and 1890, Harlan built an estimable record favoring social equality. No less than President John F. Kennedy, in his address to the nation in support of the Civil Rights Act of 1964, quoted from Justice Harlan's dissent in the *Plessy* case: "In the eye of the law there is in this country no superior, dominant, ruling class of citizens. . . . Our constitution is color-blind, and neither knows nor tolerates classes among citizens. In respect of civil rights, all citizens are equal before the law."

* * *

Leon and Joachim would have been affected by the *Plessy* ruling, both emotionally and practically, though in different ways. What they had in common, beyond more than a fifty-year friendship and surely outrage at the Court's decision, was commitment to a thriving retail operation. Before and after the Civil War and all through Reconstruction and beyond, the Black population in New Orleans had enjoyed open and equal access to all the Godchaux store's facilities.

At the time of the *Plessy* ruling, Leon was near the end of his life. Joachim Tassin was now the most experienced and valued employee that Leon Godchaux ever had. Paul Leon was far along the way to becoming the prime family member at the store: in just three years, at his father's death, Paul Leon would become the president of the Leon Godchaux Clothing Company.

When the *Plessy* decision came down, Leon, Paul Leon, and Joachim Tassin probably met within the confines of the store to evaluate its implications. They would have discussed ways in which the Supreme Court decision could adversely impact the business. Paul Leon probably asked Joachim something like, "How do you feel about continuing to encourage Black clients to shop at Godchaux's? Would your friends and clients feel unwelcomed?"

Tassin would have likely been uncharacteristically glum. He probably answered little more than, "I don't know. This is difficult. At home, we're talking about what to do too."

The three men likely discussed a revised strategy for redirecting advertising and if they should change the merchandise mix. Would Blacks now shun or even boycott the store?

Leon probably asked Tassin, "Should we continue to try to attract the New Orleans Black population to the store?

I am concerned." He would have confided, "Might there be violence aimed at us if we do?" Leon likely would have continued, "Our important black clientele are attracted because you are here, Joachim. I want you to stay. I hope you aren't thinking of leaving the store again, or even New Orleans, because of this wretched decision made in Washington."

All agreed, history was repeating itself in one of its vilest forms, but there was nothing they could do. Before the meeting ended, Joachim might well have looked straight at his old friend and benefactor seated behind his desk and said in a quiet voice, "Mr. Leon, I'm too old. It's too late to leave, and I wouldn't leave you again."

In mid-1896, the store's bathrooms, dressing rooms, and drinking fountains all had to be, to use a euphemism, reorganized. The more precise word is *segregated*.

23

How Tassin Coped

Now I want to step back in time and catch up with what had been going on in Joachim Tassin's life toward the end of Reconstruction.

The years 1884–1885, eight years after Tassin opened his independent haberdashery and five years before the beginning of the *Plessy* affair, had been fraught for Joachim Tassin. Even though his retail trade had remained stable, though not as dynamic as Godchaux's, the recent promising incoming political and civil rights tide—initially so helpful to Blacks—was draining out. So was Tassin's luck.

In 1884, Tassin's wife of twenty-one years, Marie Coustaut, died of uterine cancer at the young age of forty-eight. Whether Marie ever knew Joachim's former identity as a slave is unclear. Joachim fulfilled her long-held wish to be buried in renowned and fashionable St. Louis Cemetery No. 2, the second-oldest burial ground in New Orleans, established as a Catholic cemetery in 1823.

Fig. 38. Joachim Tassin, ca. 1895. This rare newspaper picture of formally dressed, dignified Joachim Tassin underlines his position as the successful tailor and senior member of the Godchaux organization. Courtesy of the New Orleans Item, *October 17, 1910, Part Second, p. 1.*

The next year, feeling disoriented and disconsolate, Joachim moved out of his apartment in the French Quarter that he had shared with Marie.

Joachim had lived in the French Quarter ever since being brought to New Orleans. He had lived initially on St. Ann Street near the Godchaux store, the same street where Justine worked as a young girl. When he became an independent merchant, he moved a few blocks toward the river to an apartment on Old Levee Street and lived above his own store, just as Leon had for decades.

The house Tassin bought upon leaving the French Quarter in 1885, at 1471 North Roman Street, was in the Seventh Ward, a neighborhood populated by a mixture of middle-class Whites, Creoles, *gens*, and Black residents. This residential mix suited Tassin; he would have felt comfortable on North Roman Street as a place where he belonged in the social world of New Orleans. As Godchaux had, Tassin moved, but not far away, from his store and out of the relatively congested old French Quarter, into a more placid family-oriented residential, modest, but very urban neighborhood. Tassin's new residence was within a five-minute walk of Godchaux's place on Esplanade. Joachim Tassin was now fifty-three years old.

*　　*　　*

In the fateful hot month of August 1885, a disastrous fire annihilated the J. Tassin Co. merchandise, located in rented space in the three-story brick building at 205 Old Levee (Decatur Street) corner of Iberville Street. It occurred suspiciously at eleven thirty at night. Tassin's inventory was destroyed and with it the business Tassin had owned and built for nine years. His stock in trade was valued at $10,000, but his insurance, as reported by the local newspaper after reporters checked with the

New Orleans Insurance Association and the Liverpool and London Globe Insurance, amounted to "$0000." The building itself, fully insured by his landlord, was not seriously damaged. By the time of that fire, Reconstruction had been under way for twenty years; the mood in the South was growing increasingly hostile toward the recently liberated and legally protected Black population.

Once the dreadful and devastating calamity wiped out Tassin's merchandise, he had neither adequate insurance nor capital to rebuild, to restock, to resume. He surely suspected arson in these waning days of late Reconstruction. Southern racism, always present, was again becoming more overt. In despair and awash with righteous suspicion, he probably felt helpless. On the day of the fire, Joachim Tassin would have been all but overcome with one feeling: *I'm ruined.*

While his merchandise was still smoldering, Tassin, close to panic, had probably walked to Canal Street to see his old boss. Leon would have been totally surprised to see a distraught Tassin in the store. He might not have known about the fire, which had occurred a few blocks away and only a few hours earlier during the night.

Tassin would have been so upset he probably blurted out with no preamble something like, "I think it was arson, but I cannot prove it. I have no insurance. And I doubt that I could get support in a court, even if I had a suspect."

Godchaux, stunned, would have asked a few questions, tried to learn more details about what happened. He probably would have shared Tassin's suspicion and agreed with him about his not being able to obtain justice. He might have cautioned, "Even if it is arson, Joachim, how can you prove it? Proof will be difficult to establish. The courts will not necessarily be sympathetic given the politics of the day." Leon Godchaux, still feeling betrayed, might not have initially suggested that Joachim return to work at Godchaux's.

When Leon got home and told Justine about what had happened, his wife would have likely been adamant. "You've got to take him back, Léon. Here's your chance to again employ the best fitter in New Orleans. You know that. Forget what happened years ago. Isn't it better to have him at the store than working for someone else?" Before that evening ended, Leon surely knew what he had to do. He would have sent Joachim a short note and invited him to promptly return to his old position.

Tassin would have been at once grateful and downcast, even bitter. His dream of being an independent merchant had gone up in flames.

*   *   *

The year after he returned to work for Godchaux, in 1886, now fifty-four years old, now securely back at work with a reliable salary, and a widower of several years, Tassin met Marie Pauline Millon (sometimes written as Milan or Meullon). Marie Pauline had emigrated from Bordeaux, France, to New Orleans in 1870. By the time they met, Pauline was a forty-year-old widow with two young children. Notably, she was White. Not being a Southerner, indeed being a French national, Marie Pauline did not share the aversion to people of color held by so many White Southerners. A widow with two children to care for, she was also interested in finding a partner whose life was dependable and whose income was adequate.

As their courtship matured into serious romance, Joachim would have candidly said to Pauline, as he called her (to differentiate her from his first wife, Marie), something like, "I worry that you will not want to get to know me better when you think seriously about how careful we must always be in public. Our life together is already restricted." Joachim Tassin's job was secure, but his legal standing was diminished, compromised by Jim Crow fervor. He would have confided to Pauline, "Things are changing quickly. I'm worried about our situation, you being White."

"Don't worry about that," I imagine Pauline replying. "I'm a mature Frenchwoman. I am not afraid of prejudice, and I know the situation here. Don't forget, I got to New Orleans sixteen years ago."

Their decision to marry, though legal, was fraught with social implications and challenges that only a proudly secure Black man and an idealistic White woman would have been willing to risk. The couple took up residence in Tassin's house on Roman Street.

*   *   *

Joachim and Pauline had good reason to be careful and concerned. In Louisiana, interracial marriage had long been omnipresent and simultaneously illegal. Before statehood, during the French and Spanish colonial periods, interracial marriage was illegal yet widely tolerated by way of indifferent enforcement.

After 1808, once the United States was in possession of Louisiana, until after the Civil War, interracial marriage continued to be both illegal in Louisiana and tolerated by authorities. Then in a very uncharacteristic decision for a Southern state, three years after the Civil War ended, in 1868, Louisiana became the only Southern state to repeal its antimiscegenation laws—likely because there were so many interracial relationships. This novel legal tolerance of interracial marriage in Louisiana lasted for twenty-six years, a period during which Joachim and Pauline were married.

When the Louisiana legislature fell in line in 1894 with all the other Southern states and again prohibited interracial marriage, it became the last Southern state to do so.

The twists and turns in legislation sanctioning and forbidding slave marriage and interracial marriage was of obvious consequence to Joachim Tassin. For years, he had of necessity stepped gingerly around them. He first married a free Black woman during the Civil War when he was in fact still a slave, though not recognized as such. The second time, as a Black man, he married a White woman amid the Jim Crow era.

To optimize their life together in racist-dominated New Orleans, Tassin and Pauline Millon resorted to deft legal maneuvers seasoned with a bit of purposeful misrepresentation. Official documents Tassin and Millon filed in New Orleans over the twenty years of their life together reveal how they managed the tangled complexities governing interracial relationships. When it became necessary to respond to the changing laws governing interracial marriage in Louisiana, Tassin and Millon proved particularly adept.

Two years after interracial marriage was no longer legal, in 1896, and after the *Plessy* case had been decided by the Supreme Court, the couple planned a trip outside of Louisiana, indeed, to go abroad. "We must be careful," Tassin would have warned Pauline before filing their passport application. "I am afraid for us, for both of us, given the way things are going."

They applied for passports to Europe. Based on their preliminary discussion at home, Pauline represented herself as an unmarried White lady. Tassin renewed his separate passport as a Black resident and citizen.

In 1900, Joachim answered the centennial census. He stated that he was born in Louisiana, was head of his household, owned his own home at 1471 North Roman Street in New Orleans "free and clear of any mortgage," was a Black man, married in 1886 to Pauline Tassin, a White woman. His father's and his mother's birthplace was "Louisiana."

In her own 1900 census filing, Pauline certified that she was born in France and was White. In 1900, the couple was responding to a federal census, not applying for a local license, so Tassin and Pauline felt at liberty to be candid. Besides, they had been married in 1886. The couple felt that their marriage under the more lenient Louisiana statutes prior to 1894 was sufficient protection to allow their candid responses in the federal centennial census. They could prove that they had been married back when interracial unions were legal in New Orleans. Joachim and Pauline were, so to speak, grandfathered in.

In 1904, Joachim and Pauline went together to a notarial office in New Orleans to take care of the serious business of revising Joachim's last will and testament. Three witnesses were dutifully present to certify the document. Except for minor cash bequests to a friend, to the children of another friend, and to a goddaughter, Joachim left his entire estate to Pauline. But he designated Pauline not as his wife but as my "universal legatee . . . and my testamentary executrix and detainer of my property."

By the time the census taker came around six years later in 1910, with Jim Crow sentiment more virulent than ever in New Orleans, Joachim had become "John" Tassin, his birthplace was now "Mexico," from where he "emigrated in 1835," his father and mother's birthplace was "Mexico," his naturalization status was "naturalized," and his race "mulatto." He did not own his house; rather, he was a "boarder." His marital status was "single." Pauline Milan (fifty-five) and Paul Serra (forty) were "household members." (Milan is how her name was spelled in the census; Paul Serra was probably the tenant living on the other side of Tassin's shotgun double cottage.) Tassin characterized Pauline as "unmarried."

Tassin's census declaration in 1910 could be interpreted to mean that he and Pauline had divorced at some point or that they had never in fact married. As for having declared himself a boarder, there is a possibility that since his will declared Pauline his "universal legatee," he might have found it convenient to let the United States government consider him a boarder and Pauline the property owner. Or by then, he might have signed over the deed to his house to Pauline.

Looking back at Tassin's passport and legal filings over a decade reveals his evolving state of mind. When they obtained passports, he was wary about the consequences of revealing in a local office that he was married to a White woman. Tassin's almost entirely reconstructed vital statistics by the end of his life was a carpet of craftily constructed lies. These expose his consuming fear during the heyday of the Jim Crow era, and his retreat from the sense of relative self-assured belonging that he had enjoyed as late as 1900. Toward the end of Tassin's life, the legal atmosphere and the climate of public opinion in the South had become so reactionary, so racist, so dangerous for their situation that Tassin did all that he could to protect Pauline and to cloud his own past as a formerly enslaved Black man. He had no longer been born in America, nor had his parents, who were in fact, as he well knew, a Black slave and a White plantation owner.

Joachim Tassin was introduced to the benefits of self-protective identity shrouding when he was purchased by Godchaux. Late in life, Joachim redeployed that strategy not by omission, but this time by laying down a fraudulent paper trail that began with his passport assertions in 1896 and continued for the next fourteen years, up until his death, and forever thereafter into the mythology about the Godchaux-Tassin relationship.

24

Trouble In The Fields

Leon Godchaux believed that equal wages must be paid for equal work to both Black and White people alike. Nevertheless, his conviction was anchored in its own time and place, in the competitive commercial norm of his day.

After the Civil War, with troves of men coming home and the massive enslaved population liberated, the surplus labor pool forced wages down on every Louisiana plantation. By the 1870s and 1880s, with the regional agricultural economy still crippled, the going wage rate for both White and Black agricultural labor scaled from fifty or sixty cents per day ($14–$15 today) for field workers up to a dollar a day ($29 today) for specialists in the mills. A day's work was sunup to sundown, what some locals called "from can't see to can't see."

Discontent, as might be expected, became rampant. Inspired by the trade union movement up North, a coalition of worker leaders in the South began to organize. The loosely structured groups that formed among agricultural workers in Louisiana reached out and affiliated with the Knights of Labor, officially known since its founding in 1869 in Philadelphia as the Noble and Holy Order of the Knights of Labor—the first major collective labor organization in the United States labor movement.

In south Louisiana, all through the cane belt, the Knights initiated an organizational drive to attract sugar workers. A distinctive feature of this early labor initiative was that White and Black workers congregated together in regional subdivisions called assemblies. The goals of the movement, which ultimately extended in the South far beyond the sugar industry, were higher wages, better working conditions, and "United States money" instead of "commissary pasteboard," the company store script in which so many laborers were still paid instead of cash. To safely, and surreptitiously, organize and communicate with one another in the closely supervised sugar lands, the Knights resorted to the use of code words and secret phrases. The scale and power of the movement in the sugar belt was initially nominal.

By the mid-1880s, the Knights had gained enough strength in the Louisiana sugar trade to initiate action. In October of 1887, just before the crucial grinding season, sugar plantation workers throughout Lafourche Parish demanded higher wages. Their demands were rebuffed. A massive strike ensued across the sugar belt, with equally massive reprisals.

* * *

Leaders and owners within the Louisiana planter community had been preparing for trouble for years. They had watched with alarm as freed workers began to assert their rights and their power. In 1877, a decade before the strike, a group of industry leaders formed the Louisiana Sugar Planters Association. The primary aims of the LSPA were to defuse labor collectives, to confront uprisings, and in addition to further profitability and scientific progress in an increasingly competitive industry. Beet sugar produced outside of the Louisiana sugar lands was becoming a competitive factor.

At its core, the LSPA was a collective of wealthy, politically powerful planters, centered around their personal membership in several of the most elite social clubs and business organizations in New Orleans. Upon call, state militia were available to these influential White landowners. The LSPA, with its network and influence all through the sugar parishes, was determined to crush the Knights, using every weapon, be it legislative or military. Intimidation and violence were not out of the question. Members pledged an aggressive united front.

In swift response to the 1887 uprising, the LSPA swung into action. They announced that each planter member would refuse to hire any worker discharged from another plantation or anyone who had voluntarily left the plantation on which they were employed. Furthermore, any worker discharged would be required to leave their plantation within twenty-four hours and would be subject to eviction by local authorities.

There was violence and bloodshed directed by management, executed by sheriff's posses and local militants. The strike was resolved with a slight wage increase throughout the sugar belt, without working conditions being improved. The strike was only minimally successful because the LSPA was so powerful.

Leon Godchaux, though a major figure in the industry, and by the 1880s eminently qualified by scale of landownership, was not a member of the Louisiana Sugar Planters Association. What explains his absence? Perhaps he disapproved of the LSPA's high-handed, roughshod methods. Or perhaps his social standing as an immigrant Jew, which kept him out of certain prominent clubs in New Orleans, might also have disqualified him from joining in with the planter elite.

*   *   *

By 1890, Leon Godchaux, aging and yet indefatigable, had his far-flung interests operating smoothly. His well-educated sons (more about them later) were moving into management, most of them already well beyond initial training stages. More than simply operating smoothly, his humming sugar empire out of town and his popular store and efficient clothing factory in town were operating at capacity. By 1894, with the support of roughly 350 workers, the total production at Reserve amounted to an astonishing 64,000 pounds of refined sugar a *day* during grinding season. By 1897, the total production at Reserve alone climbed to 12.3 million pounds.

*   *   *

In 1896, the editors of the *Los Angeles Times* decided that life and troubles in the far-off Louisiana sugar industry would make an interesting story. The paper sent an experienced reporter, Frank G. Carpenter, to do the job. The headline of the long report Carpenter filed was "Visit to Louisiana's Biggest Plantation and Its Immense Sugar Refinery." His lengthy subheading read "The Story of Leon Godchaux, the Sugar King, Who Began Life as a Peddler and Who Now Can Count His Wealth by the Millions—and All About How Sugar Cane Is Grown, Cut and Ground and Prepared for Our Table."

To introduce his West Coast readers to the scene, Carpenter began, "I can stand in the fields and see nothing but sugar, sugar, sugar, as far as my eyes can reach. I am on the chief sugar plantation of Leon Godchaux, and Godchaux is the sugar king of the South. He has more sugar land than any other man in Louisiana."

By the time Carpenter's report appeared, Leon was no longer involved with plantation management. That work was being conducted by his sons. Leon had retired and would die three years after Carpenter filed his story.

Carpenter provided an eyewitness on-site account of typical labor practices in the sugar industry near the end of the nineteenth century. "As they work an overseer watches them, and a timekeeper goes along beside them and sees that every man and every woman is at work. The wages are very low. They get from 60 cents to $1 a day, according to their skill and are boarded on the plantation. They sleep in cabins, several of them lying on the floor and getting their rest as best they can. The hours are from daylight until dark, and there are few stops."

25

Trouble On The River

Over the years, the marginally effective Mississippi River levees at Reserve and all along the course of the river had been built in fits and starts by settlers who had relentlessly and often ruthlessly wrested the land from its Native American inhabitants. Once he entered the sugar industry, Leon would come to know more about the irrepressible power of the Mississippi to flood its vast watershed and wantonly destroy crops, communities, and land—land the river had deposited over the eons, land that was the foundation of Leon Godchaux's fortune.

In Leon's day, rural parishes were expected to maintain their own levees along the Mississippi River. This task fell, primarily, upon local landowners. A rupture in a levee was no trifling matter. It could all too easily result in the annihilation of roads, fields, houses, and livestock, not to mention human lives—the *tout ensemble* of communities situated perilously along the river. Given the flat topography of south Louisiana, even communities miles away from the river were often in peril.

*   *   *

The flood that engaged Leon Godchaux had to do with the infamous massive Mississippi River flood tide of 1893.

Years before, two years after the Civil War ended, the *New-Orleans Times* had warned, "Planters to whom the erection and repair of our levees were formerly entrusted have been so impoverished by the war that they are wholly incapable of performing that work any longer . . . while the imminent danger of a desolating overflow stares them in the face." Aware that the war had siphoned resources previously devoted to upkeep and strengthening of the levees, the newspaper was sounding a well-founded alarm.

*   *   *

During the 1893 flood tide, the levee at Reserve sustained a puncture so severe that it amounted to one of the greatest threats to south Louisiana in the nineteenth century. The crevasse (a breach in the embankment of a river, canal, or glacier), which happened to occur precisely opposite the Reserve town center, in the vicinity of St. Peter Catholic Church, endangered not only Leon's sugar refinery but also the town itself and, indeed, vast stretches of the region.

A reporter from the New Orleans *Daily Picayune* rushed to the site. He arrived as the continually widening crevasse was near its peak. "For miles back of the river," he reported, "the water could be seen covering the fields and flowing up against the houses. The crevasse itself was terrific and magnificent in its very strength. The roaring of the rushing water could be heard for miles, and when the witness arrived at the broken levee a picture of chaos was presented. On each end of the levee were hundreds of men driving piles and making as fast as possible a line of crib work."

Days before the crevasse opened up, aware of the unusually high and still-rising tide, Leon had anticipated trouble. He would have advised his superintendent to prepare refinery workers to help. He also took an extra precautionary step: he contracted and paid for temporary help from two hundred prisoners incarcerated in nearby Major White Row Convict Camp. In addition, he arranged for additional convicts to be available on a moment's notice from the nearby Sanchez Prison.

As soon as the crevasse blew open and water poured forth, alarm bells rang from churches up and down the river road. The New Orleans *Daily Picayune* reporter noted that "Mr. V. Jorda, manager of the Reserve plantation, gathered together . . . as large a force as possible and hurried to the scene. Carts and lumber and sacks were brought, and within a few hours the work of closing the break was begun." That crew included the convicts whom Leon had kept in his employ during the high-water period who were "sent for and placed at the work."

The threat extended far beyond Reserve. As the emergency signal tolled from churches, able-bodied people from up and down the river rushed to Reserve. Among those to respond was Mr. W. H. Chaffe of Woodland Place, located five miles downriver; Dr. Sidney John Montegut, owner of the New Era plantation in La Place; and Mrs. Archille Bourgne of nearby San Francisco plantation. Each of these planters and supervisors brought men and materials including sand-filled sacks and raw lumber. As the crevasse resisted closure, professionals including United States engineer Hardee (I could not find his first name) and Captain John Millis, director of the Fourth District of the Mississippi River, under the jurisdiction of the United States Engineer Corps, rushed to the threatening scene.

Despite the marshaled labor and experts present, the murky gushing river water was bursting through the levee at a rate of 63,400 gallons per second, or 3,804,000 gallons per minute, for a full night and a day. The uncontained crevasse gaped 90–100 feet wide. As a final desperate measure, Captain Millis arranged for another three hundred convicts to be rushed to the crevasse. The combined forces, after several days and nights of urgent, continual gutwrenching work, at last managed to contain the break.

According to subsequent accounts, Leon Godchaux in *propria persona*, at the time nearly seventy years old, was on the levee directing the all-hands-on-deck effort to close—to literally plug up—the gap. It was said that he spent day and night at the site, not only supervising the operation but helping to thrust lumber and sandbags and whatever else could be mustered into the raging puncture. By the time the ordeal was over, and the community had been spared drastic flooding, Leon Godchaux had spent $100,000 (today's equivalent of about $2.8 million) on personnel and equipment to counter the flood tide. There was retroactive speculation that he had spent something even more precious—that his tireless physical effort had begun to undermine his health. Years later, Walter Godchaux Jr. recalled this incident that had become family and community lore: "All of the plantation owners from up and down the river (brought) their people and their mules and their equipment to try to close the crevasse. *Grandpère* brought his forces to the crevasse and in the process of fighting it contracted pneumonia which hastened his death in 1899."

Whether or not *grandpère* was in fact hoisting sandbags and supervising labor on the levee those fateful days and nights is questionable. But he was for sure pouring in financial resources as fast as the water was pouring out through the crevasse. There is no doubt that Leon's assistance in terms of paying for a large crew of convict labor and devoting his own plantation men and resources to the crevasse site was instrumental in helping to avoid a disastrous and fearful 1893 flood. But in contemporary reports of those desperate days on the levee, there is no documented evidence that Leon Godchaux was in fact physically present.

Leon's role in helping to prevent a human, topographical, economic, and ecological disaster of unimaginable proportions remained appreciated for years and years within the memory of people in Reserve. By 1939, when they paid tribute to Godchaux in their book *History of St. John the Baptist Parish*, published forty years after Leon's death, Monsignor Jean M. Eyraud and Donald Millet repeated what everyone locally felt, "By ingenuity, perseverance and heroic bravery, Leon Godchaux succeeded in closing the crevasse. . . . To the day of his death, [he] spoke of this incident as his greatest achievement, and justly so because even today, Reserve owes much to him for averting this great catastrophe."

*   *   *

The ready presence of convict labor available for the crevasse emergency exposes the dark underbelly of the penal system in nineteenth-century Louisiana, which Leon called upon for help. A similar institutionalized system of prisoner management existed in other Southern states.

In a practice that began long before the Civil War, and continued long after, the Louisiana State Legislature subcontracted the management and operation of the statewide penal system to private influential entrepreneurs. As early as 1844, parsimonious and indifferent Louisiana lawmakers hit upon the idea of saving state money by privatizing the state penitentiary, then located near Baton Rouge.

Prior to the Civil War, the penal system in Louisiana was a modest-sized operation whose inmates were disproportionately White men, many being foreign born. Slave crimes and misdemeanors were dealt with on the plantation. Following emancipation, 4 million slaves suddenly became subject to civil law. As the historian Lawrence Powell has said, "After slavery, black freedmen were sent to jail. This was when the 'crime problem,' in the eyes of former masters, became the 'Negro problem,' and black incarceration rates soared for infractions both serious and silly."

* * *

During Leon's day as a plantation owner, the prison system throughout the state was controlled by a single private individual and his syndicate of investors. In January of 1870, Samuel Lawrence James, an accomplished engineer and master entrepreneur, with powerful connections in the Louisiana State Legislature and with Governor Samuel McEnery, led an investor group that purchased what was known as the state-wide convict lease. James, a Tennessean by birth, a large heavy man with a muttonchops mustache, purchased the initial lease for a twenty-one-year period at the bargain price of $5,000 per year. Between 1870 and 1901, his group of investors enjoyed the exclusive legal right by legislative contract with the state of Louisiana to control the state's incarceration system and thereby to determine what every prisoner must do. As a stipulation in the lease, James had the right, whenever he saw fit, to lease men at whatever price he could negotiate, to friends, family, private businesses, and, when need arose, to respond to emergency requests for contract labor.

The prison population by then was primarily Black men. James assigned a sizable proportion of that workforce—on average 500–750 inmates per year—to labor at his own plantation called Angola. Angola had been cruelly named for the area in West Central Africa from which the last ships transporting enslaved Africans arrived just prior to abolition by Congress in 1807 of the Atlantic slave trade. Angola, boosted by free incarcerated labor, became one of Louisiana's largest agribusiness enterprises, producing abundant crops of both cotton and sugar. When James died in 1894, he was worth the equivalent of over $60 million in 2022 dollars.

Convict leasing had been sanctioned in 1865 in Louisiana as an exception to the Thirteenth Amendment, which banned enslavement or involuntary servitude except as a form of criminal punishment. The practice of convict leasing was but another example, on top of condoned debt peonage and one-sided sharecropper agreements, of state government perpetuating—now in the time of legally emancipated labor—an insidious system of exploitation of defenseless, primarily Black human beings on behalf of a dominant White-ruling hierarchy.

In some respects, the system of convict leasing was even harsher than slavery. The prisoner served exclusively as a commodity for extracting labor. The for-profit commercial beneficiary of that labor assumed no responsibility for the worker's health, well-being, or future value. During the James regime, convicts—overworked, brutalized, underfed, and poorly cared for—experienced high mortality rates at the Farm and as labor sublet to levee-building camps and railroad companies.

(The future of Angola plantation as an incarceration site did not die with James in 1894. The Louisiana Department of Public Safety and Correction took over the place in 1901 to establish Louisiana State Penitentiary, still known as Angola, but referred to by locals colloquially as "the Farm."

That prison, situated a hundred miles north of Reserve on a spread of 18,000 acres, is today the largest maximum security prison in the United States and the repository of a barbaric past.)

26

The Godchauxs' Faith

When Leon arrived in New Orleans the Jewish population was sparse. By mid-nineteenth century, there were still only one thousand to two thousand Jews in the city. No wonder that there was but a single synagogue in town. The Gates of Mercy congregation had been established in 1828, a decade or so before Leon got to New Orleans. That inaugural congregation combined the newcomer German and French Orthodox Ashkenazic people mixed in with a smattering of earlier immigrant Spanish Sephardic Jews. Gates of Mercy became the foundation Ashkenazi congregation in the city. It was devoted to perpetuation of the Orthodox ways and rituals that had prevailed in Western Europe.

(Note: The designation "Ashkenazi" did not exist before the first millennium, when it began to be used to identify people like Lion Godchot's family, the Jewish diasporic population from Israel that eventually settled in Western and Central Europe. The Ashkenazi community has expanded from around 20,000 to 25,000 in 1300 to more than 10 million today, out of a total of 14 million Jews. Globally, there are more Jews today than ever before, yet less than 0.2 percent of all people in the world are Jewish. Approximately 90 percent of American Jews and 50 percent of Jews in Israel are Ashkenazi.)

In 1846, nine years after Leon arrived, and soon after he opened his store in the city, the New Orleans Sephardic community spun off from Gates of Mercy to form its own independent sanctuary called (rather poetically) the Congregation Dispersed of Judah.

Leon did not join Gates of Mercy or any subsequent Orthodox congregation. He was not aligned with the traditional Jewish rituals and strict dicta that he had experienced as an Ashkenazi Jew in Europe. The shape of Leon's faith, he came to understand, was not anchored to his homeland, but rather configured by his experience in America.

Soon enough, he had an alternative. The Reform Jewish movement was spreading to New Orleans. In the 1830s, Reform Judaism secured a foothold in Charleston, South Carolina, then the home of the largest Jewish population in the South. The Reform notion was to make Judaism both look *and* sound less foreign. Reform proponents lobbied for an organ just as in Christian churches, for the service to be conducted in English rather than in Hebrew or German, for yarmulkes and taluses to be as little in evidence as possible, and for women and men to sit together in the sanctuary. The thrust was to move away from ancient ritual and a dead tongue within the synagogue and to abandon insular social practices within and without.

When the Reform movement eventually took hold in New Orleans, it was spearheaded by a band of progressive Jewish residents. Toward the end of 1870, 109 founding members, including the by-then prominent merchant and well-known philanthropist Leon Godchaux, ratified the constitution for the first Reform Jewish congregation in Louisiana, to be named Temple Sinai. The group was led by Rabbi James Koppel Gutheim, previously the leader of Gates of Mercy, and populated in part by Gates of Mercy adherents who sought a more liberal approach to the formal practice of their religion. The congregation was popular from the start—around two thirds of Jews in New Orleans soon identified as Reform. (To this day, the Temple Sinai congregation remains the largest and most politically and socially progressive Jewish congregation in Louisiana.)

Leon embraced the principles of Reform Judaism. His religious viewpoint aligned with Reform principles. What Leon Godchaux was seeking in America, aside from commercial opportunity and respite from oppression, was not a sequestered religious haven, but rather a civic and cultural homeland. From the beginning, he aspired to fit in, to look indistinguishable from other residents of his adopted homeland, to become successful *as an American*: in other words, to assimilate culturally. As a merchant he wanted to provide clothing that matched the everyday needs of all types of male residents citywide and out in the countryside. He was determined to remain Jewish, but on the new and very American terms of Reform Judaism.

*   *   *

What must modest Leon Godchaux have thought of the original Temple Sinai synagogue building that he and his colleagues financed? It was a sight to behold from near and far.

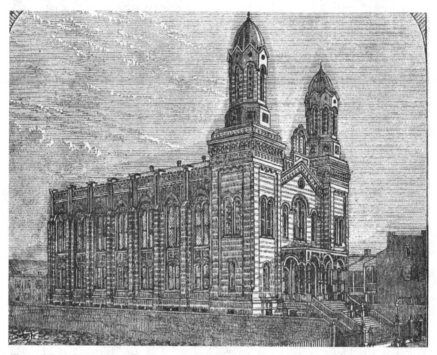

Fig. 39. New Temple Sinai, 1872. Located on Carondelet Street, between Howard Avenue and Calliope Street (now 1032 Carondelet Street), designed by architect Charles Lewis Hilger, the first Temple Sinai was imposing with its twenty-step granite staircase and was visible from near and far due to its paired 115-foot-high Roman Byzantine towers. In 1928, Temple Sinai moved uptown— following many of its Reform congregation, including members of the Godchaux family—from this statement building to a new synagogue, where it is currently located (with various additions) at the corner of St. Charles Avenue and Calhoun Street. The original Temple Sinai was demolished in the 1960s with its two iconic towers saved and repurposed. Engraving by John Williams Orr, ca. 1873/1874. Courtesy of the Historic New Orleans Collection, the L. Kemper and Leilia Moore Williams Founders Collection, acc. no. 1951.41.12.

Designed by a local German American architect, Charles Lewis Hilger, and erected on a lot purchased from the Grand Lodge of the Masons of Louisiana, this statement building was completed in 1872. Its paired 115-foot-high towers replete with Roman Byzantine details rose above most structures in the low-rise city. The interior of the temple was approached by a lofty, broad twenty-step granite staircase. The sanctuary seated up to 1,500 people. The building was given its full (and possibly snide) due in *The Historical Sketch Book and Guide to New Orleans and Environs*: "On each side of the entrance rises an octagonal tower [with] eight windows, and countless lesser eyelets . . . fringed with all the circles, curves and scallops of Byzantine and Gothic architecture, and capped by mosque-like green minarets."

Those looming totemic towers, visible from near and far, the building's gaudy striped red and yellow brick exterior, its intrusive and forbidding twenty-step podium entrance, and voluminous interior, taken together loudly proclaimed to predominantly Catholic New Orleans that the Jews are here—to stay.

That first Sinai temple (Reform-speak for "synagogue") was located on Carondelet Street, between Howard Avenue and Calliope Street (now 1032 Carondelet Street). It stood at the seam between old congested downtown where Leon and Justine lived and the newer more spacious community then forming farther uptown. (What was considered uptown in those days is now part of contemporary downtown—so it goes.)

A fragment of family lore passed down by Tommy Godchaux, Leon and Justine's great grandson, lights up the religious terrain that Leon and his wife were content to inhabit: "Justine, aware of the 612 strictures guiding Jewish conduct, recalled that Jewish persons were traditionally forbidden to travel on the Sabbath. The one practical exception to this rule is travel over the water, to allow for sea voyages. The independent and unconventional Justine, who loved to travel about town in her carriage, showed a playful creativity in her approach to this problem. She had . . . a basin (installed) under her carriage . . . so that Justine could adhere to religious law while maintaining her social schedule. From her Esplanade Avenue home, Justine and her washbasin traveled, unaccompanied, to the library and to lectures and concerts, and to her friends' homes." To the couple, Orthodox rules were not entirely forgotten, but they were no longer determinative by a long shot.

*   *   *

Leon's philanthropic devotion to Jewish causes was clear and bountifully expressed, far beyond his generosity to Temple Sinai. He was a major benefactor of the Jewish Widows & Orphans Home, an institution that was particularly dear to his heart.

Fig. 40. Jewish Widows & Orphans Home, 1867. This institution, founded to aid victims of the devastating 1855 yellow fever epidemic, appealed to both Leon and Justine, who were major supporters. Designed by Will Freret and dedicated in 1856, this handsome building stood at the corner of Jackson Avenue and Chippawa Street. In the 1880s, following the many Jews who emigrated uptown, a replacement Victorian building designed by Thomas Sully was erected on St. Charles Avenue at Peters Avenue (now Jefferson Avenue, the present location of the Jewish Community Center). The home, which provided both Reform Jewish education and a progressive secular education, became the inspiration for the founding of the Isadore Newman School at which orphans would be educated among children of more privileged, established New Orleans families. When the organization stopped admitting widows in the 1880s, its name was changed to the Jewish Orphans' Home. Photograph 1867 by Theodore Lilienthal. Courtesy of Tulane University Special Collections and Napoleon III Museum, Arenenberg, Switzerland.

The Jewish Widows & Orphans Home had been founded to aid victims of yellow fever epidemics. Leon had survived the scourge, living during two especially virulent episodes in 1853 and 1855. Yellow fever remained a feared threat in New Orleans throughout Leon's life (and for many years thereafter).

In 1887, Thomas Sully designed a new building for the association, which moved far uptown to the corner of St. Charles and Peters Avenue (Jefferson Avenue). That corner is today the location of the Jewish Community Center, built around 1963.

* * *

Above all his other philanthropic preoccupations, Leon was devoted to the success of Touro Infirmary. In his day Touro was the most prominent hospital in New Orleans, to which he donated generously and served as a director. Touro, as it is still known, had been founded by an endowment in 1852 from Judah Touro to aid Jewish immigrants. Because Leon had once been a Jewish immigrant, it drew his steadfast interest.

Soon after Leon's death, Touro's board decided to expand the hospital. It began a $225,000 campaign. Leon's heirs, following in their father's way, signed on as substantial contributors. Alas, as building projects will, this one broke the budget's bottom line even before it broke ground. The need was dire, construction ready. The *Jewish Ledger* issue of June 1905 reports what happened: "Just at the time when everything seemed most auspicious, and steps had been already taken to begin the work of construction, the Board realized that there would be a shortage of $50,000. Neither the Board nor the members of the Association aware of the conditions had formed plans how to secure the additional amount."

Salvation was at hand. As the *Ledger* went on to recount, "Last Sabbath day, June 10, the anniversary of the natal day of the lamented Leon Godchaux, and on that day . . . Chairman Rabbi I. L. Leucht received the following letter dated June 10, 1905: 'My Dear Doctor -Today being the anniversary of my father's birth (he would have been eighty-one), my mother, sisters, brothers and myself, desiring to commemorate his memory in some way to the benefit of the city and State where he spent the greater portion of his life, have instructed me to increase our subscription to the new Touro building fund to the amount of $50,000 [approximately $1.5 millionto day]. Yours very truly, CHARLES GODCHAUX, Executor.'"

A MUNIFICENT GIFT.

The Widow and Children of the late Leon Godchaux Contribute Fifty Thousand Dollars to the Building Fund of the Touro Infirmary.

"The Leon Godchaux Memorial Pavilion" to Occupy the Place of Honor.

A pen Picture of the Life and Career of a Self-made man whose name will be Perpetuated with that of Judah Touro.

M. LEON GODCHAUX.

MRS. LEON GODCHAUX.

Fig. 41. Mr. Leon Godchaux and Mrs. Leon Godchaux, published when Touro Infirmary gift was announced. A Godchaux family gift in the amount of $50,000 to the infirmary was announced in 1905 to commemorate Leon's birthday six years after his death. The trigger for the enhanced family donation was an expected emergency construction gap at Touro Infirmary that had arisen even before the hospital's expansion program began. The surprised, relieved, and grateful Touro board resolved to dedicate the hospital's new and magnificent entrance pavilion to Leon Godchaux "so that his memory shall be forever linked with the institution." That entrance and pavilion have long since been demolished. Courtesy of the Louisiana State Museum Historical Center, the Leon Godchaux Family Collection, Record Group 138.

The board, overwhelmed by this act of spontaneous generosity, notified Charles at once that it had "unanimously resolved to name the center pavilion of the new hospital the 'Leon Godchaux Memorial Pavilion' . . . so that his memory shall be forever linked with the institution." The *Ledger* hastened to inform its readers that the pavilion in question would be the "most imposing part of the proposed structure, its center, whence wards and rooms and operating rooms would ramify."

Within the year, true to the plans and board's promise, the front building of the hospital complex was demolished and replaced by the handsome Leon Godchaux Pavilion. The Godchaux Pavilion became the central element of the hospital façade facing Prytania Street.

Fig. 42. Touro Infirmary expansion plan, ca. 1905. The hospital was entered through the Leon Godchaux Memorial Pavilion facing Prytania Street, seen at the center of the front of the project. Courtesy of Florence Jumonville and Touro Infirmary Archives at the Historic New Orleans Collection.

Fig. 43. Touro Infirmary Godchaux Memorial Pavilion hospital entrance on Prytania Street. The pavilion doorway evoked a rusticated stone gateway to a grand country estate. Photograph by C. Bennette Moore. Courtesy of Florence Jumonville and Touro Infirmary Archives at the Historic New Orleans Collection, acc. no. 2021.0020.

Fig. 44. Touro Infirmary Godchaux Memorial Pavilion lobby. A simple and dignified gateway to the expanded hospital. Photograph by C. Bennette Moore. Courtesy of Florence Jumonville and Touro Infirmary Archives at the Historic New Orleans Collection, acc. no. 2021.0020.

The new Godchaux Pavilion exterior looked like an embellished, rusticated stone gateway that evoked the entrance to a grand country estate, iconography that Leon would not have countenanced even though the result was every bit as dignified as he would have approved of. A massive plaque, measuring seven feet long and three feet wide, was mounted above the door: "Touro Infirmary— The Leon Godchaux Memorial Pavilion."

The popularity of the hospital did not abate. To accommodate further expansion, beginning in 1934, the entrance to Touro Infirmary was again reconfigured and then again several times. The Leon Godchaux Pavilion was soon no longer an identifiable entity as such, though the space remained in use. In turns, the once-gracious Leon Godchaux Memorial Pavilion became a bulbous corridor connecting waiting room to the new X-ray facility and later a space folded into the outpatient clinic. Today, according to Florence Jumonville, the former Touro archivist, the Godchaux plaque is affixed to an exterior wall "three stories up and mostly obscured by the bridge across Prytania Street from the hospital to the medical office building and parking garage."

*   *   *

Like the family founder, Leon's children and grandchildren, for the most part, identified as Reform Jews (see Appendix I: Immediate and Not So Immediate Descendants). Most who continued to live in New Orleans remained members of the Temple Sinai congregation as nonobservant secular Jews. Leon and Justine wanted to express their Jewish faith and Jewish backgrounds in a modern way. Abandoning Judaism was the last thing they had in mind. But like so many other Jewish families in America, and Reform Judaism itself, assimilation has long been gnawing away at the core acreage, with the same inevitability as the rising tides and powerful coastal storm surges deplete the Louisiana coastline.

Today, more than half of Leon and Justine's descendants are no longer practicing Jews. Of the sixty-four men and women from around the country directly descended from Leon Godchaux who attended the November 1993 Godchaux family reunion in New Orleans, only 38 percent readily identified as Jewish, 34 percent professed no religious affiliation, 14 percent were Protestant, and a further 14 percent practiced a range of other religions. Of the spouses of direct descendants, 37 percent were Jewish.

Incidentally, the Godchaux reunion hospitality room was in the Marriott Hotel, where most of the out-of-town visitors stayed. That unappealing streetscape-demeaning hotel rises astride the corner of Canal and Chartres streets. It occupies the precise location where Leon's retail and office emporium had dignified the area with its resemblance to elegant nineteenth-century Parisian department stores. When the Marriott opened in 1972, the preservationist-minded weekly newspaper the *Vieux Carré Courier* gave it its "Worst Skyscraper" Award, lambasting it as the "Quarter's Worst Disaster," a cross between "a 42-story Scarlett O'Hara drag show and a Walt Disney Mississippi gambler's riverboat."

* * *

The size of the Jewish population in New Orleans has scarcely fluctuated over the years. By the outbreak of World War II, the city's Jewish population dwindled to about 6,500, a mere 1.4 percent of the total. In a postwar resurgence, by the mid-1950s, that number expanded to just over 9,000, which still accounted for only 1.5 percent of the city's population, a figure close to the national average.

* * *

Had it not been for Lion's determination and courage as a child, members of his family in future generations would likely have had a very different destiny. Those who remained in the French-German Rhinish borderlands would have been caught in the maelstrom as the world around them grew ever darker: first the French-German conflicts of the 1870s; the next generation tangled into the Allied-German conflict of World War I; only twenty years later, the onslaught would have probably culminated in a gruesome fate for the European Godchots—like so many other Jewish families—herded into churches and then railcars and then sent east, likely condemned to death by hard labor or extermination.

27

"Death, As It Must To All Men . . ."

The family assembled for a formal studio portrait around 1890.

Fig. 45. Leon Godchaux family, ca. 1890. Seated left to right: Edward, Justine Lamm Godchaux, Leon Godchaux, Leonie (Mrs. Gus Mayer), Paul Leon, Blanche (Mrs. Leon Fellman). Standing left to right: Jules, Anna (Mrs. David Danziger), Emile, Walter, Charles, Albert. Courtesy of Dick McCarthy, Amanda Chustz, and the Louisiana Historical Center, the Leon Godchaux Collection, Record Group 496.

The men wore dark well-tailored suits, vests tightly buttoned, crisp white collars (in assorted styles) just visible above close-fitting jackets. The collar configuration was the least uniform aspect of the men's attire: Leon's and four of his sons' collars were closed by dark bow ties while the other three sons displayed a jaunty variety of well-tied cravats. On both the men and women, the collars were high and tight, terminating under the chin. The ladies wore demure long dresses with ruffled tops. Everyone was dressed with simplicity and elegance in late Victorian high style, as would befit the family of the Duke of Clothing, emulating the latest fashion in Paris, London, and New York. Leon and five of his sons sport fashionably flourishing mustaches.

Apart from Leon, each family member stared unwaveringly into the camera lens as if in response to "Hold still now!" Leon Godchaux gazed slightly to his right and marginally downward, as if reflecting on his lifelong difficult, complex struggle that brought his family to this quiet, serene moment.

The family was arranged in a three-layered composition with Leon, as would be expected, seated at the center, Justine positioned to his immediate right, her shoulders squared, her gaze determined and alert.

* * *

By the time this studio photograph was taken, Leon had seen to the practical education of his sons. He was determined to judiciously transfer managerial responsibility within his multifarious enterprises to them. It took them all to manage the far-flung and diverse business he'd established. At the same time, for all his forward-looking care, though not unusual for the day, he automatically excluded his daughters from his educational priorities and from any future role in his businesses. He did include them with equal shares in his financial legacy. That is how it was—then.

Eldest son Paul Leon had been pulled out of Riverside Academy in Ossining, New York, at the age of sixteen to apprentice at the clothing store. He was now in charge of the retail, wholesale, and manufacturing clothing operations. Paul Leon would succeed his father as head of the clothing company.

Jules, following prep school at Exeter and college at Tulane and MIT, was placed at Raceland, where he soon assumed management of the Raceland refinery.

Walter, after graduating from Yale, was sent to Napoleonville to run the Elm Hall group, where he also headed agricultural research for Godchaux Sugars Inc.

Edward, after graduating from Tulane and subsequent specialized education in agriculture at LSU, began his career at Reserve. In time, he assumed control of the plantation and refinery there.

Emile graduated from Tulane and Yale Law School. Soon after Leon's death he established the New Orleans firm of Hornor and Godchaux. That firm later merged into what became the distinguished law practice of Milling, Godchaux, Saal, and Milling. Emile, for some years, took over managing the Godchaux family legal business.

Charles, after graduation from Exeter and Tulane, initially joined the family clothing business with his brother Paul Leon. After training at the store, Charles moved on to enter the world of finance, rising to become the second president of the Whitney Central bank in New Orleans (later, Whitney National Bank). Charles became the family financial point person. He also served as the last family chairman at Reserve and executor for both of his parents' estates.

Albert, after graduating from Exeter and MIT, trained at the store tutored by Paul Leon. He eventually fell out of the family line of businesses and opened his own insurance agency, Godchaux and Meyer.

Leon's daughters would become established as prominent women married into successful Jewish families in New Orleans. As they are not fundamental to the Godchaux business enterprise thread, I will say more about them later. (For greater detail about the lives, careers, and families of the ten Godchaux children, see Appendix I: Immediate and Not So Immediate Descendants.)

Another photograph of Leon Godchaux, possibly taken while the family was in the photographer's studio, one of the few that exists of Leon as an individual portrait subject, shows the entrepreneur staring into space in three-quarter view, head level, averting the camera's gaze (see frontispiece photo). In this photograph, Leon is caught in a moment of contemplation as if remembering all that he has been through and wondering what will become of his wife and their ten children. He is resolute and calm as if his normally busy mind has drifted out of the portrait studio, drifted into a quiet moment unlike so much of his life, almost as if he'd taken the opportunity, in this place dedicated to permanent remembrance, to engage in his own meditation.

*   *   *

On May 17, 1899, Leon might have visited his big new store on Canal Street, its completion one of his ambitions of a lifetime. That evening, he visited the Louisiana Industrial Fair with one of his sons where he "examined critically the horses on exhibition, expressing his preference for the finest." The next morning, a Thursday, he felt unwell and became gripped by a fever. Though free from pain, he rapidly grew weak. He died at home at 3:45 that afternoon, surrounded by his family. One obituary writer reported, "His death . . . was as easy and quiet as falling asleep. . . . It seemed indeed as if he but closed his eyes and rested his head against the pillow for a sleep of but a few hours' duration." Godchaux had no history of disease and had not otherwise been ill. He was seventy-five years old.

Leon Godchaux's heavily attended funeral that began a few days later at 4:00 P.M. "passed through Esplanade avenue en-route to Metairie Cemetery. It attracted much attention because of its size . . . and many were the comments . . . eulogistic in the extreme." Dr. Max Heller, rabbi of Temple Sinai, presided over the service. Speaking to people of all walks at the funeral—prominent city denizens, all of the Godchaux family, and employees and former employee beneficiaries of the Godchaux benevolent organization—Dr. Heller said, "That your loss is the loss of this large city, nay of the whole State, is testified to by the men and women who have gathered here. The general voice attests with one accord that here lies a man whose conspicuous prominence was due to native powers, to a supremacy of talent which marked him out a leader in the much contested sphere of industry and commerce. . . . He was a plain and unassuming man. His entire conduct refuted and rebuked the charge that the Jew loves display. His manner was the simplest, his tastes the most modest and unostentatious. He was the same to the humblest laborer as he was to the richest and highest of his fellowmen."

Leon had prescribed Joachim Tassin to serve as one of his sixteen honorary pallbearers. By designating Tassin a member of this small group of immediate family and selected friends, Godchaux made his high regard and warm feelings toward Joachim clear to the world on that day in 1899. Amid the Jim Crow South, Leon Godchaux saw to it that the once-enslaved boy and now free Black man was honored. The fiction of Joachim Tassin's guarded past followed Leon to the grave and into the press evermore thereafter.

* * *

In fulsome obituaries, Leon Godchaux was lauded as a financial genius and a humane businessman. "Mr. Godchaux never speculated," the *Daily Picayune* recalled. "His fortune was made by hard work and careful investment. He was very much respected by the small planters with whom he dealt. . . . Although he had more money in sugar than anyone in the state, he paid bigger prices to the small planters. He always secured the best—the best chemists and the best machinists, and put in the latest machinery. . . . He made friends wherever he went. . . . If he leaves any enemies, they must be very few. . . . Mr. Godchaux's employees were much attached to him and were always well treated. . . . He had a large number of people in the store and at times more than 2,000 on the plantations. . . . There is a benevolent organization existing among the employees of the store."

Leon also left, in addition to few if any enemies, an estate estimated by the *Daily Picayune* at $8 million ($245 million today), which placed him among the state's very wealthiest citizens. Other sources estimated his fortune at $6 million, adding, "Although of course that is more or less a matter of conjecture."

Leon Godchaux's last will and testament was dictated on December 8, 1898, to his friend, notary Felix J. Dreyfous. Requisite witnesses surrounded him, with Leon "sitting in a chair in the second room on the upper floor of his residence No. 1240 Esplanade Avenue corner of Liberty Street" (Today Treme Street). Leon left three lifetime annuities: $100 a month to his sister Pauline Blum; $50 a month to her daughter, his niece, Jeanne Marx; and to his sister-in-law, Jennie Lamm, $100 a month. The balance of Leon's considerable estate was left in equal shares to his ten children. Justine was not left out; on the contrary, she was entitled to enjoy all his assets other than the three annuities for her lifetime. He dictated, "I give and bequeath to my wife Justine Lamm the usufruct (usufruct is the right to enjoy the use and advantages of another's property) and enjoyment during the term of her natural life of all the residue of my estate without Bond." He named son Charles his sole executor.

Eleven years after his death, on October 17, 1910, still in awe of the man and his achievements, the *New Orleans Item* reminded its readers in an article about Godchaux, "When Leon Godchaux died on May 18, 1899, his obituary crowded the news of the day aside in the newspapers. The dramatic incidents of his career were telegraphed to the East and West and the far Pacific slope. Information of his career was in demand for his name was widely known. . . . Barely able to read or write, Leon Godchaux was the pioneer of modern sugar planting methods, the father of the central refinery system, the largest sugar producer in the South, and the heaviest taxpayer in Louisiana. Scarcely able to keep his own accounts, he was the most able manager of sugar estates in America and made his fourteen sugar plantations models for others to follow. Opposed to speculation and avoiding bonds as paying too little, he placed his money where it gave employment to 3,000 people and made others rich as it enriched him."

Headlining its 1910 Godchaux story "Poor French Boy's Ambition Have Fruited into Great Enterprises," the *New Orleans Item* published photographs of Leon's most celebrated early employees, Joachim Tassin "first employee," Carl Wedderin "the accountant," Charles Steidinger "salesman," and Rosemond Champagne. Leon himself, in a "photo by Moses," was set off in the foreground in front of his grand emporium.

Fig. 46. Retrospective celebration of Leon Godchaux's success, 1910. Leon Godchaux in a "photo by Moses" stands out before his grand emporium. With him are Joachim Tassin, "first employee," Carl Wedderin, "the accountant," Charles Steidinger, "salesman," and Rosemond Champagne. Still in awe of the man and his outsized achievements, eleven years after his death, the Item published a long retrospective piece about Leon, his astonishing career, and his most prominent employees. The newspaper reminded its readers "his obituary crowded the news of the day aside. . . . The dramatic incidents of his career were telegraphed to the East and West and the far Pacific slopes." Courtesy of Greg Osborn, New Orleans City Archives and Special Collections and the New Orleans Item, October 17, 1910, Part Second, page 1.

The *Item* story is filled with the commonplace errors of the day about Godchaux and his Creole colleague. It describes Tassin as "first employee." Nevertheless, part of the long two-page report serves as an extended memorial to Joachim Tassin, who had died a mere five months before the lengthy piece was published.

* * *

A year after Leon's death, Justine made the weighty decision to abandon Esplanade Avenue, pack up her former life with Leon in the Creole part of town, and move uptown. She wanted to be nearer her sons Charles and Edward, who were moving into grand houses on stately St. Charles Avenue. Justine, now a widow, wanted to live near her children.

Fig. 47. Charles Godchaux house, 5700 St. Charles Avenue, 2021. Built by Charles Godchaux in 1901 to the design of architects Favrot and Livaudais in keeping with the stately houses that were beginning to populate St. Charles Avenue in uptown New Orleans. After a serious fire in late 1941 damaged the building, the Charles Godchaux family moved permanently to 8 Garden Lane. Courtesy of the author.

Fig. 48. Edward Godchaux house, 5726 St. Charles Avenue, ca. 1890. Built in 1889 to the design of architect Louis Lambert, this house was purchased by Edward Godchaux in 1899. This view of the original house reveals, on its Nashville Avenue side, its Eastlake-style raked porte cochere and second-floor dormer porch. Facing St. Charles Avenue, upheld on whimsical columns, was a baywide entrance porch overhung by a jaunty protruding roof. Edward hired his brother's architects, Favrot and Livaudais, to make various changes, including exterior alterations to the house. This photograph was reproduced in the series New Orleans Architecture, *Volume VIII, "The University Section," compiled by the Friends of the Cabildo, Pelican Publishing Company, Gretna, Louisiana, 1997.*

Fig. 49. Edward Godchaux house, 5726 St. Charles Avenue, 2021.
The house today harbors embedded in its profile reminiscences of
the original. The Godchaux brothers' houses are still there on the
riverside of St. Charles Avenue between Arabella Street and Nashville
Avenue with one house between them. Courtesy of the author.

Justine purchased a far larger home on St. Charles
Avenue, at the corner of Constantinople Street, about fifteen
blocks uptown from her sons. She proceeded, in the words
of *her* obituary, to turn it into "one of the most elegant and
thoroughly furnished houses in the city." (The site today,
alas, is occupied by a low-slung block-long and block-deep

two-story brick apartment house of no architectural distinction whatsoever.)

The splendid houses on the river side of St. Charles Avenue owned by Charles and Edward (5700 and 5726 St. Charles) were situated on prime real estate in uptown New Orleans. Charles's occupied the corner of Arabella Street, and Edward's the corner of Nashville Avenue, with but a single lot separating their properties. Edward's Victorian mansion was designed in 1899, the year of Leon's death, by local architect Louis Lambert. Though renovated several times, it is now included on the National Register of Historic Places.

Comparing the site of Leon's house on Esplanade where Charles and Edward grew up with the location of their own far grander establishments on St. Charles Avenue, it is obvious that street-type-wise, the sons had not ventured all that far from home.

Fig. 50. Down Esplanade Avenue from the 1200 block (location near Leon's house). Esplanade Avenue, in Leon's day, was one of the handsomest streets in the city and the center of the French and Creole community. It was lined by cafés and pleasure gardens, its neutral ground planted with a double row of trees. The neighborhood was serviced by a mule-drawn omnibus. Photograph by Nancy Ewing Miner, ca. 1928. Courtesy of the Historic New Orleans Collection, acc. no. 1979.325.5249.

Fig. 51. Down St. Charles Avenue. Charles and Edward Godchaux found a place to live in the burgeoning American sector on another stunning street much like the one where they grew up, including fine neutral ground landscaping and streetcar transit at the door. Photograph by Nancy Ewing Miner, ca. 1928. Courtesy of the Historic New Orleans Collection, the Charles L. Franck Studio Collection, acc. no. 1979.325.5250.

Both Esplanade and St. Charles avenues were exceptionally wide boulevards, with a parklike "neutral ground" brimming with azalea bushes and a diversity of trees and other primarily indigenous vegetation—including palm, magnolia, crepe myrtle, and live oak, whose moss-covered limbs arch over the street, creating the iconic photogenic effect of a bower that so many love about New Orleans. The boys managed to move far from home, into the center of the trendier reaches of newer Anglo New Orleans, without relinquishing inhabiting a street of exceptional beauty in which, by the way, a light-rail line ran, just as it had in Esplanade Avenue in their day as children.

*　　*　　*

Justine lived in her uptown house until her death in 1906. She was buried next to her lifelong beloved husband, side by side, in the family plot in Metairie Cemetery.

During her life, like her husband in his philanthropic endeavors, Justine Lamm Godchaux devoted herself primarily to Jewish causes, most notably the Jewish Widows & Orphans Home, where she was a matron. "Few knew of her good deeds," one obituary noted, "because she was not inclined to have them made public." Justine, an avid reader, designed her own bookplate. There is one tucked away in an archive box at Tulane University.

Fig. 52. Justine Godchaux's bookplate. Unlike her husband, Justine was well educated and literate in both French and English. Framed by a live oak tree, so present in New Orleans, her bookplate features a slight single-masted sailing vessel underway—a reference to her immigrant past or to the small pleasure craft that plied the waters of Lake Pontchartrain. Courtesy of Tulane University Special Collections.

Justine's funeral, conducted by Dr. Max Heller, rabbi of Temple Sinai, took place at her St. Charles Avenue house. She lay in an open coffin surrounded not just by family members, but also by over three hundred floral arrangements that arrived all through the day, sent by friends, family, and admirers. Justine's pallbearers were her seven sons, her two sons-in-law (Leon Fellman and Gus Mayer), and one grandson (Walter Denziger). She was described by various obituary writers in various formats as "one whose life had amounted to something, one who had striven to uplift and benefit others." A solemn cortege proceeded from her residence out to Metairie Cemetery, where Justine was interred next to Leon.

In her own hand, Mrs. Godchaux declared how her estate would be distributed, memoralization of the end of the first generation of the Leon Godchaux family in New Orleans:

> I give to Armide Lamm, my sister, an annuity during her life time of $100 per month, which annuity, however, only to begin at the death of her mother, my sister-in-law, Mrs. Jenny Lamm, who is now in receipt of a like annuity under the will of my late husband, Leon Godchaux. . . .
>
> To my daughter Blanche, wife of Leon Fellman, I give my entire house-hold effects contained in my residence, 4007 St. Charles Avenue, and grant her the privilege of purchasing said residence as it now exists for the original purchase price paid for same. I request my executor to divide my jewelry amongst my three daughters. I give the balance of my estate to my children . . . share and share alike. . . .
>
> I appoint my son Charles Godchaux executor. . . . This wholly dated, written and signed by me with my own hand at New

Orleans this thirteenth day of June, 1903 (signed) Justine Lamm Godchaux.

*   *   *

Leon and Justine's burial site in Metairie Cemetery occupies ground that was formerly part of Metairie Racecourse.

Fig. 53. Metairie Racecourse, ca. 1867. The elliptical mile-long track and grandstand were parallel to Metairie Road on the south, bounded on the east by Shell Road and the New Basin Canal. The track had opened in 1838, the year after Leon arrived in New Orleans. After it closed in 1872, new development opportunities occurred. The recently organized Temple Sinai congregation was looking for burial ground for its members. Photograph by Theodore Lilienthal. Courtesy of Tulane University Special Collections and the Napoleon III Museum, Arenenberg, Switzerland.

By 1872, the last race was run, the racecourse had folded, and the land was soon sold for development—specifically as a Christian cemetery. Most of the other cemeteries in town were managed by the Catholic archdiocese. For Jews, Gates of Prayer and Dispersed of Judah had their own cemeteries. Temple Sinai's congregants had no dedicated burial space.

A new cemetery in town with abundant land caught the attention of the newly established Temple Sinai board, itself on the hunt for cemetery space for its own people. Leon Godchaux was then a forty-eight-year-old congregation member. The new owners of the racetrack property, after due deliberation, generously offered forty plots to the Sinai supplicants. Leon became one of those first Sinai congregants to subscribe to a burial plot in the Jewish burial ground within Metairie Cemetery.

*   *   *

Justine and Leon's gray granite tombstone ensemble sits alongside a curved road in an area not designated as such, but surely is the "Jewish section" of Metairie Cemetery. Names of the entombed all around them are family members and members of the city's early Reform Jewish community. Their comparatively modest grave site, designated Section 84, Lots 18 and 19, is approached by two short steps. The steps rise onto a grass-covered mounded plinth erected to keep the memorial area above the high-water table. Their slightly elevated terrain was an alternative to the traditional elaborately sculpted and constructed aboveground, often ornamented stone tomb structures so common in New Orleans. Their simple upright plaque raised on the elevated plinth reads:

LEON GODCHAUX
Born in France June 10, 1824
Died in New Orleans, LA May 18, 1899

JUSTINE LAMM GODCHAUX
Born in France April 18, 1838
Died in New Orleans, LA December 29, 1906

There is no florid quote, no sentimental statement, no comment of remembrance.

Fig. 54. Metairie Cemetery, Leon and Justine's burial site. A modest stone stairway leads up to their simple tomb monument seen in the background. The burial site is elevated to raise their graves above the water table. Courtesy of the author.

Fig. 55 Metairie Cemetery, Leon Godchaux and Justine Lamm Godchaux's tomb monument. Eschewing an elaborate sepulcher, traditional among prominent New Orleans families in their day (and still today), in which bodies would be housed, Leon and Justine's grave site is marked only by a straightforward cenotaph. The monument, erected above their separate in-ground graves, summarizes in the simplest terms their lifetime journey. Their gravestones, a few yards from the monument (not shown) are simple, small, rectangular marble plaques set in the ground inscribed with only their names. Courtesy of the author.

* * *

Through the years, Joachim Tassin's devotion to the Godchaux clothing business never flagged, save for his brief experiment as an independent merchant. In time, his importance to the Godchaux mercantile enterprise was memorialized in the press. Just months after his death, during the Jim Crow era, the *Picayune* ran the previously mentioned Godchaux story that incorporated a shoulder-length three-quarter view of Tassin, formally attired in a stiff wing-tipped collar shirt, black bow tie, and dinner jacket. The image of Tassin was prominently inset on the page just beneath a larger equally formal, dignified picture of Leon Godchaux; both portraits were projected in front of a photograph of the façade of the new Canal Street store.

Fig. 56. Leon Godchaux, Joachim Tassin, and the Godchaux building. Tassin's key role at the store was emphasized by his prominent position in this detail of a newspaper illustration, which also included portraits of other important store employees (see Fig. 46). The New Orleans Item, *October 17, 1910, part 2, page 1. Courtesy of the Louisiana State Museum Historical Center. Leon Godchaux Family Collection, Record Group 138.*

Joachim remained actively engaged in work at Godchaux's for nine years beyond Leon's lifetime. Before retiring, he helped to train the next family generation. Upon retirement, he drew a generous pension from the firm. During the two years between Tassin's retirement and his death, Godchaux's was such a deep part of Joachim Tassin's life that the pensioned, elderly Creole gentleman, dressed smartly as if going to work, would frequently wander over to the store to visit his friends and lifelong colleagues.

Joachim Tassin died on May 2, 1910. He was described in his *Daily Picayune* obituary as "a native of Jamaica." His reported life story began (inaccurately), "It was sixty-five years ago when Mr. Tassin began his career with the late Leon Godchaux. It was about that time that Mr. Godchaux, as a peddler, began his career. His first employee was Tassin who assisted him with his pack and bundles."

Joachim Tassin was interred beside his first wife, Marie, in the handsome tomb that he had purchased in Square 2 of St. Louis Cemetery No. 2.

Fig. 57. Joachim Tassin's tomb, St. Louis Cemetery No. 2. Tassin chose to be buried alongside his first wife, Marie-Madeleine-Elene Coustaut. Their tomb is listed by the Archdiocese of New Orleans, which oversees the cemetery, as "elevated tomb No. 1 in the 1st alley to the right facing the sun." Photograph courtesy of Jari C. Honora.

*   *   *

The succession Tassin left for Marie Pauline Millon included an impressive list of properties. There was a narrow sixteen-foot-wide by one-hundred-foot-deep lot on Roman Street with a house on it, purchased the year before his death. Tassin had bought another house and lot in his neighborhood in 1902, this one twice as wide with the standard one-hundred-foot depth. In his earliest foray as a real estate entrepreneur in his own neighborhood, Tassin had purchased from Albert Godchaux, Leon's fourth son, "a certain lot of ground of about thirty feet wide by one hundred feet deep, together with the buildings and improvements thereon." These were all rental property investments that Tassin managed from home and kept an eye on. He also left Pauline the plot in St. Louis Cemetery No. 2 that he had purchased back in 1870. Of course, his estate did not include the house on Roman Street in which he and Pauline lived, the house in which he declared his own "relation to head of house" to be a "boarder." That property was already hers, the deed probably transferred to Pauline prior to his 1910 census responses.

In October of 1910, five months after Joachim's death, and eleven years after Leon's, the *New Orleans Item* included the previously mentioned lavish two-page spread to "celebrate the 70th anniversary in the new world and in Southern trade by the great Canal Street establishment which is the first direct accretion of a young French immigrant's first scant stock of goods." Leon's life and deeds and Tassin's life and deeds were still known firsthand to the reporter and to others all over town. News reports so soon after Tassin's death expose a contemporary knowledgeable journalist's account of what everyone believed about Tassin's past, including his role and his interaction with Godchaux. The reporter informed his readers: "Leon Godchaux's first employee was Joachim Tassin, a native of the West Indies believed to have been born in Kingston, Jamaica, in 1825. . . . Tassin carried Mr. Godchaux's pack seventy years ago when he was a peddler on the river front. . . . When his employer went up in the world, Tassin went up with him. . . . Four generations of New Orleans citizens and citizens to be have had their clothes fitted to them by Tassin. It was no unusual thing for aged men to bring in little tots to have their first trousers put on by Tassin, who had done the same for their grandfathers. . . . Whenever any doubt arose on a business matter, if Mr. Godchaux was not about, Tassin would be consulted by the other employees and the difficulty was over."

In a rueful personal comment, the *Item* reporter seemed unable to refrain from adding, "Tassin who died last May leaves his second wife and two stepchildren. . . . Joachim Tassin would have died a richer man but for the eight years he spent in a store of his own."

* * *

During the more than sixty years that he lived in New Orleans, Joachim Tassin managed a complex life through a complex period, especially adverse for a Black man, much less a slave. Through arduous work, skill, and intelligence, he gained success and notoriety and wealth far beyond anything he could have possibly imagined as he sat alone, a frightened slave boy, in the back of Leon and Mayer's wagon.

28

Leon In Memoriam

When Leon Godchaux's life and achievements are assessed, a number of consistent themes emerge.

Sound judgment, forward thinking, an instinct for consolidation, a penchant for adaptation to scientific advances, and a knack for efficiency each contributed to Leon Godchaux's success in both the clothing and sugar trades. Over many years in the retail industry, he transformed his business from the ancient practice of offering one-off handmade goods, initially from a pack on his back, to vertical manufacturing and mass production of clothing that could be sold retail as well as wholesale. In time, he adopted those same ideas to reach the top of the sugar industry.

Large-dimensioned success at the store and at the manufacturing plant in New Orleans, as well as on his far-flung agricultural lands, was arguably achieved because there was no racial or class discord between employees and management within his enterprises. Sensitive to the racial divide in his workforce and in his culture, Godchaux was dedicated to a fair-mindedness that satisfied people who worked for him.

Leon Godchaux had an incisive, imaginative mind, liberated from reliance on past practices. He was forward thinking enough to hire modern engineers and chemists—unlike his competitors, who scoffed at the idea. He had sufficient courage to commit capital to a vision of the future of sugar refining with no assurance of success.

Leon learned adroitly from others and from his own experience and then skillfully and swiftly adopted what he learned. He was at once conservative and an adventurous risk-taker who backed his hunches with his own labor and his own hard-earned wherewithal.

*   *   *

Leon Godchaux's involvement with slavery has been misunderstood. At the end of his life, most obituaries asserted that Leon Godchaux never owned a slave. A one-line exception in the New Orleans *Times-Democrat* at the time of his death mentioned that "Leon did own slaves but freed them [implying immediately] because he believed it to be wrong to possess other human beings." All later published commentators, as well as Leon's descendants, vehemently denied that Leon Godchaux ever owned a slave.

It is notable that in the era when slavery was legal and rampant, no slave worked in Leon's manufacturing or wholesale business and, with the marked and extraordinary exception of Joachim Tassin, none in his retail operation. In his commercial for-profit endeavors as a successful entrepreneur, where and when he could have used slave labor, as his peers did eagerly and routinely, as was ordinary at the time, he did not. He did, however, use slave labor for child care and household help.

How to understand Leon's apparent aversion to slavery when it was a commonplace aspect of commercial life? Part of the answer may be Leon's Jewishness and humble background. He felt a profound if secular connection to his race, one that had suffered exploitation over centuries. Since birth, he had known the rudiments—lessons embedded in the emblematic Passover story—which would have reminded him that he belonged to a once-enslaved race.

Beyond this, Leon Godchaux was a thoroughly ethical man. His moral compass, a guiding impulse that set his aversion to commercial exploitation of slavery, proved to be one of the keys to his prosperity. The very notion of the Lost Cause that suffused New Orleans from the end of the Civil War far past the end of Leon Godchaux's life held no attraction whatsoever for him.

*   *   *

Leon Godchaux's own personal relationship to risk-taking is another aspect of his character that helps to explain his outsized success. He was commercially adventurous; he developed sufficient courage and self-confidence to assume risks, but he never gambled recklessly.

Leon's approach to risk varied in fundamental ways from the approach of the great tycoons of his American generation such as John D. Rockefeller, Henry Clay Frick, Andrew Carnegie, J. P. Morgan, Jay Gould, and the Lehmans. They were preeminent masters of risk who sought to lever their wealth and proprietary information, sometimes ruthlessly, to make fortunes. To those adroit entrepreneurs, daily business included high-wire finance—operations that bordered on gambling. They constructed derivatives, floated bonds, bought and sold (and yes, sometimes manipulated) securities on listed exchanges and in unlisted backrooms. They broke unions, sold off pieces of their companies, formed advantageous partnerships, and often leveraged the capital of partners, investors, and banking houses at home and abroad.

Leon's horizon line was lower, but nevertheless one lit by driving ambition. His ambition extended only across his own geographic region, an indisputable and creative ambition constrained in scope by his cautious nature. His vision led down a more conservative and narrowly focused path than Morgan's, Frick's, or Carnegie's. Godchaux's inclination was to expand carefully into realms and at a scale where he could retain hands-on contact with the enterprise and with the people working within it. He depended upon his own capital. His mindset was that of a French bourgeois rather than a freewheeling mogul industrialist.

Unlike many of the great American industrialists of his day, and the most successful entrepreneurs in the South, Leon Godchaux was not an exploiter of labor, Black or White, in a time when labor exploitation was the norm. He was not stingy with wages. Leon had experienced hand-to-mouth survival for many a year. He had lived on the edge of financial oblivion.

*　　*　　*

As Godchaux's self-confidence became ever more sturdy, he proved to be practical but not timid. Though he became the largest taxpayer in the state, one of its largest landowners, and one of the wealthiest and most prominent men in the South, he was guided by his humble past while far outstripping it. Leon Godchaux quietly and inconspicuously assimilated socially and culturally into a turbulent culture without, for the most part, being morally compromised by it.

Modesty was another hallmark that defined the man. Even after becoming wealthy and a major landowner, Leon never thought of himself as a landed aristocrat. He never attempted to have his name publicly proclaimed because of a charitable act. He regarded his plantations as a business rather than as a pretext and stage set devoted to a bygone way of life. He never dreamed of building a symbolically grand mansion to live in on his abundant landholdings, even to visit as a privileged weekend retreat where he could impress others. He did not erect a be-columned stage set mansion sited at the end of a long, stately allée of gigantic live oaks, surrounded by a cluster of kitchens, root cellars, and icehouses, not to mention the symbolic remnants of inhumanly overcrowded slave quarters. Leon did not share the ethos of the traditional Southern planter—their cult of neomedievalism and feudal nostalgia. Indeed, he chose never to live at any of his plantations. When he was at Reserve, his favorite property, he worked out of a modest office on the second floor.

The Godchaux store and building at Canal and Chartres is a life's end departure from Leon's hallmark modesty. Built in the last years of his life, avowedly impressive and grand in scale, the building expresses the man in full, and yet is still traditional in style, a bow to his never abandoned French heritage. And there was nothing symbolic about it: this was a place to work.

* * *

Leon Godchaux launched a revolution in the sugar industry that spread worldwide. In the factories, he replaced antiquated labor methods with science-based refining. In the fields, he introduced modern trams to eliminate backbreaking work and improve efficiency. Recognized in his own day as a transformative industrial pioneer, Leon was celebrated, far and wide, as the "Sugar King of Louisiana."

How he would have bristled at that soubriquet, Sugar *King* with its overtones in his day of European royalty.

The initiatives and innovations Leon Godchaux created within the nationally significant enterprise of sugar refining continued to bear fruit after his death. By the early twentieth century, Godchaux Sugars (as the company was eventually called) became for a time the largest sugar producer from cane in the United States. The centralized sugar factories at Reserve, Raceland, and Elm Hall were grinding collectively more than 500,000 *tons* of cane annually and processing it into nearly 50 million *pounds* of sugar. The Godchaux sugar operation was recognized as the very model of what today would be called an exemplary, scientifically sophisticated, vertically integrated industrial prototype.

On a salient day in 1904, William Howard Taft, then the secretary of war in the administration of President Theodore Roosevelt, visited Reserve to review its renowned operation. He brought upriver with him a small fleet. On board to view the Godchaux operation was an entourage of one hundred diplomats, politicians, and prominent New Orleans businessmen and a group of prominent individuals associated with building the Panama Canal. This stately occasion was commemorated in a photograph taken on the front steps of the Godchaux house.

Fig. 58. William Howard Taft and his entourage visit Reserve plantation, 1904. Taft, secretary of war, stands in front of the column on the left with Albert Godchaux at his side. Secretary Taft came to Reserve with a large entourage of businesspeople and government officials to observe a heralded modern model plantation operation. Taft and the others were spending the weekend in New Orleans while waiting for a naval ship to take them to Panama. The photograph has often been reproduced with an erroneous caption misidentifying the year as 1909 and describing Taft as president of the United States. Photograph by John Norris Teunnison. Courtesy of Brooke Robichaux/L'Observateur.

*   *   *

Leon Godchaux was intensely and forever French, forever and intensely a French provincial, Lion Godchot from Herbéviller, Lorraine. When he left home, Leon selected a destination where French was spoken and where French ways and laws had been established many years before. He could have emigrated to New York, Galveston, Baltimore, or Boston as so many French Jews did. He wanted to change his life, but he did not want to relinquish everything French about it.

When Leon opened his first store in New Orleans, he called it Leon Godchaux, French and American Clothier. The young merchant on Old Levee Street was proud of his French heritage. When his brother joined, it became *frères*.

When it came time to marry, the twenty-seven-year-old proprietor singled out a sixteen-year-old French seamstress émigrée, also born in Lorraine. Being a hardworking, cautious French provincial, it took Leon years of frugal saving before he would agree to move from his French Quarter bachelor apartment above the store at the port. The neighborhood he selected to move into was smack in the middle of the French and Creole community. Not until he was forty-seven years old, thirty-four years after arriving in America, did Leon renounce his French citizenship to become a naturalized American. Each of Leon and Justine's children were given proper names that would have found resonance in Herbéviller: Paul Leon (namesake of Leon's father), Anna, Blanche, Edward Isaac, Charles, Jules, Emile Prosper, Albert Charles, Walter, and Michelette Leonie (always known as Leonie), namesake of Leon's mother and her own father. His grandchildren called him *grandpère*. At home, the family spoke French.

*   *   *

Leon experienced life as an outsider. He was a poor village boy who plunged into a sophisticated, cosmopolitan urban world. He was a Jew residing in a Catholic city. He was an immigrant in a community that valued ancestry, bloodline, and tradition. At a time when slaveholders—Black, White, and Creole—were recognized as the most successful citizens, he barely participated. He was an illiterate peddler who vaulted himself into becoming a large-scale merchant. He was a Jewish city merchant who became a plantation owner with no aspiration toward the landed life. His native language was French in a community that was increasingly English speaking. If he could read and write, which is doubtful, he did so haltingly amid a culture that was literate. Even after he became wealthy, he shunned ostentation during the glamorous belle époque.

*   *   *

Lasting tributes to Leon continued to memorialize his birthday. To celebrate the memory of her father's one hundredth year, his daughter Michelette Leonie (Mrs. Gus Mayer) sponsored the Leon Godchaux centenary scholarship at Tulane, announced by President Dinwiddie, and reported by the *Times-Picayune* in its edition of June10, 1924. The award was to be devoted to a selected Louisiana boy, preferably a student in industrial chemistry.

It took until 1934 for Leon Godchaux to be officially honored by the United States government. That year, the U.S. Maritime Commission contracted with the Delta Shipbuilding Company of New Orleans to build a tanker ship to be christened the SS *Leon Godchaux*.

Fig. 59. Launching the SS Leon Godchaux. *Commissioned in 1934, the ship was present in Manila Bay when Japan surrendered on August 15, 1945, V-J Day, ending World War II. Some thirty years later, she was broken up for scrap. Courtesy of Jane Godchaux Emke.*

World War II imposed its own plans on the vessel: in October 1943, she was assigned to the navy, converted to a dual-purpose ship called a stag class distilling ship useful for troop or cargo transport. Renamed USS *Wildcat*, she was launched again on January 7, 1944, entering the Mississippi near the spot where the packet *Indus* had landed in 1837, almost a hundred years earlier, depositing Lion Godchot in America.

The USS *Wildcat* joined the Asia Pacific theater. She was anchored in Manila Bay until Japan's surrender on August 15, 1945 (V-J Day). Reassigned to Joint Task Force 1, she went on to participate in the July 1946 atomic bomb tests, known as Operation Crossroads, at Bikini Atoll. In January 1947, she was decommissioned and reassigned to the National Defense Reserve Fleet for layup at Olympia, Washington. In June of 1965, her name, as if in shadowy memory of more peaceful days, reverted to the SS *Leon Godchaux*. No matter, she was soon deemed obsolete and sold in January of 1968 by the U.S. government to Zidell Explorations Inc., based in Portland, Oregon, only to be broken up for scrap in the mid-1970s. In a way unknowable by the United States government, her trajectory—from glory to eradication—served as a poignant metaphor for the fate of Leon Godchaux's landholdings, refineries, and retail operations.

* * *

In 1975, the New Orleans Kings Klub honored "Great Men of Louisiana" as the theme of its Mardi Gras Krewe of SUNEV (Venus spelled backward). Leon's bust was prominently blazoned on separate commerative dubloons in each of the Mardi Gras ceremonial colors—purple, gold, and green. Above his image was imprinted HONORING GREAT MEN OF LOUISIANA. And below it, LEON GODCHAUX LOUISIANA'S SUGAR KING. The Duke of Clothing had come a long way.

Fig. 60. New Orleans Kings Klub Mardi Gras dubloon. In 1975 the Krewe of SUNEV (Venus) honored "Great Men of Louisiana" as its theme. Leon Godchaux's image in three-quarter profile was imprinted on gold, green, and purple dubloons, the traditional Mardi Gras colors, along with his birth and death years, stylized sugar stalks, and his long-established popular title, LEON GODCHAUX LOUISIANA'S SUGAR KING. Courtesy of Cynthia Johnson Hebert

*   *   *

Most recently, and only briefly, in September 1976, Leon's legacy was celebrated by a scholarly account of his life. The sixteen-page article appeared as one of the essays about the most important American Jewish businessmen, published in the *American Jewish Historical Quarterly*. Bennet H. Wall, author of the assessment, concluded his generally accurate account (with important exceptions) of Godchaux's life, "His origins were humble, and his education limited. . . . He rose to become, in his lifetime, the best known citizen of New Orleans. . . . His impact on Louisiana cannot be measured. . . . It is possible to say that he was the most important person in the economy of that state in the nineteenth century."

29

Collapse Of The Store

After Leon's death in 1899, Paul Leon, who had worked at the store in close collaboration with Joachim Tassin for over a decade, took over in earnest. At the age of forty-two, he became president and for the next twenty years, despite World War I, it was business as usual at the store.

Over the years, quality retailing kept moving farther away from the river, away from lower Canal Street, where Leon had built, owned, and moved his mercantile operations into the grand Godchaux building emporium.

By the early 1920s, the most popular Canal Street locations for upscale retailing had shifted to the 800 and 900 blocks, farther away from the river. Closely attuned to trends, Paul Leon sold Leon's prized grand emporium. It was time to move.

Paul Leon leased the Macheca Building at 826-828 Canal, on the other side of Canal, situated near the corner of Baronne Street, in the heart of the evolving now-most-desirable retail location in town. He immediately began renovations on the turn-of-the-nineteenth-century seven-story office building and opened for business there in 1924. It was no accident that the site Paul Leon chose was practically across Canal Street from Godchaux's main rivals, Maison Blanche, opened in 1897 by Isidore Newman, and a block away long-established competitor D. H. Holmes.

(I cannot write "D. H. Homes" without recalling Ignatius J. Reilly, the spectacular comic character in John Kennedy Toole's *Confederacy of Dunces*, as he makes his first appearance under the clock at the entrance to D. H. Holmes.)

Once renovations were completed to Paul Leon's satisfaction, the newly repurposed Godchaux flagship store topped out at seven stories, which made it one of the tallest buildings in town—a comparative skyscraper. It is notable that Paul Leon—more conservative, less comfortable with risk than his father—did not purchase the Macheca building, even though ample proceeds were available from the sale of the grand Godchaux building on Canal at Chartres.

Fig. 61. Godchaux's 826-828 Canal Street, ca. 1935. This was the penultimate headquarters store of the Leon Godchaux Clothing Co. Limited. Original architects of the Macheca Building, completed in 1901, were Toledano & Wogan. Reconstruction architects working under the guidance of Paul Leon Godchaux were Andry and Bendernagel, together with contractor Lionel Favret and esteemed architect Emile Weil who focused on the ground floor large display windows and iconic pedestrian arcade. Renovation completed in 1924, the firm moved in, forever a tenant at this site until bankruptcy in 1986. The building is now listed on the National Register of Historic Places. Photograph by Charles L. Frank, ca. 1935. Courtesy of the Historic New Orleans Collection, the Charles L. Frank Studio Collection, acc. no. 1979.325.1644.

At its new location, Godchaux's no longer catered exclusively to men and boys. It became an extremely successful top quality full-service department store, offering clothing and accessories for men, women, and children. Meanwhile, the manufacturing division continued to operate elsewhere but was eventually shut down after World War II.

After Paul Leon died in 1924, his modest, quiet, even more cautious, and very capable son, Leon Godchaux Jr., became president of the store. Leon Godchaux Jr., who had worked at the store since graduating from Yale in 1909, completed the renovation his father had begun and during his tenure maintained the top-quality merchandise and service at this one building Godchaux's had been long known for. (This is the same building in which my father, after graduating from Yale in 1931 and working a stint at the Godchaux factory, was in training to become an executive before he joined the wartime air force; where my mother worked during World War II; and where, in the summer of 1950, I had my first summer job as a distinctly junior clerk in the back office.)

*   *   *

Just before the dire years of World War II, on March 1, 1940, Godchaux's celebrated its one hundredth anniversary, marking Leon's opening a country store in Convent back in 1840 as the inauguration of the family's continuous stewardship through Civil War, Reconstruction, and modern times as successful merchants.

Together with the Godchaux family, the *Times-Picayune* underwrote and orchestrated a daylong citywide wonder of a celebration for a business that had become an iconic landmark in the commercial life of New Orleans. The newspaper published a special "Godchaux's Section." Below the banner headline "STORE OBSERVES 100TH BIRTHDAY TODAY," the center of the page was taken up by three photographs: an image of the then-current flagship store on Canal Street, a smaller picture of the original Godchaux store on Old Levee Street, and an oval inset of the store's current president, Leon Godchaux Jr.

Headlines of the individual stories that filled the pages of the paper promised information about the following:

Godchaux's Unusual History Dates Back to Youth with Pack

Godchaux's to Mark Arrival of Founder with Special Events

Godchaux Began Humbly, Rose to Financial Peaks

Easter Bonnets to Be Prizes in Millinery Test

Octave, Godchaux Footman, Proves Adept at Many Services

It's Lucky Friday Today for First Babies Born Here

At Godchaux's Today

Clothing Plant Executives Plan Visit to Godchaux

Rare, Historic Exhibits Arranged for 100th Anniversary of Godchaux

Pony Express Due to Arrive at 4 P.M. from Lakefront

The store went so far as to stage two elaborate historical reenactments. At 9:45 A.M., people who happened to be on the Mississippi River dock at the foot of Canal Street would have seen the once young urchin now all dressed up in period costume alight from a tugboat, step onto the dock, and from there travel by awaiting horse and carriage the ten blocks down Canal Street to the Godchaux store.

Fig. 62. On opening day of the elaborate 100th anniversary celebration of Godchaux's, 1940, Walter Laroque impersonated Leon Godchaux alighting from his carriage carrying an immigrant's carpetbag. (For some unexplained reason, one sign above the store entrance claims it is 1950.) Courtesy of the Louisiana Historical Center, the Leon Godchaux Collection, Record Group 496.

To top off the one hundredth anniversary celebration, at 4:00 P.M., a horse-drawn Pony Express wagon took delivery of a variety of goods at the New Orleans airport and hauled them downtown to the store "to represent mode of travel used to bring newest styles to Godchaux's years ago."

Inside the store, the sales staff was decked out in period costume. All six retail floors were reorganized the better to display samples of Godchaux's collection of vintage clothing, shoes, and accessories. On the first floor, one could get a whiff of "Madame Schiaparelli's newest perfume, 'Sleeping'" and, on the fifth, an eyeful of "Historic Costumes Worn by New Orleans Women."

In the same year as the one hundredth anniversary celebration, to help support the U.S. war bond drive, Godchaux management obtained special permission from the U.S. Treasury Department to have an American flag fabricated and draped across the store's façade, which it did from time to time during the war. Permission was needed because the flag was extraordinary: eighty feet long, fifty-five feet wide, and composed of seven hundred square yards of U.S. regulation bunting.

During its 105th year, to celebrate V-E Day, toward the end of World War II, Godchaux's again went all out in the flag-raising department. On May 9, 1945, the day after Germany's unconditional surrender, the company hosted its flag again, possibly the largest ever seen in New Orleans, to mark one of the most triumphant days in American history. The flag was again festooned across the Godchaux's façade to memorialize the end of the war on V-J Day.

Fig. 63. The Godchaux's American flag celebrating the end of World War II, 1945. The gigantic flag, possibly the largest ever seen in New Orleans, was seven stories high. Permission had been obtained from the Treasury Department to have the flag fabricated and draped across the store's Canal Street façade. Courtesy of the Louisiana Historical Center, the Leon Godchaux Collection, Record Group 496.

*   *   *

As to the destiny of Leon's original Canal Street emporium, the district continued to falter. By the 1960s, occupants in the former Godchaux store on Canal Street near the river included pawnshops, franchise restaurants, and especially wholesale goods sellers. In 1969, the grand fin de siècle Godchaux building, along with some of its nineteenth-century neighbors, was demolished to pave the way for the unfortunate Marriott hotel complex I mentioned previously.

*   *   *

In 1968, Leon Godchaux Jr.'s son, Leon Godchaux II (known by friends and family as "Pee Wee"), after a long stint connected with the Godchaux sugar company (see next chapter), moved over as president to run the Godchaux clothing business, a post he held until 1982. He pursued an expansionist policy, opening elegant new stores in suburban malls and regional cities.

At its merchandising peak, in the mid-1980s, Godchaux's spread far beyond its Canal Street flagship store. It operated six stores in the greater New Orleans area and had expanded into the suburbs and into nearby regional towns such as Houma and Biloxi. To fund this suburban-driven expansion, management loaded the company with debt far beyond previous comfortable levels. Under the appearance of robust health, there was trouble.

After his fourteen-year term as president of Godchaux's clothing, Leon II pushed himself upstairs to become chairman of the board. In an inner-family switcheroo, his cousin Thomas Godchaux assumed the post of president. Tommy became president of an overly expanded department store business, hopelessly struggling, saddled with debt, and under attack by experienced national merchants.

On January 6, 1986, the company declared bankruptcy. Leon Godchaux II, as chairman of the board, wrote to stockholders: "The continuing loss of sales and volume, and consequent loss of profits have produced such a drain on our financial resources that drastic steps have to be taken."

The company had gone down fast. Fifteen years earlier, in celebration of its 130th year of operation, Godchaux's sponsored a full-page proclamation in the *New Orleans Item* headlined "QUIETLY AND WITH PRIDE, WE'RE CELEBRATING OUR 130TH ANNIVERSARY YEAR." In a nostalgic tone that seems in retrospect to foreshadow what was to come, the store's statement began, "There aren't many of us left—the independently-owned and operated, medium-sized business. These have been the backbone of America for many years; we're proud to maintain our position in that category, and we're of the opinion that we're the oldest business of our kind (of any substance), in the country, which is still owned and actively managed by the founding family." Above this fateful statement were pictures of Leon and Paul Leon, "the Godchauxs who started it all." Shown below them "is the Godchaux family that is continuing a great tradition" where we find Leon Jr. (chairman of the board) seated, and standing behind him (among others) Leon Godchaux II (president) and Leon "Lee" Godchaux III, his son, then in training.

When the flagship store at 826-828 Canal Street closed, along with all the newer branches and retail stores, bankruptcy ended forever Leon Godchaux's heritage in the clothing business.

*   *   *

The demise of Leon Godchaux's hard-won achievements in the clothing business could be ascribed to family-owned and managed retail establishments' being a casualty of both the oil bust in south Louisiana and competition from powerful, directly competitive national retail chain stores that moved into New Orleans such as Saks Fifth Avenue, Macy's, and Brooks Brothers. And surely these were powerful forces working against the old, locally focused retail establishments. Parallel trends doomed similar legacy stores in towns across America. In New Orleans, Maison Blanche, no longer family owned but rather part of the City Stores group, collapsed into bankruptcy protection in 1979, thereafter revived when purchased in 1982 as a division of the (unrelated) Goudchaux mercantile group based in Baton Rouge. D. H. Holmes lost its independent status when sold in 1989 to Dillard's, a diverse national chain of department stores.

In the case of Godchaux's, there was no second act. As in other cases of family-owned department stores across the country, the loss of the enterprise was the result of failed anticipation by management of large trends in communication, transportation, regional warehousing, national advertising, and late-stage suburbanized merchandising sweeping America. Loss of the Godchaux clothing business through bankruptcy must also be ascribed in part to failure of imagination about how to capitalize on more than a century of goodwill, brand recognition, and a sterling reputation for quality, service, and integrity. It is notable and unfortunate that through all those years of good times and abundant profits, going back to Paul Leon himself, that the well-located desirable real estate held by the company in a prime location on Canal Street was never purchased. That asset alone could have provided funds for a civically focused foundation operating in the generous spirit of Leon Godchaux and of so many of his descendants.

On the last day of the bankruptcy, a final clearance sale was held at the Canal Street store. I was there. The elegant display consoles of dark mahogany and glass-topped sales cases no longer contained fine jewelry and colorful cosmetics: they were piled high with distress merchandise offered at knockdown prices. Eager customers descended like vultures picking over roadkill.

30

Catastrophe At The Sugar Company

Ever the thoughtful manager and planner, the year before he died, being a prudent founder and sole owner, Leon Godchaux consolidated his sugar empire and transferred ownership of it to Leon Godchaux Co. Ltd. The managing board consisted solely of his sons. Mindful of his advanced age and in good health, Leon wanted to assure his family's ability to continue fruitful operation of the large, thriving, profitable sugar company, his second great enterprise. Various sons were now experienced in the business and in place at key points of its operation: Jules was firmly in charge of Raceland Central, Edward had assumed control of operations at Reserve, and Walter was seasoned enough to run Elm Hall.

Fifteen years after Leon's death, the exclusively in-family ownership format changed once again. By act of sale in June 1914, the year that World War I broke out, Leon's sons transferred the Godchaux sugar holdings and operations to a successor corporation, Godchaux Company,

Inc. The new corporation issued half preferred and half common stock, all family held. The primary purpose of this asset transfer was to place Godchaux sugar holdings within the flexible, protective shield of a corporation.

Three years later, in 1917, just before the end of the war, a fire tore through the refinery at Reserve and devoured it. The company, being competently run by Edward, expeditiously built a new enlarged and more advanced, retooled factory able to process even greater capacity. It attracted more third-party growers, some from as far away as the Caribbean. There was now seemingly nothing in the way of end-demand sugar products that it could not produce. The company's stunning array of widely advertised offerings included "standard granulated, extra-fine granulated, coarse, medium, sanding, fruit granulated, superior-fine granulated, confectioner's, dark brown, and light brown, yellow and canary." Plus, Golden Star syrup!

*　　*　　*

When peace again prevailed across the Western world, business was better than ever; indeed the Godchaux sugar business had become one of the most productive in the country.

The Godchaux boys decided in 1919—only twenty years after Leon's death—to shoot for the big-time corporate structure financially speaking. Whereas heretofore the sugar company had been entirely family owned, they decided to go public. By now the three brothers responsible for the three divisions of the sugar company were settled and seasoned. Edward, in charge at Reserve, now fifty-two, was an expert in agronomy and sugar chemistry. Jules, forty-seven, had been trained in mechanical engineering and was running the Raceland operation. Walter, interested in recycling underused products and in charge of Elm Hall, was at forty-three the youngest of Leon's children sugar company executives.

As a first step, Godchaux Company Inc. was sold to Godchaux Sugars Inc., an entity incorporated in New York in July of 1919. The express purpose of this change in organizational form was to list the company shares in the public markets. First and second preferred and common stock were issued. Now, corporate stock of Godchaux Sugars Inc. could be bought and sold by any willing seller to any willing buyer.

Fig. 64. Godchaux Sugars Inc. Preferred Stock Certificate #461 owned by Charles Godchaux. Once stock was issued on the public markets, control of the sugar company was soon lost. This canceled stock certificate was found bundled with hundreds of others moldering on the damp, dark ground floor of the Godchaux-Reserve House— graveyard of the sugar company corporation's stock certificates. Courtesy of the author.

The boys had their reasons. The public market offered liquidity to anyone in the family who wanted to convert their ownership interest to cash. Being listed in the public markets opened new avenues for financing operations and expansion. At this stage, the family kept control of management and members of the Godchaux clan owned the majority of the company's stock.

As a condition of conversion to a public company, it was incumbent upon Godchaux management to provide a notarized certification of all of the assets that underpinned the value of the enterprise, the first ever enumerated. Beyond simply naming the plantations, the scale of each property and its boundaries were detailed. The largest by at least 50 percent was Reserve plantation. The other sugar-producing plantations and landholdings were listed as: Star Plantation, Badoil, Madere Tract, Belle Point and Labranche, Church Tract, Lasseigne Tract, Dufresne Tract, Perilloux Tract, Keller Tract, Vicknair Tract, De La Neville Tract, LaPlace Property, and Dutch Bayou Tract.

Entering the internationally traded commercial markets by floating the company's stock was celebrated by the Godchaux managers. The company posted a formal announcement in the *New York Times* of their intention on June 24, 1919, announcing the company's forthcoming listing and consolidation into a New York corporation. A week later, on July 1, 1919, in the *New York Times* and on the same day in the *Washington Post* management published a display advertisement proudly listing the array of Godchaux's commercial sugar products.

Into the early 1920s, the company continued to be controlled and run by the family. The 1921 *Moody's Manual of Railroads and Corporation Securities* documented the continuing tight Godchaux family management structure. The officers of the corporation consisted of five of Leon's sons: Charles served as president, Paul Leon as treasurer, Emile as secretary, and Edward and Jules as directors. Edward, known familiarly and affectionately to the Reserve community as "Mr. Eddie," remained the on-site refinery manager at Reserve.

The *Moody's Manual* revealed additional details about the accumulated hard assets and expanded production capacity of the company in the early 1920s: "37,365 acres in fee simple in Parishes of St. John the Baptist [location of Reserve], St. Charles, LaFourche, Assumption, St. Bernard and Madison, LA., 17,499 acres of which are in actual cultivation; three sugar factories with an aggregate daily grinding capacity of 5,500 tons of cane; two sugar refineries with an aggregate daily capacity of 1,400,000 lbs. of refined sugar; 63.82 miles of railroad on the properties, together with the complete equipment including 16 locomotives and 790 cane cars. These properties are situated on or near the Mississippi River within an average of 40 miles of New Orleans." According to *Moody's*, total sugar company assets in 1920 were $17,814,496 ($229 million today), with a net annual profit of $1,404,079 ($18 million today). The company was asset rich with large landholdings fronting or near the Mississippi River in southeast Louisiana, near New Orleans.

Though the company had a challenging time in the dark days of the Depression, even suspending its dividend (which no doubt upset family members and new stockholders), by 1933, with the nation on its way out of the Depression, Godchaux Sugars Inc. was again profitable and growing. Post–Depression profits were down from over $1 million per year to about $240,000. Yet all property, operating facilities, and landholdings had been kept intact. Production was recovering, up to 2 million pounds of sugar per day. The well-run company was described in industry literature as "the largest producer of raw cane sugar in the United

States." In that same year, industry publications admiringly reported that Godchaux's Sugars produced raw sugar from its own lands, from other planters in Louisiana, "but also large amounts of foreign 'raws' delivered through the port of New Orleans . . . [and distributed] through the territory of twenty-two states."

By the mid-1930s, the company was again functioning as a profitable, well-run enterprise with assets and processing operations, strategically and rationally divided into the three factory-focused groups as first envisioned by Leon, together with one cluster of land assets downriver:

1. The River group, with headquarters, cane mill, and refinery at Reserve, four plantations, about thirty-eight miles west of New Orleans, with a total area of 12,403 acres.
2. The Raceland group in Lafourche Parish, forty miles southwest of New Orleans, five plantations, with a large cane mill at Raceland, with an area of 10,341 acres.
3. The Elm Hall group in Assumption Parish near the town of Napoleonville, fifty-five miles west of New Orleans, three plantations, with a land area of 8,100 acres.
4. In St. Bernard Parish, twenty-five miles downriver from New Orleans, 4,476 acres.

*   *   *

In the heyday of production between the world wars, the company published its own promotional brochure. Titled

The Story of Godchaux's Pure Cane Sugar: Nationally Known for Superior Quality, the pamphlet touted the diverse forms in which "pure cane sugar" was available from the company to satisfy the eager needs of any and every retail consumer: a five-pound bag of "Extra Fine Granulated—wrapped in 'kitchen towel bag'; a one-pound box of 'Confectioners XXXX'; a one-pound box of 'Brown Sugar'; and a one- or two-pound box—or bag—of 'Extra Fine Granulated.'"

In Leon's time, and well into the first decades of the twentieth century, there was little if any awareness of the adverse effects of sugar on human health. The promotional literature had no reason to be circumspect or apologetic. Just the opposite. That same Godchaux booklet proceeded to treat the reader to a capsule history of sugar, written like a children's story, complete with illustrations of ancient kings' being paid tribute with sugar. "Travelers," it asserted, "went on long and perilous journeys, across unmapped mountains and dangerous seas, just to bring back a few ounces of the sparkling substance that was worth hundreds of times its weight in gold. . . . In those distant days . . . only the fabulously wealthy could afford to sweeten things with [sugar]. . . . [Today] for only a few pennies we may have a luxury that would have delighted a Roman emperor. Modern refining methods have placed it within the reach of us all. Nowhere can we better observe these modern methods . . . than at the Godchaux Sugar Refinery in Reserve, Louisiana."

At its center, the *Story of Godchaux's* brochure included a variety of recipes for the householder, each of course required a portion of sugar. The pamphlet concluded with a compendium of helpful household tips of every conceivable (and some hitherto inconceivable) kind. We learn that "old silk stockings make good dry mop," plus how to "keep goldfish cool," "mend glass," and "keep buttons on underwear and pajamas." To receive a copy of the brochure gratis—and what, then or now, could be counted sweeter?—one had simply to fill out the coupon in the back of the pamphlet and mail it to the home office in the Masonic Temple Building in New Orleans together with "a Godchaux Insignia cut from a Godchaux sugar carton, or cotton bag, and six cents in stamps."

Though surviving the Great Depression and two world wars, after World War II, Godchaux Sugars Inc. encountered enhanced national competition. To remain a top producer, the company inaugurated a major upgrade expansion in 1950 and underwrote continual efforts at modernization of its plants and equipment. As a result, the company remained financially healthy and commercially up to date going into the second half of the 1950s. Its Annual Report to Stockholders dated January 31, 1956, covering the prior two years, showed an earned surplus after all dividends were paid at the end of 1955 of nearly $6 million, about the same as the end of 1954. Though annual profits for 1955 were down from 1954, net year-end profit was still at a respectable level, more than covering dividend obligations. As a sign of its corporate health, long-term debt continued to be liquidated. At the time, according to U.S. government documents, "Godchaux Sugars, Inc. ranked seventh in size among all sugar refineries in the United

States and fifth in size among sugar refiners operating east of the Mississippi. . . . In addition to its own sugar the company's refinery handled a large amount of Cuban and Puerto Rican sugar imported through the port of New Orleans. . . . Products were distributed under the brand name 'GODCHAUX' and 'Raceland' through jobbers and wholesale grocers in twenty-one states, principally in the southern and central . . . territories. These brand names had become well established over a long period of time."

*   *   *

After Charles Godchaux retired in the early 1950s, Godchaux Sugars Inc. was run by Leon Godchaux's great grandson, Paul Leon Godchaux II. A tall, lean man known as Leon, or to everyone who knew him well, he was called Pee Wee. For clarity's sake, I'll call him Leon II. He was only in his late thirties when he assumed the presidency of Godchaux Sugars Inc.

A graduate of Exeter with chemical engineering degrees from Yale and Iowa State University, after service in the navy during World War II, Leon II began work in the research department of Godchaux Sugars Inc.

By the time Leon II took over as president, the original capable and respected children of Leon Godchaux were no longer involved in management of the sugar company. Edward had died in 1926; Jules died in 1951; Walter in 1952; and Charles in 1954. The next generation was in charge.

By 1955, problems at Reserve were brewing, even bubbling as if in a giant heated sugar kettle. The company faced labor unrest. The United Packinghouse Workers of America local 1124, representing Reserve's 850 employees, asked for a wage increase to bring compensation into parity with wages at other refineries in the area. The demand was for an increase of ten cents per hour, plus fringe benefits amounting to four and a half cents an hour.

The board, led by Leon II refused. It countered with a compromise offer of five cents per hour. Relationships with the workforce, heretofore peaceful and paternalistic in the way of a company town since the days of Leon and his sons, broke into explosive discord. There was more than anger and disappointment: vandalism, beatings, even several murders ensued as workers in favor of settlement confronted those employees in favor of holding out. During the devastating nine-month strike from April until December, 95 percent of all breadwinners in the town of Reserve were out of work; some were forced to vacate company-owned houses. The strike was so violent and so destructive to the community that it reached headline proportions in the regional press.

Finally, the Godchaux management's offer was bitterly accepted. But during the strike interval, the previously peaceful and harmonious community of Reserve was ripped apart. Dr. Gerald Keller, the town's historian whose entire family once worked at the refinery, told me, "The workers settled for the original Godchaux offer, but it was never the same. It was bitter, very bitter. Reserve has never been the same." At the same time, profitability in the sugar business was on the decline.

*   *   *

Then something even more long-lasting happened. Months after the strike was settled, in late January of 1956—quietly, without fanfare, surreptitiously, perhaps exhausted, and disheartened after the bitter strike— Godchaux sugar company management made a fateful move. In one fell swoop, Leon II, together with a couple of other Godchaux family members involved with the sugar business management, along with several nonfamily insider stockholders and directors who had accumulated shares since the company went public, sold an option to purchase *all* of their stock in the company. The option entitled the purchaser to obtain a closely held block of stock that constituted a majority of shares outstanding—in other words, a controlling interest.

The option was sold to a private unlisted corporation set up for the express purpose of gaining control of Godchaux's Sugars Inc. called benignly and simply the 52026 Corporation. Behind the surrogate veil of the unlisted corporation, the actual purchaser was the notorious real estate developer magnate and speculator William Zeckendorf Sr., his son William Jr., and their cohorts. Zeckendorf chose to remain unidentified, at least at first.

Zeckendorf's 52026 Corporation, a private holding vehicle not traded on any exchange, was created by Zeckendorf for one reason only—to cleverly and effectively, without disclosing his name, carry out his investment plan to take over Godchaux Sugars Inc. Even though the sugar company was itself a public company, Zeckendorf devised a way to gain control of it outside of the troublesome gaze and interference of public market regulators by setting up a private unregulated corporation as the purchaser. Nor was he obliged to bid in the marketplace for the controlling shares.

*   *   *

By the time he set his sights on the Godchaux assets, and for years before and after, Zeckendorf was known all over the country as the controlling force behind the powerful real estate development firm of Webb & Knapp Inc. At the time of the Godchaux deal, Zeckendorf was no beginner in the real estate game. In thirteen years, he had leveraged Webb & Knapp Inc. from a tiny unprofitable real estate consulting firm into a publicly held empire that owned and operated, through a maze of subsidiaries, buildings and property from New York to San Francisco. He had become a proven big-time finder of great opportunity in undervalued real estate.

William Zeckendorf Sr. knew how to identify a soft spot and swoop in. Zeckendorf had owned the East River site in New York that he sold to Wallace Harrison and Nelson Rockefeller that eventually became the United Nations headquarters. He had advantageously purchased and profitably sold in New York the iconic Chrysler Building situated on the East Side near Grand Central Terminal, and the venerable Hotel Astor in Times Square. He'd also been a major player in the Chicago Lakeshore Drive's Miracle Mile real estate market, in the development of Disneyland, and on Zeckendorf property, he enabled development of theme parks in Colorado, Massachusetts, New York, and Texas.

In Los Angeles, taking advantage of a needy period for 20th Century-Fox (now a subsidiary of the Walt Disney Studios), he purchased the acreage that he famously developed into the film studio complex known as Century City.

Zeckendorf's plan to take over Godchaux Sugars was well crafted. It was farsighted as well. It did not stop at taking ownership of Godchaux Sugars Inc. That was only step one. Step two was to spin off the operating sugar company together with a nominal amount of land to an operator in the sugar business. Indeed, Zeckendorf arranged as early as May 10, 1956, to sell the operating sugar company to the National Sugar Refining Company. National, in turn, was a subsidiary of the American Sugar Refinery Company, the behemoth of the sugar industry in America, listed on the New York Stock Exchange, founded in 1891 by Henry Osborne Havemeyer. The ASRC owned the massive 162-foot tall Filter House in what was then the industrial district along the river in the French Quarter. It was the second tallest building ever to be put up there. Zeckendorf's goal was to make money or to at least break even on disposing of the sugar-producing assets and then to exploit the remaining vast valuable acreage along the Mississippi River in south Louisiana held by Godchaux Sugars Inc.

Zeckendorf's stealth strategy was seemingly accomplished without resistance—indeed with complicity—from Godchaux Sugars' management.

* * *

The insider Godchaux family members and associates who sold out before any public announcement remained anonymous for as long as possible. They had George F. Scanlon, an independent investor who was only recently appointed chairman of the board of directors of Godchaux Sugars Inc., to cover for them. It was Scanlon, the *Wall Street Journal* revealed, "who heads a group of stockholders with whom the agreement was made."

Leading up to the fateful sale of the private option, the management of Godchaux Sugars Inc. had been ripe for manipulation. Leon Godchaux's son Charles, longtime chairman but not any longer involved in daily company operations, had died in 1954, the last of the founder's children to be associated with the company.

Robert B. Holland Sr. was elected as board chairman in 1954 to succeed Charles Godchaux. Holland, a lawyer who lived in Dallas, was prominent in the rice industry, but hardly a full-time hands-on chairman who knew the sugar industry.

At the time that Holland was elected, a new executive committee was created to run the company. This inner management group was composed of only Holland, Leon Godchaux II, and the company's largest stockholder, George Scanlon. Two of those members, then, were in effect outside directors who came to town for meetings. Leon Godchaux II was both president of the company, worked at the company, and the only resident member of the executive committee.

Holland died suddenly in New York on April 24, 1955, after less than a year on the job.

George Scanlon was selected by the board to replace Holland as chairman. Scanlon was well known to the Godchaux men who were running Godchaux Sugars. He had been elected a director of the company back in 1945, just after the end of World War II. In his earlier business dealings before the war, Scanlon had been slapped with an injunction order from the Supreme Court of the State of New York and enjoined—because of his illegal business transgressions—from acting, as he had been in the past, as a securities salesman and asset manager. By war's end, George Scanlon, a businessman with a checkered past in finance, was making his living as a director of several companies around the country and functioned simultaneously as a well-off private investor. He was what you might call, in this, the latter part of his career, a professional director—an amiable, well-known businessman who earns fees serving as a corporate director while he looks out for his own investments. He was not involved in the working operations of the company. Most notably it was Godchaux family insiders, not Scanlon, who were running the company.

*   *   *

In late January of 1956, the *New York Times,* the *Wall Street Journal,* and the *Times-Picayune* reported on the deal citing a statement by "George F. Scanlon, Chairman of Godchaux, who heads a group of stockholders with whom the agreement was made." No names named, no details about who was in the selling group. The account in the *Wall Street Journal* went on to say that the deal "was later confirmed by Webb & Knapp, and by Leon Godchaux II, company president. . . . Under the terms of the pact, the controlling stock interest in the sugar firm will be acquired by a wholly-owned Webb & Knapp subsidiary, 52026 Corp."

At the time of the sale, the board of Godchaux Sugars Inc. was composed of Scanlon and otherwise by a few family members, including Walter Godchaux Jr., Leon's grandson, and Richard McCarthy Jr., Charles Godchaux's son-in-law. It was led by board president Leon Godchaux II.

* * *

After the backroom confidential deal was made, effectively selling out to Zeckendorf, it was time for public disclosure. By notice dated June 13, 1956, some six months after Zeckendorf had privately bought control of Godchaux Sugars Inc. and arranged to spin off the sugar-production assets, Godchaux's management, led by Leon II, called "A Special Meeting of Stockholders." Investors were informed, or so the notice implied, that they would soon be asked to make a crucial decision about the future of the company.

The special meeting notice, a letter sent to all shareholders, was a document to behold! It characterized the upcoming meeting as advisory and simultaneously solicited proxies from anyone unable to attend. It advised that the special meeting would take place in twelve days, in New York at the Godchaux Sugars Inc. offices at 120 Broadway, Room 332 at 11:00 A.M.

The lengthy meeting notice—full of charts, tables, and arcane legalese—surely dictated by Zeckendorf's lawyers, but mailed under the Godchaux letterhead, would have been a staggering surprise to most Godchaux stockholders. Less than two weeks was hardly enough time for anyone to do the careful research needed to evaluate the sale proposition, confer with legal and accounting sources, or to investigate what was going on with this possible sale of the company, much less make any reasonable decisions or arrangements to travel to New York from New Orleans, where a good deal of the stock was held or to organize resistance or alternate proposals. Recipients of the solicitation letter were informed that "the proxies received will be voted . . . in the absence of contrary specifications, in favor of the sale to The National Sugar Refining Company of the Corporation's [meaning Godchaux Sugars Inc.] sugar refining, milling and by-products operations at Reserve Louisiana and in favor of changing the name of the Corporation to Gulf States Land & Industries, Inc." This one loaded sentence was asking for approval of two different enormously weighty matters: to sell the profitable ninety-year-old sugar business to National, and second, to extinguish the name Godchaux Sugars Inc. The remaining prize acreage, all the assets not sold to National, would be called henceforth Gulf States Land & Industries Inc.

The driving motivation behind targeting Godchaux Sugars Inc. for a corporate raid was openly admitted in the notice: "Although the Corporation is primarily engaged in the sugar business, its assets include more than 33,000 acres of real estate in Louisiana. It was these substantial real estate holdings that led Webb & Knapp, Inc. to become interested in acquiring control of the Corporation and to arrange for 52026 Corporation to purchase a majority of the Corporation's outstanding stock."

Reading a bit further, any sensible stockholder would recognize that although their approval was sought, as legally required, their approval was not necessary. Zeckendorf had the sale all sewn up: "As of June 1, 1956, 52026 Corporation owned the following shares of the Corporation's [Godchaux Sugars Inc.] stock, none of which has been recorded but was nevertheless owned for the Beneficial interest of 52026 Corporation: 63,501 shares or 74.7% of the Class A stock and 72,743 shares or 87.2% of the Class B stock. . . . 52026 Corporation purchased these shares from the holders thereof in May 1956." In what amounted to memorialization of a stealth corporate takeover, as likely Zeckendorf's lawyers insisted, the Godchaux notice included this statement: "The consent of the holders of two-thirds of the Corporation's outstanding stock is sought for authorization of the sale. The shares of Corporation stock owned by 52026 Corporation (consisting of more than the specified two-thirds) will . . . be voted in favor of such sale."

The letter also revealed that "half of the outstanding common stock (constituting all of the voting stock) of 52026 Corporation is owned by Webb & Knapp, Inc., a real estate company, and half (non-voting) by Alleghany Corporation, an investment company."

Zeckendorf both came out of hiding and revealed his silent financial partner. Alleghany had lent Zeckendorf the money to finance the Godchaux deal and got in return valuable options to buy Webb & Knapp stock. A few years before this deal, Alleghany, a cash-rich investment holding company, had gained control in a proxy fight of the New York Central Railroad and then made Webb & Knapp administrator of the railroad's Manhattan properties.

*   *   *

The Special Meeting Proxy Solicitation Notice also asked for ratification of a *new* board of directors, which would become the board of Gulf States. This succession board of fifteen members included the three Godchaux family members who had been involved for years in the management of Godchaux Sugars Inc.: Leon Godchaux II would become "President, Director and member Executive Committee"; Walter Godchaux Jr. was designated as "Vice President and Director"; and Richard McCarthy Jr. (married to Justine, daughter of Charles Godchaux) scheduled to become "Vice President and Director."

When reading this lineup of the proposed new board, a Godchaux stockholder might have assumed that there would be continuation of significant Godchaux family management of Gulf States. However, in other accompanying details, it is made clear that neither the new president nor either of these new two vice presidents—the Godchaux family members—would become owners of any form of Gulf States Land & Industries corporate stock or of Webb & Knapp Inc. stock. The Godchaux men agreed to be listed in prominent roles of the successor company. They would draw a salary—perhaps a substantial one—yet function as paid employees without any ownership interest. All the new voting stock in Gulf States Land & Industries would be held by directors connected with Webb & Knapp Inc. or their associates.

Leon Godchaux II, as mentioned earlier, did not leave Gulf States Land until 1968. In that year, he moved over to head, as president, the other major enterprise built by his great grandfather, the Godchaux's department store business. It, as we have seen, was eventually wiped out and closed bankrupt, while he was chairman of the board.

* * *

Sophisticated investors quickly expressed their dismay at the published per share price at which Leon Godchaux's sugar business and abundant acreage had been sold. The assets sold were everything—all the operations, all the improvements, all the land, and, in addition, 100 percent of the potentially enormously valuable subterranean mineral rights on all that acreage.

Shareholders were advised that the sellout stock price was based "on the values as carried on the books of the Corporation . . . but no representation is made that these are the actual values of such items." The other justification for the share price accepted by Godchaux management was the average exchange traded price of Godchaux Sugars Inc. in the months before the buyout. Before the deal was struck, management had not insisted upon an independent appraisal of the company.

Both of the employed measures of value accepted by management were flawed and surely inadequate to derive a fair price for the company. Book value generally materially understates the actual value of a company, especially a company loaded with unappraised passive assets that are not currently producing significant income. This is particularly the case when the company possesses thousands of acres of land laden with below-surface mineral rights in an area where producing oil and gas wells are in plain sight.

The second stock price justification—the recently traded average value of Godchaux's sugar company stock over a series of prior months—also, quite sensibly, struck the savvy outside investors as a questionable basis for setting the true value of the Godchaux sugar company. On the stock exchange, an industrial company such as Godchaux Sugars Inc. would have traded based primarily on current earnings, its record of paying a dividend, and potential earnings as a manufacturing enterprise over the next several years. Its share price would not have fully reflected the full long-term inherent and heretofore unrealized value of its land assets.

Zeckendorf was a tough and skilled real estate operator. He understood that asset-rich companies like Godchaux Sugars Inc., holding 33,000 acres of land—much of it developable, much of it in the midst of proven oil and gas reserves, and some of it the site of enormously valuable pine and cypress forests, situated along the Mississippi River and served by numerous commercially active bayous and roads and railroads, and with who knew what other assets below the surface—would have an *intrinsic value* far higher than its value reflected on the company's books or in the public markets.

*　　*　　*

Once he gained control, on June 27, 1956, Zeckendorf's 52026 Corporation promptly completed the spin-off of the sugar refinery and sugar-production "assets, properties, business and goodwill relating to the Corporation's sugar refining, milling and by-products operations" to the National Sugar Refining Company, New York. Webb & Knapp hauled in $14 million from the sale, about $6 million being for the fixed assets plus some $8 million for accounts receivable, inventories, and manufacturing supplies.

At Reserve, home of Leon's most cherished and first plantation, National acquired a robust assemblage of well-maintained sugar-producing and related assets. These were included in the sale inventory:

1. *Sugar refinery.* Capacity 2.5 million pounds of cane per 24 hours.
2. *Cane mill.* Grinding capacity approximately 3,300 tons per 24 hours.
3. *Servall plant.* By-product plant to process bagasse.
4. *Sugar storage and packing facilities.* Four warehouses with aggregate capacity for 20 million pounds of raw and refined sugar and mechanized packinghouse and three concrete silos with storage capacity for 23 million pounds of bulk refined sugar.
5. *Residential and recreational facilities.* For use by employees. (These included at Reserve the employees' club building, pool, playing fields, house as well as the Godchaux house).
6. *Land.* Approximately 235 acres on which the buildings referred to in "items 1–5 are located."

In addition, the act of sale included, not mentioned in this inventory, approximately 765 acres of nearby land, the guest house, Reserve's dock and port facilities, as well as twenty-two miles of rail tramway.

The prepackaged deal between the nationally dominant sugar behemoth American Sugar Refining Company and real estate tycoon William Zeckendorf served both of their purposes to a tee.

But there was almost a slipup, one likely anticipated by the commercially sophisticated buyers, one they were willing to risk given the high payoff if the deal worked. On July 25, 1957, a couple of months after the Godchaux sale was announced, the federal government intervened based on antitrust concerns. The Federal Trade Commission claimed the obvious—that the acquisition would eliminate Godchaux as an independent refiner and remove it as a competitive factor in the country. What managements of American, National, and Zeckendorf understood all along, and the government only came to recognize when the deal was sealed, is that though National sold its output in twenty-eight states and accounted for 13 percent of U.S. sugar production, it did not have a strong presence in the South and Southwest. Godchaux, on the other hand, sold sugar in twenty-one states, principally in the Southern and Central freight rate territories, and was the seventh largest refiner of sugar in the country with only 4 percent of the market. Combined with American, the largest refiner at nearly 30 percent, and National second in the nation at over 13 percent, by adding Godchaux, they would account for 47 percent of sugar production in America. The combination would control nearly half of all sugar output in the United States. A commanding national market share that could dictate prices is what American and National wanted, just as Zeckendorf wanted Godchaux's land. The sale went forward. The government's antitrust case dragged on. It would take years to resolve.

*　*　*

Gulf States Land & Industries, Inc. benefited from all that the Godchaux management had neglected to imagine. Here is the stunning array of assets, long ago assembled by Leon Godchaux, turned over to Zeckendorf in the guise of Gulf States Land & Industries:

1. *Cane mill at Raceland.* Grinding capacity of 4,000 tons of cane per 24 hours.
2. *Servall plant at Raceland.* By-product to process bagasse.
3. *Warehouses at Raceland.* Storage capacity for 21 million pounds of turbinado sugar.
4. *Other structures.* Residential housing for employees and agriculture buildings and plantations.
5. *Land.* Total acreage approximately 33,240 acres.

   (i)　*Agricultural land.* Approximately 10,000 acres plus agricultural buildings and equipment used in the plantation operations in three Louisiana parishes.
   (ii)　*Land and buildings used for subdivision and residential purposes.* Located principally in vicinity of existing industrial facilities.

(iii) *Wood and swamp lands.* Undeveloped.

(iv) *Mineral rights.* On all retained acreage, about 18,900 acres being under lease to oil companies and about 14,340 acres being open.

* * *

The Zeckendorf-Godchaux deal was big enough and surprising enough to draw national attention. An enterprising reporter at the *Wall Street Journal*, John S. Tomkins, filed his story on July 5, 1956, only two weeks after the charade of a Special Meeting of Godchaux Sugars Inc. took place in New York. "Late last year," Tomkins found out, "a New Orleans real estate broker named Harry Latter discovered that officers and investors close to Godchaux wanted to sell their stock. . . . He brought the deal to Charles F. Noyes Co., Inc., a New York real estate firm. Acting as co-brokers they brought the Godchaux situation to Mr. Zeckendorf . . . and got substantial broker's and finder's fees for their trouble. The Noyes firm also got seventy-five cents a share commission for delivering a block of over 103,000 class A and B shares owned by George F. Scanlon, Godchaux's chairman, and 17 other private and institutional holders."

This fact-checked report, released in a nationally respected financially focused newspaper, made it clear that the deal was hatched privately in New Orleans among the broker Harry Latter and "officers and investors close to Godchaux." Harry Latter was an engaging and effective real estate broker and founder of the largest real estate brokerage firm in New Orleans. He was also a close friend of several members of the Godchaux family. There is no way that he would have guessed that family members and insiders were eager to liquidate the company. He probably had been informed; indeed, his efforts to find a buyer likely solicited.

*   *   *

Most stockholders, imagining no alternative, tendered their shares at the price negotiated by Godchaux management. But not everyone went along meekly. To some professionals in the investment community, the price offered of $60.50 a share for class A stock and $55 for class B stock seemed no less than outrageous and they challenged it in court.

A coterie of independent investors, primarily domiciled in New York, refused to tender their stock at the offering price. On June 10, a month after the price was established, a group of nonfamily aggrieved stockholders, including seven New York–based brokerage houses that served as custodians for their clients, brought an action in the New York State Supreme Court to obtain a higher price for their stock. They sought "to have the value of their stock determined by an appointed appraiser making such directions in regard to the proceedings as the Court shall deem proper." The petitioners had obtained their own estimation of value and told the Court, ". . . petitioners claim $163.90 for their Class A shares and $149 a share for their Class B. shares." The investment professionals believed that their Godchaux stock was worth 270 percent more than negotiated by Godchaux management.

As the case dragged on during the summer of 1956, the Zeckendorf faction refused to enter into further negotiations. At one point, in exasperation, the lawyer for the petitioners simply stated, "We are . . . instructed to advise you . . . that the said offer ($60.50 and $55) is hereby rejected as being materially less than the true value of said shares." The petitioners won the right in New York State Supreme Court in August of 1956 to have a thorough independent appraisal conducted. This decision was vigorously appealed by Zeckendorf, surely because he knew that he had made an outstanding deal. On October 1, 1956, the court refused to render an opinion, and the matter was not pursued any further by the frustrated petitioners.

When the sale of the sugar company was going on, none of Leon's children were still alive, except for childless Michelette, who would die the next year. But a veritable dynasty of grandchildren and other descendants were stockholders in Godchaux Sugars Inc. Not one in the family petitioned for a proper due-diligence process or a proper in-depth appraisal.

The *New Orleans States* diligently reported just how good a deal Mr. Zeckendorf pulled off. Webb & Knapp, as of May 22, 1956, had bought 85 percent of the class A and class B shares of Godchaux common stock "for approximately $8,243,000 as a first step." The spin-off to National of the sugar-refining business was expected to bring "around $9,500,000." According to Gregory Beadle, the former manager of the Godchaux refinery at Reserve,

"Webb & Knapp ultimately sold the Godchaux refinery and business to National Sugar, including 1,000 acres for a combined total of $14,000,000." Zeckendorf retained all the rest of the land at zero cost, on top of a multimillion-dollar profit on the sugar assets.

*   *   *

As soon as he gained effective control in January of 1956, Zeckendorf initiated planning for the land his group retained in the guise of Gulf States. Twelve days after the deal to National was certain and his control of Godchaux Sugars Inc. was certain, Zeckendorf revealed in New York and in New Orleans his grand scheme for the land portion of the Godchaux property. The *New Orleans States* reported under a bold top-of-the-page headline, **"Firm May Build 'New City' Between New Orleans, BR (Baton Rouge)."** Readers in New Orleans learned that "Zeckendorf said the firm plans to develop some 33,000 acres of property now owned by Godchaux Sugars, Inc., . . . (into) residential units and shopping centers. . . . Planning may call for some office buildings to take care of the new industries which may locate in the area. . . . Much of the Godchaux property constitutes an area of great industrial potential . . . and preliminary talks already have been held with companies in the petrochemical and metallurgical fields." The newspaper also quotes Zeckendorf in the same article saying, "Webb and Knapp also is interested in the mineral resources—chiefly natural gas. . . . All but 16,000 acres already are under lease to such companies as Humble Oil & Gas Co., Shell Oil Co. and Superior Oil Co."

By April of 1957, Zeckendorf announced plans for an entire new community on former Godchaux land to be developed just south of Reserve and just north of New Orleans. Plans for the small parcel of Leon's property he targeted, situated on the Airline Highway at LaPlace (now a thriving suburban area close to the New Orleans city limits and the international airport) were far enough along for a public relations photo-op to be sent around to newspapers. The picture featured Percy Herbert, sheriff of St. John the Baptist Parish, and Hannon J. Barre, president of the parish police jury (a powerful local political post), beside an awaiting bulldozer. The new city, to be composed of over 4,000 home sites, was to be called—no doubt for local public relations purposes—Godchaux Community. The developer was, as announced in the press release and photo, "the Mississippi River Development Corp., an affiliate of Webb & Knapp Inc., of New York City." By the time the 4,000-plus-home project got under way several years later, and the name value of the formerly well-known Godchaux dynasty no longer thought to be essential, the development was renamed Riverlands. Another nearby portion of Godchaux property was developed as the residential subdivision called Carrollwood. Today, Riverlands and Carrollwood are thriving subdivisions on a marginal speck of Leon's property.

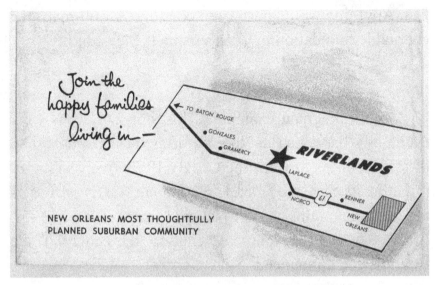

Fig. 65. Riverlands promotional brochure, 1950s. This diagrammatic map shows the Riverlands subdivision location on former Godchaux property near LaPlace, between New Orleans and Reserve. Unlimited opportunities for Godchaux Sugars shareholders were lost when the thousands of acres assembled by Leon Godchaux were sold, together with their mineral rights, to real estate speculator and developer William Zeckendorf Sr. Courtesy of Louisiana State Museum Historical Center, Leon Godchaux Collection, Record Group 138.

These large subdivisions provide an example of what Godchaux management could have done by forming a partnership with residential property development experts, hopefully insisting upon a more responsible planning approach.

Within the family, the opportunity for partnerships with developers and firms in other businesses for the long term and constructive use of land Leon assembled was lost. Anything would have been possible. A well-managed charitable foundation in Leon's name the least of it.

* * *

A more poignant example of lost opportunity is what eventually happened at Reserve after it was spun off to the National Sugar Refining Co. By 1962, five years after initiating its case, the federal government finally proved its antitrust complaint against National Sugar, filed in 1957. In its preamble to a long case citation, the Federal Trade Commission announced,

"THE NATIONAL SUGAR REFINING COMPANY
CONSENT ORDER ETC. IN REGARD
TO THE ALLEGED VIOLATION OF
SEC. 7 OF THE CLAYTON ACT
Docket 6852—Complaint July 25, 1957;
Decision February 1, 1962

Consent order requiring the nation's second largest domestic sugar refiner to sell within six months and so as to restore the former competitive standing, the assets including refinery and sugar mill at Reserve, La. of the seventh largest—fifth largest east of the Mississippi— refiner which it acquired in June of 1956."

Once National was compelled to sell the Godchaux assets at Reserve, that decision set in motion the evolving future of Leon's first and most revered sugar property.

National Sugar sold the Reserve refinery to the flamboyant Cuban sugar speculator-tycoon-financier and once the most powerful sugar broker in the world, Julio Lobo, and his partner David C. Bintliff of Houston. In 1959–1960 Lobo had been driven out of Cuba by Fidel Castro. They operated the Reserve property under the name of Godchaux Sugar Refining Company. In 1965, Bintliff foreclosed Lobo's indebtedness and assumed operation of the refinery. A year later, Bintliff sold out to Southern Industries of Mobile, Alabama, which had previously acquired a company called Henderson Sugar Refiners Inc. in the early 1960s. The sugar company operating at Reserve was again renamed, this time in 1966, as Godchaux Henderson Sugar Co. Inc. Godchaux-Henderson operated for a few years until it was purchased in 1975 by Great Western Sugar Co., a Denver, Colorado outfit, owned by the recklessly speculative Texas-based Hunt brothers. The Hunt brothers were primarily interested in real estate development, not refining sugar. A decade later, in around 1985, due to poor profitability in the sugar market, and their own widely publicized speculative losses in the silver market, the Hunts shut down the refinery. In March of 1992 they sold Reserve for $11.5 million to an ambitious industrial service company called the Port of South Louisiana.

The Port of South Louisiana had a plan to use Godchaux's valuable stretch of riverfront property to build what is now called the Globalplex Intermodal Terminal. And develop they did! By the time they were finished, the Port of South Louisiana owned and operated a public terminal and maritime industrial park situated on 335 acres, "formerly a sugar refining complex." The Globalplex morphed into a premier sea gateway for U.S. export and import traffic—4,000 oceangoing vessels and 55,000 barges call at the Port of South Louisiana each year, making it the top-ranked port in the country for import tonnage and total tonnage.

All this and more could have been realized at Leon's Reserve, with more patient and prescient management.

31

The Restoration Of A Legacy

As the Globalplex master plan evolved, the Godchaux house, by then a derelict empty frame building of faded and ever-fading substance, remained unwanted on their property, once the residential center of Leon's Reserve.

Fig. 66. The derelict Godchaux-Reserve House, November 5, 2014. To the Port of South Louisiana managers, intent upon developing its Globalplex Intermodal Terminal at Reserve, the principal house on the Reserve place was an expendable nuisance. The port's agenda was to develop a massive regional industrial park, not historic or cultural preservation. Long abandoned, the house had fallen into deplorable condition. At the last moment, preservationists took an active interest. Courtesy of the author.

*   *   *

The old Godchaux house's plainness, disrepair, and its lack of appeal to the port planners did not mean that the frame building and property were inconsequential. Use of the house as a residence by French, German, and free people of color dated to early in the eighteenth century. The central core of the house reached back to 1764, when two simple wooden rooms heated by a fireplace were built by a French soldier, Jean Baptiste Laubel, who purchased the site from a German settler called Jacques Hofmann, who had originally purchased the site in about 1722. (So many early immigrant settlers from Germany sought out the rich farming land in that area along the Mississippi that it became known as the German Coast.) Hofmann's purchase is murky. It was likely the "purchase" of land stolen from Native Americans. After Laubel died in 1774, his widow and two sons continued to work their rice and corn farm for nearly forty years. The Laubel heirs enlarged the main house. In 1810, the Laubel sons sold out to a local German farmer, Christome Borne, who six years later sold the property to Jean Baptiste Fleming and Jeanette Teinter, the first free people of color to own the property. In 1821, the house and the land changed hands yet again. The Creole brothers (we have previously met), Francois and Elisée Rillieux—free people of color from a prominent New Orleans family—took possession. The Rillieux family operated Reserve as a successful sugar plantation, selling off occasional parcels and property in 1830. That sale included twenty-nine slaves. In 1833, the succession of Francois Rillieux sold out to Boudousquié and Andry. As we have seen, Leon Godchaux subsequently took title to the place from Sophie Boudousquié in 1869. At that time, the main house at Reserve stood near the river at the entrance to the sugar refinery, facing the long and wide entrance to the factory.

Fig. 67. The Godchaux-Reserve House in its original location. Inhabited by plant managers, the house is positioned in this photograph where Leon found it near the river. It faced the long entrance road leading to the sugar refinery, which was lined by workers' and executives' houses. Courtesy of Stephen Guidry.

Sometime between 1882 and 1894, to avoid threatened destruction by river flooding, Leon moved his house from the riverfront to a safer site within the Reserve factory complex, where the Port found it. None of its prior owners, including Leon Godchaux, viewed the main house as anything more than the utilitarian main residence of a working agricultural enterprise.

*　　*　　*

In recent years, preservationists recognized that the house was of historic significance and worth saving. Its original rooms ranked among the oldest, if not indeed *the* oldest, in the vast Mississippi River watershed. Architectural historians date the earliest core of the extant house to circa 1760, as evidenced by its enormous hand-hewn beams. The house had assumed most of its present size in the 1820s, when Francois and Elisee Rillieux owned the property. The fact that past owners of the property—German, French, Blacks, Creoles, free people of color, and a Jewish immigrant from Alsace-Lorraine—mirrored the mixed-race history of the region attached to the house an engaging and compelling immigration and racial diversity story. Yet the old wood-frame structure, lived in by plant managers and superintendents, and rented out as a duplex in the 1970s, sat abandoned, ignored, falling apart in the early 1990s. In the dark corners of the moldy lower level of the building is where I found stacks of soaked, broken bundles of limp canceled stock certificates issued in the halcyon days of Godchaux Sugars Inc., some drilled through with punched holes and others torn at the corner, others stamped "Retired" or "Void." This was the burial ground of the thousands of shares of Godchaux Sugars Inc. that had been tendered and permanently retired in the Zeckendorf deal.

*   *   *

To the rescue, and just in time, came the River Road Historical Society (RRHS), a regional nonprofit preservation organization focused on the east bank of the Mississippi River along the "German coast." The RRHS had previously salvaged and restored several plantation buildings in the area. Aware that demolition of the old house by Globalplex was eminent, the RRHS stepped in with emergency assistance. In a heroic outreach, even though strapped for funds, the RRHS took possession of the abysmally deteriorating, abandoned Godchaux house. For its part, the Port was reasonable: it donated the building to the St. John School Board, which in turn transferred it to the RRHS. As a condition of its donation, which closed on July 27, 1993, the Port imposed one condition. The house had to be moved out of the Port's way, out of its area of planned development.

The hulk that had to be relocated was dismal and fragile. The building's main supports were all but rotted, as wood-frame structures will. Exposed cypress beams were unstable; walls a-crumble; mortar missing; scarcely pointed bare brick chimney stacks were unstable; broken windows and shattered glass everywhere; a caved-in roof revealed rafters harrowingly exposed.

The house had become the sort of place that the soulful Southern photographer Clarence John Laughlin would doubtless have seen fit to include in his evocative book of haunting photographs so aptly titled *Ghosts Along the Mississippi*. Laughlin's elegiac 1948 masterpiece, a collection of black-and-white photographs exquisitely printed with many double exposures, is inhabited by all manner of abandoned plantation buildings, replete with wild-grass-encrusted statues and overgrown gardens— much of it shot at strange angles. Laughlin had a deft eye for spooky surrealism and knew how to present it magnificently. At the time he was creating his portraits of those "lost, and by the wind grieved, ghosts," the house at Reserve was still too presentable for his purposes and likely in its bones not grand enough.

The RRHS contrived to roll the fragile hulk of a house a half mile to a 0.8-acre levee-facing lot at the corner of the River Road and West Tenth Street, where the building stands today. In anticipation of the forced move, the RRHS had purchased the vacant riverfront lot the previous April for $22,000. The house would again be facing the river, as it had originally.

When the River Road Historical Society providently stepped in, the house had been sitting unoccupied and untended since 1971. It was a wreck barely standing, situated in a desolate landscape of shuttered factory buildings. Irony of ironies, just a few blocks away, tourist-laden tour buses whizzed past daily, ferrying people from all over the country, even from all over the world, eager to visit nearby restored plantation houses such as Destrehan, San Francisco, Oak Alley, Houmas House, and Laurel.

The spectacle of this frame wreck being rolled toward its new site and life once again facing the river drew crowds of onlookers. Jonathan Fricker, director of the Louisiana State Division of Historic Preservation, drove from Baton Rouge to witness the risky move. Shortly afterward, he recorded the big event for the state's preservation magazine, *Preservation in Print*: "Moving day, September 25, 1993, drew a big crowd to witness the spectacle. An enormous steel girder chassis on wheels was erected under the house. The move was quite a feat. With its brick between posts and *bousillage* construction, the house was very heavy—over three hundred tons. As it was winched along, inch by inch, thick boards that had been placed to keep the wheels from sinking into the turf snapped like match sticks. . . . The project still has a long way to go. But given the fact that the house came so close to demolition, we are fortunate to be as far along as we are."

The River Road Historical Society added its own postscript to Director Fricker's report: "The River Road Historical Society thanks all who donated funds, time and effort—especially the Godchaux Family Fund. Without its contribution of matching funds, the project would not be as, to quote Mr. Fricker, 'far along.'"

*   *   *

Financing the house relocation and restoration was slow and difficult. The locally savvy but cash-strapped RRHS had entered into a crucial initial agreement with the Louisiana Division of Historic Preservation: in exchange for a $30,000 loan and adding funds of its own, it would assume responsibility for restoring the house, a project estimated at the time to cost well over $500,000.

Late in 1993, toward the end of the year that the River Road Historical Society purchased the house, an opportunity arose to harness Godchaux family support for the restoration of the building. During Thanksgiving weekend, the extended Leon Godchaux family held a long-planned mega all-hands reunion in New Orleans. More than a hundred people attended, sixty-four being Leon's bloodline descendants, about half of all those alive.

Fig. 68. Godchaux family reunion, New Orleans, 1993. About half of Leon and Justine's living direct descendants attended. Thirty-four percent identified as Jewish, 14 percent as Protestants, and 14 percent as members of other religious groups. Thirty-four percent, the same proportion as Jews, professed no religious affiliation. Reunion headquarters were in the Marriott Hotel, now occupant of land assembled by Leon for his grand emporium store, the Godchaux building. Courtesy of the Godchaux Reunion.

An optional field trip to Reserve was planned as part of the reunion program. A healthy contingent of attendees traveled by chartered bus to Reserve—some admitted never having so much as seen the property. It turned out to be a chatty group of men, women, and children from across the country, some strangers to one another, all full of curiosity about their mutual connection and separate lives, with only Leon Godchaux in common. The group wandered through the few safe parts of the building, many aghast at what they saw.

On the return trip to town, it became painfully obvious that most of the family members in the coach were content to let the past remain just that: in their view, the plantations had been lost long ago, the storied acreage had been snatched out of family hands now for generations, the retail stores in New Orleans and the region were history, the family name had faded into indistinction, so what, pray tell, was the point?

Nevertheless, a handful of family members were unable to let go of a vision. At my suggestion, a group that included my sister Gail, Jane Godchaux Emke, John Godchaux, Richard McCarthy III, Anne Polack, Ben Eiseman, and Leon Godchaux II, and a few other stalwart equally nostalgic family members, proceeded to form the Godchaux Reserve Plantation Fund. Our first meeting was held in New Orleans on December 28, 1993, barely a month after the reunion and four months after the RRHS had gained possession of the building. Our goal was to raise awareness within the family and to obtain substantial financial support to help the RRHS salvage and eventually preserve this now-acknowledged historic treasure. A symbolic icon, this building beyond its historic significance, embodied all that remained of Leon Godchaux's physical legacy.

Over the next few months, as acknowledged by the RRHS, we succeeded in raising funds sufficient to help stabilize the lower floor where those soggy canceled stock certificates were still moldering. Additional modest funds helped the RRHS provide matching funds essential to obtaining grants. Nevertheless, the goal of establishing an ongoing long-term pool of money to support the restoration, maintenance, and operation of the house was not to be realized: broad family interest and support proved to be inadequate.

Meanwhile, in 1994, following archival investigations, documentation, inspections, and application, the house was accepted to be listed on the protective and prestigious National Register of Historic Places. It was initially designated as the "Godchaux-Reserve Plantation House." Its description in that imprimatur listing noted that the interior contained "some of the state's finest Federal woodwork," a description that particularly referred to the four hand-carved cypress mantels that long predated Leon's ownership. Soon after, cognizant of the negative implications of the word *plantation* and its inappropriateness to the actual nature of the structure, the RRHS petitioned to have the formal name of the house officially changed to the Godchaux-Reserve House.

THIS IS TO CERTIFY THAT

GODCHAUX-RESERVE PLANTATION HOUSE
WAS ENTERED INTO THE

NATIONAL REGISTER OF HISTORIC PLACES

UNDER THE PROVISIONS OF THE

NATIONAL HISTORIC PRESERVATION ACT OF 1966

21st DAY OF   JANUARY,   1994

KEEPER OF THE NATIONAL REGISTER   STATE HISTORIC PRESERVATION OFFICER

Fig. 69. National Register of Historic Places Certificate, 1994. This certificate for the Godchaux-Reserve Plantation House, dated January 21, 1994, helped to protect the Godchaux-Reserve Plantation House while other efforts were being initiated and before its designated name was modified to the Godchaux-Reserve House. Courtesy of the State of Louisiana, Division of Historic Preservation.

By the summer of 1995, there was palpable restoration progress, particularly on the lower floor. The exterior support columns that held up the building were restored in original brick. Downstairs, the floor that had been sagging into the Louisiana muck was cleared of a century of infested debris and then properly underpinned and bricked. Cypress doors, handsome new windows, and perfect replicas of the original shutters and hardware were installed. Upstairs, the falling-apart gallery flooring was replaced, and the roof temporarily tarped over. That initial work protected the skeletal remains from weather and intruders.

*   *   *

In 1996, three years after the regionally focused River Road Historical Society stepped in to rescue the house, a new nonprofit organization of concerned citizens based in and around Reserve formed to replace the RRHS.

The new Godchaux-Reserve House Historical Society (GRHHS) was laser focused. The founding officers of the new organization included Reserve businessman and builder Stephen Guidry (president); former Reserve town councilperson Julia Remondet (secretary); and scholar author, former school board superintendent Gerald Keller (vice president). Mark Sandoval, a descendant of the Boudousquié family; Jane Godchaux Emke; and I were asked to serve as honorary members.

The sole mission of the GRHHS was to assure the successful future of the Godchaux house and in doing so to enhance the cultural life and attraction of St. John the Baptist Parish. The board recognized that the building and its story had the capacity to attract commercial activity and diversity to their community.

By the time the GRHHS got down to work, it possessed the documentation necessary to bring this ambitious project to responsible fruition. Archival research had already been sponsored in conjunction with the River Road Historical Society. The Louisiana Division of Historic Preservation had assisted. Tulane students under the experienced guidance of Professor John Stubbs, at the time director of the Tulane University School of Architecture, master in preservation studies program, had produced pro bono in-depth investigations about construction and materials. Among many other notable contributions in their comprehensive report, the Tulane architects-in-training figured out and presented graphic diagrams of the approximate evolution of the façade of the house from the 1760s through to the Leon Godchaux period.

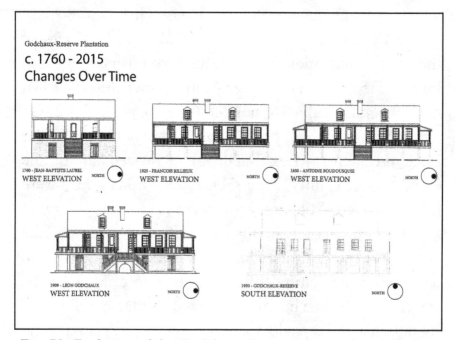

Fig. 70. Evolution of the Godchaux-Reserve House façade design, 1760–1909. These architectural diagrams document the evolution of the west elevation (the formal façade facing the river) over the years of ownership by the Laubel, Rillieux, Boudousquié, and Godchaux families. During the Godchaux tenure, the entrance stairway was reconfigured and access to the ground floor much enhanced. Courtesy of Tulane University, School of Architecture, Preservation Studies Program.

Since the GRHHS's founding, outstanding progress has been made. The board, assisted by Reserve residents, worked with modest funds to bring back the house. Many individuals in Reserve contributed their time and professional skill. Stephen Guidry obtained hundreds of feet of mature precious cypress logs to replace rotted beams. The timber he obtained had been felled on a former Godchaux property during the clearing of rights-of-way by utility and oil and gas exploration companies. Guidry set up a large table saw in the front yard of the house—visible for all to see from the River Road—then personally milled the gigantic beams to replace, *in kind* and *in situ*, the supporting beams and struts that had rotted. Leon's prescient purchase of swamplands replete with cypress stands allowed his once former timber to be cycled back into his once former Reserve house.

To commemorate completion of phase 1 of the restoration, on October 16, 2018, a communitywide ceremony took place in a large tent next to the now renamed Godchaux-Reserve House. On that sunny clear fall day, on a tour of the house that preceded formal remarks, guests witnessed a revived and once again dignified structure.

Fig. 71. The Godchaux-Reserve House phase 1 restoration at completion, 2018. In step with contemporary social trends, the designation "plantation" (as described on the National Register in 1994) was no longer associated with the house or with the preservation organization dedicated to its restoration. Painting by Dwain Richard. Courtesy of the Godchaux-Reserve House Historical Society.

The roof was rebuilt to its original profile and again doing its job. Replaced dormer windows looked just as they had in Leon's day. All the sidewalls were freshly enclosed, chimneys and gallery surfaces refinished. The once soggy, dank, subsiding lower floor was now composed of stable, carefully preserved old brick. The ground-level antique redbrick floors, walls, walks, and column supports were precisely pointed and aligned to assure a stable future. The bright upper floor exterior of the house radiated a new vibrancy, shining in its coat of creamy yellow walls and bright white trim, a life revived. The delicate upper-floor white railings and support columns shimmered in the soft, warm sunlight as they etched an outline against the deep-blue sky. Reserve's and Leon's finely proportioned Creole cottage was once again alive. Even the iconic double-staircase entrance stoop, the setting for the original photograph of Secretary Taft and his massive entourage's visit in 1904, was emulated, though not yet precisely replicated. To celebrate the occasion, a good-humored costumed reenactment of Taft's photo-op was staged, populated by Reserve townsfolk and Godchaux family members.

Fig. 72. Reenactment photograph at Godchaux-Reserve House, October 16, 2018. More than a century after the William Howard Taft visit, regional officials and residents of Reserve, joined by several members of the Godchaux family, staged a costumed reenactment of the Taft visit photograph (see Fig. 58). The tableau photograph was part of the festivities to celebrate completion of the phase 1 renovation of the Godchaux-Reserve House. Local ladies provided home-cooked regional delicacies for a buffet under the tent adjacent to the house. Speakers memorialized the event. Courtesy of Brooke Robichaux/L'Observateur.

Not to be forgotten, Godchaux No. 3, polished and enhanced, was visible snugly under a nearby protective roof. The GRHHS plans to eventually display the locomotive near the house, wheels clinging to a short section of original narrow-gauge rail track.

*　　*　　*

Once renovation is complete—delayed because of a direct hit to the roof and side walls by hurricane Ida in 2021—the house will assume a new, useful life. Current plans are for each room dressed with appropriate period furnishings to tell the story of one owner. The diversity of races and religions and countries of origin will be highlighted. A portion of the building may become a museum focused on the sugar industry in south Louisiana. Plantation tour buses should not be whizzing past for much longer.

The logo aptly created by the GRHHS and now used on its stationery and memorabilia is a crisp engraving of the Godchaux-Reserve House. The building is surrounded by a heartfelt motto that encapsulates what residents of Reserve still feel today about Leon Godchaux's and his children's long-ago stewardship: "The House That Grew a Community."

Fig. 73. Sign at Godchaux-Reserve House phase 1 completion celebration, October 16, 2018. "The House That Grew a Community" became the motto of the Godchaux-Reserve House Historical Society. It expresses the appreciation for years of Godchaux community stewardship. The warm cream color, sparkling white trim, and restored roof, galleries, railings, windows, and doors of the renovated exterior of the house appear in the background. Courtesy of the author.

* * *

Leon's notorious humility, combined with his third- and fourth-generation successor's inability, have left nothing except the Godchaux-Reserve House as a tangible vestige of Leon Godchaux's vast and multifarious achievements. Within a hundred years of Leon's death, his retail stores, his clothing-manufacturing operation, his extensive country properties, and the sugar refineries are no longer. Like a whiff of the sweet scent of night-blooming jasmine upon the morning breeze, they are gone.

Appendix I

Immediate And Not So Immediate Descendants

In his own inimitable way, Leon assured his legacy. He left his individual unmistakable genetic signature within the family he founded, an imprint that reached all the way back in time to the story of Jewish emigration from Judah. It simultaneously flowed forward and was destined to spread widely. Leon and Justine left behind a dynasty of ten children, born approximately two years apart, over a twenty-six-year span. The span of the children's own lifetimes extended for a century, from the firstborn, Paul Leon Godchaux, in 1857, to the last to die, Michelette Leonie Godchaux, in 1957.

By no means comprehensive, below are thumbnail sketches of Leon's children and of particular Leon Godchaux descendants most of whom appear in this biography.

* * *

Paul Leon Godchaux (1857–1924). Leon's first surviving child (and my great grandfather) was born before the Civil War, at a time when the future of New Orleans, and indeed commerce throughout the South, was growing tenuous. Paul Leon was born over a decade before Leon entered the sugar industry. His parents lived in the apartment above the store on Old Levee Street. His birth certificate was registered as "Godchot." Paul Leon attended grammar school in New Orleans after the family returned from New York. At thirteen, five years after the Civil War, Paul Leon was sent "up east" to study at Riverside Academy in Sing Sing (now Ossining), New York. Leon's determination that his male children receive a fine education is first exposed in sending his first son at a young age so far out of town. In his late teens, Paul Leon traveled abroad to spend time in Strasbourg, the capital of Alsace-Lorraine, his parents' homeland. Leon wanted to be certain at this stage of his career in the 1870s that his progeny remained linked to their European heritage, to their Lorraine relatives, and fluent in French. As Leon became increasingly committed to life in New Orleans, and attachment to his homeland diminished, none of the later-born siblings was sent off to Europe.

At this stage in his own development, the illiterate merchant believed that a few years of good education out of town would be sufficient to assure advancement in life. At age sixteen, Paul Leon was yanked out of school to begin his apprenticeship in his father's clothing company. After Leon's death in 1899, Paul Leon succeeded to the presidency of the Leon Godchaux Clothing Co. Ltd., where he served in that capacity until he died in 1924.

Paul Leon married Henrietta "Retta" Weis on November 6, 1884.

Fig. 74. Paul Leon Godchaux (1857–1924) and his wife, Henrietta "Retta" Weis (1868–1942). Paul Leon was Leon's first child and his successor as president of Godchaux's Clothing Company, Ltd. Through his marriage to Retta Weis (daughter of Julius Weis and Caroline Mayer), the Godchaux and Weis families were united. Courtesy of Carrie Godchaux Wolf and the author.

They proceeded to have five children. Their first was my grandmother Carrie "Gram," born in 1885.

Fig. 75. Carrie Godchaux Wolf (1885–1974). She was Paul Leon and Retta's first child and Leon's first grandchild. Courtesy of Carrie Godchaux Wolf and the author.

The children who came after were given—to continue the tradition—familiar family names: Leon Jr., Justine, Juliette, and Paul Leon Jr., known generally as "Paul."

Hardworking and a personable hands-on manager, Paul Leon (as he was known throughout the family and the New Orleans community) was recognized for his diligence, dedication, and attention to every detail of the clothing enterprise. His youngest son, Paul, remembered his father as "neat, methodical, conservative, super courteous; imbued with a know-how for gracious customer hand-shaking. . . . He believed in personal charity. . . . He wore the same style of suits made from the same patterns of the same goods, summer and winter, the same solid blue bow ties. . . . He dried the wash basin after he washed his hands—so meticulous, neat, and tidy. He was a symbol of good manners."

Under Paul Leon's distinctive leadership, as previously mentioned, the clothing business thrived. He notably oversaw the last phases of construction of his father's dream project, the Godchaux store and building at Canal and Chartres.

Paul Leon was also a civic activist. In 1912, he founded the New Orleans Retailers' Credit Bureau, at first financing it himself. Eventually, Paul Leon's fellow New Orleans merchants recognized the need for a credit clearinghouse as their businesses expanded and their clientele became, more often than not, strangers in the growing city. Paul Leon also served as treasurer of Godchaux Sugars Inc. Like his father, he belonged to the Young Men's Hebrew Association, served as a director of Touro Infirmary, and actively supported the Jewish Widows & Orphans Asylum.

Also like his father and mother, Paul Leon loved music. While his sisters took up piano, he took lessons on the violoncello as a pastime, an instrument that his own youngest son, Paul, would learn to play with considerable skill.

*   *   *

Paul Leon's eldest son, Leon Godchaux Jr., attended Exeter and Yale. He was put into position directly from his 1909 graduation in New Haven to work at the Leon Godchaux Clothing Co. Ltd., acceding to the presidency in

1924 after his father's death. During his long and successful tenure, Leon Godchaux Jr., as previously mentioned, had the foresight to move the store from Canal and Chartres to Canal near Baronne Street. He oversaw the renovation of the Macheca Building at 826-828 Canal, a leased seven-story medical office building, into which the flagship store moved in 1924. He later leased and connected to the store two adjacent buildings on Baronne Street. These provided Godchaux's with a second entrance and additional display and selling space.

Leon Godchaux Jr. developed strong and distinct habits. One of them was to walk routinely at lunchtime three blocks from the store, cross Canal Street, then turn left into Bourbon Street before entering the inviting, mirrored, bistro-like first floor dining room of Galatoire's. The restaurant had opened in 1905 when Jean Galatoire, the founder, brought family-style recipes and traditions from his French village of Pardies. Mr. Galatoire never imagined that one day his establishment would become one of the most sought-out restaurants in America. Once seated at his regular table, Leon Godchaux Jr., a slight man about five foot six or seven, cast in the Godchaux family physical mold, routinely asked for his own special unlisted salad. His signature requested ingredients consisted of lumps of jumbo-crab meat, large peeled boiled Gulf shrimp, anchovies, sliced fresh tomatoes, topped by a chopped boiled egg, all served on crispy iceberg lettuce lightly dressed with a Creole mustard vinaigrette. In time the "Godchaux Salad" was elevated to a mainstay on Galatoire's menu. It is still today.

Like his grandfather and father, Leon Jr. was attracted to classical music. He became adept at the violin. As an adult, Leon Jr. formed a chamber music group that met in his house on Everette Place on Sunday afternoons. The group was of sufficient caliber to attract players from the New Orleans Symphony Orchestra, of which Leon Jr. served as president. Leon Jr. was also adept at woodworking. He crafted masterful pieces in his basement shop. Among other objects, he built elegant polished mahogany music stands for his home salon. In keeping with his deep interest in music, Leon Jr. organized in 1946 the New Orleans summer "pops" concert series and served as the organization's first president.

Leon Jr. married Hortense Elma Shlenker. They had three children: Susan O. Godchaux, Paul Leon Godchaux II, and Anne Godchaux.

*   *   *

Leon Jr.'s middle child, Paul Leon Godchaux II, known by friends and family as Pee Wee since childhood, was born in 1917. He graduated from Exeter, went on to Yale majoring in chemical engineering before earning a master's degree in the same subject at Iowa State University. Leon II, after service in the navy during World War II, and marriage to Marion Kahn, first worked in research at the sugar company and then became president of Godchaux Sugars Inc. in the early 1950s. As president he was instrumental in advancing the poorly conceived sale of the sugar company in 1956 when it was sold out to the Zeckendorf interests.

After a decade as president of Gulf States Land, controlled by the Zeckendorf interests, in 1968 Leon II was elected president of the Godchaux Clothing Company. During his fourteen years at the helm, Leon II oversaw a dramatic expansion of the enterprise, opening elegant branch stores in newly developed shopping centers and regional cities. In 1982—the company already in trouble—he relinquished the presidency to his cousin Tommy and assumed the role of board chair. Four years later, the Godchaux's Clothing Company dissolved in bankruptcy. A total loss.

In later years, Leon II assumed the presidency of the Franklin Realty Company, a family real estate holding company where he presided until forced to give up his position due to failing health.

Leon II, like his father and grandfather and great grandfather, while nurturing a family, led an active civic life. He served as president of the Touro Infirmary board, the Downtown Development District organization, and the New Orleans Philharmonic Symphony Orchestra board.

*   *   *

Albert Jacob Wolf (1881–1968) and Carrie Godchaux (1885–1974). Albert J. Wolf entered the Leon Godchaux story when, in 1906, he married Paul Leon's daughter, Carrie. Carrie Godchaux, born in New Orleans in 1885, was Paul Leon and Henrietta "Retta" Weis's first child and Leon Godchaux's first grandchild.

Albert was born and raised amid the tumult of Bayou Sara, a rowdy cotton port tenuously clinging to the muddy east bank of the Mississippi River, a hundred miles north of New Orleans. The thriving stopover port along the river-trade route was perched below the steep bluff on which St. Francisville was located. Once flood and fire destroyed Bayou Sara, like most Bayou Sara businesses, and inhabitants, the Wolf family moved up the steep bluff to St. Francisville.

Albert Wolf was the son of Morris Wolf and the grandson of their German Jewish family founder, Jacob Wolf (1825–1857). Morris Wolf had three siblings, Sarah, Morris, and Emanuel. Sarah married Julius Freyhan, born in Breslau, Germany (1832–1904), who emigrated to Bayou Sara at a young age. He became a successful local businessman. Freyhan invited his wife's siblings, Morris and Emanuel, to join in his various far-flung and ultimately highly successful commercial enterprises. The brothers prospered as a partner in Freyhan's businesses located in Bayou Sara and in St. Francisville. Eventually, after years of working together, and after Julius Freyhan moved to New Orleans, and shortly before he died in 1904, Morris and Emanuel purchased, by contract dated June 22, 1903, Mr. Freyhan's extensive business interests and properties in and around West Feliciana Parish, where St. Francisville is located.

Three years before Albert married into the Godchaux family, the vast scale of property holdings that his father and uncle had purchased included the following:

All the Land & Improvements on
which their Store, Warehouses, Gin House,

and Connections stand in the town of St. Francisville & Bayou Sara, La.

The Store Building known as Serbovitch Store in St. Francisville;

The Vacant Lot, Brasseaux Property;

The Vacant Lot, Tom White in Bayou Sara;

The Applewhite Swamp Land, Cat Island, in West Feliciana Parish;

The Rogillio Swamp Land;

The Richardson Tract of Land in West Feliciana Parish;

The Sanders Tract of Land in West Feliciana Parish;

The Gibbons Tract of Land in West Feliciana Parish;

The Wright Tract of Land in West Feliciana Parish;

The Polly Jones Place in West Feliciana Parish;

The Anthony Connell Place in East Feliciana Parish;

The Dan Beryhill Place in East Feliciana Parish;

The S. Miller Gin House Property in East Baton Rouge, State of Louisiana.

Obviously, Freyhan and the Wolf brothers had been sufficiently solvent after the Civil War to accumulate an array of assets that owners could no longer afford to hold.

Albert's father, Morris, moved to New Orleans sometime between 1885 and 1895 together with his wife and children. His brother, Emanuel, remained in St. Francisville to oversee family holdings in the area.

Morris surely knew the original Leon Godchaux. It is not beyond reason to think that young Albert would as well have been in Leon's presence from time to time. By the time Morris had relocated to New Orleans, both Morris Wolf and Leon Godchaux were prosperous merchants, both had family origins along the banks of the Rhine, and both were members of the Temple Sinai congregation.

Albert Jacob Wolf forged his own distinguished path. After one year at Harvard, he returned home to Tulane, where he earned his BA in 1901. His relocation to Tulane was triggered by his father's premature death. Initially engaged in the thriving New Orleans business of cotton export, Albert became in time—through a merger between firms in New Orleans and New York—a founding member and partner of Merrill, Lynch, Pierce, Fenner & Beane, which became in its day the largest and most successful securities brokerage firm in America. Albert's charitable work included membership on the board of the National Heart Council; he was a director of Godchaux's Clothing Company, a board member of the New Orleans Cotton Exchange, and president of Touro Infirmary. Like Leon, he loved horses and horse racing, visiting races in Paris, London, and Louisville.

Albert and Carrie's first son was named Morris Wolf II, my father. Their other children, Caroline and Albert J. Wolf Jr., built solid careers in teaching and architecture.

Fig. 76. Albert Jacob Wolf (1881–1968). Albert J. Wolf married Leon Godchaux's first grandchild, Carrie Godchaux, in 1906. They proceeded to have three children and thereby eventually became the author's grandparents. Courtesy of Carrie Godchaux Wolf and the author.

* * *

Edward Isaac Godchaux (1867–1926). Leon's second son was born two years after the end of the Civil War, a decade after Paul Leon, his two sisters, Anna and Blanche, having been born in the interim. (More about the daughters to follow.)

Before his family responsibilities descended upon the young man, Edward was permitted to matriculate and remain in college, but also to go on to graduate work. He attended the University of Louisiana (now Tulane University). After graduation, Edward entered Louisiana

State University Agricultural and Mechanical College in Baton Rouge (by that time the state capital) to pursue courses in agronomy. He had been instructed to learn something practical connected to the sugar enterprise where his father was a rank beginner. Edward became particularly knowledgeable about the rudiments of sugar chemistry. The LSU Agricultural and Mechanical College had been established by an act of the legislature in 1874 to carry out the provisions of the progressive United States Morrill Act of 1862, which providentially granted lands in each state for the furthering of agricultural education. That institution merged three years later with Louisiana State University, taking its name. Edward acquired specialized knowledge in the chemistry of sugar and earned an advanced degree. Leon promptly appointed him manager of operations at both Reserve and for a while at Raceland plantations, a role in which he excelled.

Edward became the soul of the second Godchaux generation at Reserve. A popular and dashing young man, he was known in Reserve and its environs for his skilled horsemanship. Historian Laura Renée Westbrook writes of Edward's having been "raised in a climate of popular reverence for his generous, thoughtful, and successful father, whom he chose as his model of the courtly, responsible gentleman he wished to become. Leon Godchaux reared his son with the expectation that he would be suited to take over the family sugar operation at the beloved Reserve Plantation. Edward was able to fulfill his father's hopes for him, to succeed within his father's lifetime, and to realize his own abilities."

In 1893, Edward married nineteen-year-old Ophelia Gumbel, daughter of a prominent New Orleans Jewish family. Like the Godchauxs, the Gumbels were charitable and civic minded—members of Temple Sinai and supporters of Touro Infirmary. The principal beneficiary of Gumbel's largesse was Audubon Park, the 350 acres of a majestic assortment of watercourses and oak-tree-lined pedestrian ways amid the fast-growing uptown area of New Orleans. A vibrant, elaborate, spacious memorial fountain, installed in 1918 near the park's entrance on St. Charles Avenue commemorated the philanthropic endeavors of the Gumbel family.

The city had purchased the property in 1871, originally part of the Foucher and Boré plantations, to prepare a suitable site for the 1884 World's Industrial and Cotton Centennial Exposition. Once that spectacle closed, planning was sought for the precious property that extended from St. Charles Avenue to the river. In 1886, New City Park was renamed Audubon Park to honor the famous artist/naturalist John James Audubon who had lived and worked in New Orleans in the 1820s. A final design was executed in around 1896 under the direction of John Charles Olmsted, senior partner of the by-then heralded landscape architecture firm Olmsted Brothers. John's younger half brother and partner, Frederick Law Olmsted, had become by then the most celebrated landscape architect of his era. The firm, led by Frederick, had designed, among others, New York's Central Park. Audubon Park in New Orleans became a luscious, magical magnet of oak bowers and waterways, replete with diverse foliage and generous winding trails. It drew many second- and third-generation Godchaux family members to live in its proximity.

Edward turned out to be everything his father wished, and more. His commitment to Reserve was far more than financial—it was social and emotional as well. Edward arranged for management to provide favorable loans to workers in need. He built rental housing, including dormitories for single men.

Edward became a significant benefactor of St. Peter's Catholic Church in Reserve, the spiritual and social focal point of the descendants of the early German, Acadian, and European settlers of St. John the Baptist Parish. Donations from Edward personally and from the sugar company, matched by a local subscription, made possible in 1922 the rewiring and refurbishment of the church interior. Less than thirty years earlier, Leon's men and others fought the crevasse near the church and avoided an epical flood. In 1930, four years after Edward's death, the board of St. Peter's Catholic Church memorialized Edward with three new stained-glass windows (they were destroyed in 1965, along with the rest of the building, by a violent act of God named hurricane Betsy).

Ever the agronomist, late in his career, Edward allocated nine hundred acres of the former Belle Pointe plantation—land Leon Godchaux had acquired in St. John the Baptist Parish near Reserve—to the operation of a dairy farm. Opened in 1914, Belle Pointe Dairy boasted over four hundred head of fine Jersey, Holstein, and Guernsey cattle.

Birds-eye View of Godchaux's Belle Pointe Dairy—One of America's Finest and Cleanest Dairies

Special milk—from ONE DAIRY ONLY—controlled quality.
600 acres green pastures—12 months each year.
Loafing Barns for contented cows.
Separate Cow Washing Barn—clean cows.
Scientific feeding—milk richer in vitamins and food elements.
Milking Parlor, glazed, screened, ventilated.
Daily weight record of each cow's production.
Silos—for better milk and healthier cows.
Healthy employees, in clean uniforms.
Milk bottles double capped and sealed—protects pouring lip.
Bottles and equipment sterilized with steam.

Milk protects health of mother and child.
Milk promotes growth.
Milk builds strong bones and teeth.
Milk builds resistance to disease.
Milk helps protect against rickets.
Milk increases the expectancy of life.
Milk helps to maintain health at optimum level.
Milk Corrects the deficiencies of the modern American diet.
Milk furnishes the best quality of the greatest number of necessary food elements at the lowest possible cost.
Milk nature's greatest source of calcium.

"Guaranteed" by Godchaux—For more than half a century a name that has stood for Quality.

Fig. 77. Belle Pointe Dairy opened in 1914. Nine hundred acres of Godchaux land were converted from sugarcane to producing Belle Point milk of "rich and surpassing flavor" overseen by dedicated agronomist Edward Godchaux, Leon and Justine's fourth child. The milk from a combination of Jerseys, Holsteins, and Guernseys was blended to make Belle Pointe Special Milk. Courtesy of the Louisiana State Museum Historical Center, Leon Godchaux Collection, Record Group 496.

As explained in the company's brochure, "Jerseys, noted for their rich milk. Holsteins for their delicious, easily digested milk. Guernseys for their rich, golden colored milk. All three are combined to make BELLE POINTE SPECIAL MILK, rich and of surpassing flavor." The bovines were said to have been fed a special proprietary diet invented by Edward to ensure that the 450 gallons of milk they collectively produced daily would be both healthful and flavorful. The dairy grew into a major enterprise, with seven general-purpose barns, two milking barns, a veterinary hospital, three storage silos, refrigeration and cooling plants, a testing laboratory, and a dedicated fleet of delivery trucks servicing a territory that extended all the way to New Orleans. In 1947, the sugar company liquidated the dairy to again devote the acreage to sugar production.

Fleet of Home Delivery Trucks

This same fresh, cold, safeguarded milk, double capped and iced is at your door within a few hours after it is produced, in these new and clean delivery units, purchased in 1936.

Know the source of your milk supply.

Every drop of this SPECIAL MILK is produced *ONLY AT BELLE POINTE DAIRY*.

Fig. 78. Belle Pointe Dairy delivery trucks. The dairy serviced an extensive area that ranged all the way to New Orleans. In 1947, Godchaux management returned the land to sugarcane production. Courtesy of the Louisiana State Museum Historical Center, Leon Godchaux Collection, Record Group 138.

(In due course, in the wake of Zeckendorf's take-over, the Belle Pointe property—along with others along the

Mississippi River corridor, including some that Leon Godchaux once owned—eventually became the site of noxious, polluting chemical plants and refineries, so concentrated and so environmentally dangerous that the area became widely known as Cancer Alley.)

Edward died in 1926. His life was celebrated in two funerals, one in New Orleans and the other in Reserve, at St. Peter's Catholic Church. Both occasions were covered by the *Daily Picayune*. Of the one in Reserve, the paper reported, "In keeping with the life of the deceased philanthropist, creedal ties were withdrawn and men, women and children of all races and religions—men, women and children who had known and loved Edward Godchaux—crowded the church for the services." The depth of the segregation that persisted in the rural South for more than half a century after the Civil War can be read between those lines.

Edward Godchaux's support of a non-Jewish congregation at Reserve was not merely a case of sensible corporate public relations. His ecumenical footprint was heartfelt. Edward and his wife, like most of Leon's immediate descendants, celebrated Christmas (and in some cases Hanukkah as well) while remaining without ambiguity 100 percent secular Jews. As a family exception, two of Edward and Ophelia's children, Leon Gumbel and Lucille, never joined a synagogue.

*   *   *

Elma Godchaux (1896–1941). Edward's second daughter, a writer, turned out to be quite unlike any other family member before or after her time—both fiercely independent and wildly eccentric. The most publicly noticed of any of Leon's children or grandchildren, Elma was inquisitive, vivacious, and like her grandmother just five feet tall. Like her father and grandfather, she developed an ardent interest in horses, becoming a committed equestrienne in New Orleans and at Reserve. Following in her father's civil convictions, she devoted a lifetime in her own work to social and racial justice.

Edward and Ophelia encouraged their children to be thoroughly educated and bilingual—they employed a French governess and preferred that French be spoken at home. By the third generation, education for the girls in Leon's family was being accorded the same priority as for the boys. Not satisfied with the poorly funded neighborhood high school in New Orleans, Edward and Ophelia sent Elma to the girls-only H. Sophie Newcomb High School on Washington Avenue. There the demanding curriculum included chemistry, drawing, English, French, German, history, Latin, mathematics, "physical geography" and physiology, and athletics (five-foot-tall Elma, for a wonder, was on the basketball team).

Like some of her uncles, Elma went east to college—Wellesley, in Massachusetts. She was both an ardent student and an active participant in social life. Her cousin Irving Gumbel was a student at Harvard at the time and introduced her to a classmate of his from Louisville—Walter Kahn. A romantic relationship developed, and Elma transferred to Harvard's then sister college, Radcliffe. She studied both classical and contemporary literature and had the added good fortune to personally encounter such literary luminaries as Robert Frost, Ernest Hemingway, and Archibald MacLeish.

Elma married Walter in New Orleans in 1916 when she was still at Radcliffe while he was in graduate school and a teaching instructor at Harvard. Walter enlisted in 1918 and was sent to France, whereupon Elma and their infant daughter, Charlotte, moved back to Reserve, where her father was managing the Godchaux property and sugar business. After the war, Elma and Walter returned to Cambridge, where he completed his education at Harvard.

But Mammon beckoned. Walter soon forsook academe for the world of investment banking, going to work on Wall Street for Lazard Frères. Elma, ever the rebel, was not wildly content with Walter's decision. Walter's work increasingly required that he spend long intervals in Europe, during which Elma regularly returned to New Orleans. There she played a high-spirited role in the French Quarter's bohemian scene, frequented by participants in the legendary Southern Renaissance such as William Faulkner, Sherwood Anderson, Katherine Anne Porter, Louis Armstrong, and Jelly Roll Morton.

Through her cousin Paul Leon Godchaux Jr, who was its publisher and business manager, and Julius Weis Friend its editor (to whom she was also related), Elma gained easy access to the avant-garde circle that had formed around the New Orleans literary magazine the *Double Dealer*. Founded in 1921, it billed itself as "A National Magazine for the South" and indeed ended up publishing many of the notable writers of the day, such as William Faulkner,

Ernest Hemingway, Ezra Pound, Robert Graves, Robert Penn Warren, Thornton Wilder, Edmund Wilson, Amy Lowell, and Hart Crane. Though the magazine lasted only five years, it is still remembered for its championing of modernist literature. Elma, more than an appreciator and a spectator, was sometimes romantically involved among those literary denizens.

By 1933, Elma and Walter made the decision to separate. Upon their divorce a year later, she and Charlotte moved permanently to New Orleans. When Charlotte left for Radcliffe in 1935, Elma moved to a courtyard apartment on Chartres Street, deep in the French Quarter, not far from the site of Leon's first New Orleans store.

There she launched a writing career. She quickly became a socially engaged writer. Elma produced progressive and locally incendiary short stories as well as one widely noticed novel, *Stubborn Roots*. In her work, she was determined to explore—and expose—the plight of disadvantaged Southerners, Black and White alike. An aversion to the exploitation and disenfranchisement of Black people, after all, ran in her blood—an inheritance from her grandfather and her father, to whom she was especially close. In 1998, Elma's daughter, Charlotte, in an interview with the social historian Laura Westbrook, described her mother as having been "passionate about the plight of Negroes. Had she been alive during the Civil Rights movement, I'm sure she would have been involved."

Elma did join Temple Sinai, but she preferred Black Baptist churches. The preaching—and the dynamic music—were more to her liking. She celebrated not only

Christmas but also Easter. Her grandchildren were raised in the Catholic faith.

Elma's stories, originally published in journals such as the *Southern Review* and the *Frontier and Midland*, at once excited admiration and caused consternation, even outrage, in the deep south. "Wild Nigger" was included in *Best Short Stories of 1935*. "Chains," whose protagonist was a Cajun with but a small patch of swampland to his name, was published in the *O. Henry Memorial Award Prize Stories of 1936* and republished in *Louisiana in the Short Story*. "The Horn That Called Bambine" was reproduced in several anthologies. Elma's novel, *Stubborn Roots*, dedicated to "the memory of Edward Godchaux, Louisiana planter," was set at a sugarcane plantation in the 1800s. Published in England as well as America, it was commended by the *Times* of London for its bold depiction of characters and saluted by the *Saturday Review of Literature* as "a remarkable novel."

After her divorce, Elma had romantic relationships with several creative artists, including writers Thomas Wolfe and Lyle Saxon and the New Orleans sculptor Enrique Alférez. Toward the end of her short life, depleted by adult diabetes, she moved uptown to a house on Octavia Street near where more conventional members of her family had lived for two generations. Ailing and weakened, she would also be closer to Touro Infirmary, the hospital so intimately associated with the Godchaux family going back to her grandfather's day. Elma died on April 3, 1941, at the age of forty-five. She was buried next to her father in the family plot in Metairie Cemetery.

* * *

Charles Godchaux (1869–1954). After the war, as Union and Confederate hostilities began to fade, and as Leon prospered, his dream of an educated family and his ambition for the best for his children became palpable. Charles, number three son, born in 1869, first attended University of Louisiana (now Tulane University) preparatory school at age ten, and was subsequently sent to the notoriously rigorous long-established eastern prep school Phillips Exeter Academy (class of 1887), 1,600 miles away "up north" in New Hampshire. Leon's decision to send Charles to Exeter inaugurated a Godchaux family tradition followed by many other Godchaux family members over the years. How or why Leon chose this rigorous boys' prep school way up in New Hampshire is unknown, but suffice it to say the choice is consistent with Leon's devotion to rigor and excellence.

When Charles took that trip, it was a long and complex travel experience for an inexperienced young adolescent boy. (It was still when I became an Exonian at fifteen, in 1951.) Two days and nights on the Crescent Limited—the rail line Charles took—brought him to New York. There he had to be met by someone to help transfer trains and stations for the 250-mile journey into cold and rural New Hampshire, landing at the Exeter station, where again he had to be met and escorted to a school so much larger and so much more sophisticated than anything he had experienced, much less imagined. Exeter was educational boot camp, with all the trimmings.

Charles was not allowed to remain away from family and the Godchaux enterprises through college. Once home he was assigned an apprenticeship in his father's retail operation and later elected a director of the company. At the same time, Leon was grooming Charles to enter particular aspects of the sugar business, schooling him in the intricacies of production and management. He was also active in the affairs of the Leon Godchaux Clothing Co. and was a vice president and a director of that company at the time of his death. For most of his career, Charles enjoyed an exceptionally long run as president of Godchaux Sugars Inc., managing that enterprise from its incorporation in 1919 to 1953, when he was elected chairman of the board. During his tenure, Charles modernized the factory and oversaw in 1950 a major expansion of the refinery. Soon after Charles retired, the company was on a slippery downward slope into oblivion.

Earlier in his career, Charles had ventured into banking. In 1895, at the age of twenty-six, he founded the Central Trust and Savings Bank. Almost immediately he merged it with the Whitney and Germania Banks to form the Whitney Central Bank. He became its first vice president. In time, Whitney Central became Whitney National Bank, an enterprise that rose to become one of the institutional financial backbones of the city's economy. Upon the death of George Q. Whitney, Charles became the second president of the bank in 1907, only to resign in 1914 to devote full time to Godchaux family enterprises, particularly Godchaux Sugars Inc. and to serve as the family's principal financier.

Charles Godchaux's interests and engagement in New Orleans civic affairs were both diverse and committed. Like his father, Charles served on the board of directors and was active in the affairs of both Touro Infirmary and the Jewish Children's Home. He displayed his own novel charitable streak as well. Charles became a stalwart of the New Orleans Mid-Winter Sports Association, the group that launched the inaugural Sugar Bowl Football Classic in 1934 and that later added a medley of more diverse amateur Sugar Bowl winter sports attractions such as sailing and tennis. Charles was also a founder of International House, a key organization to this day, dedicated to promoting international trade through New Orleans. He was a member of the New Orleans Country Club and Lakewood Country Club, as well as the Round Table Club in New Orleans.

Charles married Bonita Hyman Hiller in New Orleans in 1899, the year Leon died. They had three children: Charles Jr. (who died at age five), Lillian (Mrs. Thomas Jefferson Feibleman), and Justine (Mrs. Richard McCarthy Jr.). Justine's husband was present at and part of the unwinding of Godchaux Sugars Inc.

After a fire destroyed their stately family residence at 5700 St. Charles Avenue in 1941, Charles and Bonita moved to 8 Garden Lane.

In 1944, during the tumultuous years of World War II, because of his pristine reputation and known effectiveness, Charles, then seventy-five years old, was appointed president of the citywide United Community Fund and War Chest.

In recollections and obituaries of Charles, who is buried in Metairie Cemetery together with his wife and family members, descriptions such as "courtly demeanor; graciousness; personal charm; mannered grace of the vanished past; many benefactions; unfailing kindness" are sprinkled throughout the manifold tributes.

* * *

Jules Godchaux (1872–1951). The full scope of Leon's ambition for his male children's education was allowed to bloom by the time son number four, Jules, became an adolescent. Following in the footsteps of his brother Charles, Jules attended Exeter, graduating in 1888, and then Tulane. He was sent to graduate study in mechanical engineering at the renowned Boston (later Massachusetts) Institute of Technology to acquire skills that would be extremely useful in the sugar-refining business. Jules inaugurated the Godchaux family's affiliation with MIT, which continued from time to time down through the generations. For the first time, Leon, now in his sixties and more secure, prosperous, and worldly, allowed a child to be university educated beyond the well-known confines of New Orleans.

After graduation, Jules was made a vice president at Godchaux Sugars Inc. He quickly became the go-to person for all things mechanical. Not only did he oversee the updating of the sugarhouses on the Godchaux plantations, but he also encouraged inauguration of the transformative steam-powered tramway and rail lines across those properties. In the process, he became head of the Sterling

Central and the Franklin and Abbeville Railroad. During his career, true to his education, Jules founded the Louisiana Engineering Society. He also served as chairman of the Raceland Bank and Trust Company and as a director of the Louisiana Agriculture Association.

Jules also engaged in some freelance consulting. Utilizing his specialized education and accumulated experience, Jules oversaw the construction of a huge sugar mill at Baraguá, Cuba.

Jules married Cora Dorothy Tanner in New Orleans in 1901. They had no children.

*　　*　　*

Emile Prosper Godchaux (1874–1950). After Jules, the other three sons were set free to complete their university educations outside of New Orleans. Emile matriculated at Yale, where he earned a BA. In doing so, he began another enduring Godchaux family educational tradition—this time at Yale. Emile graduated from the college in 1896 and from Yale Law School two years later, the year before Leon's death.

Emile went to work for a New Orleans law firm that would become the powerhouse Milling, Godchaux, Saal, and Milling, where he concentrated on Godchaux business. In 1910, Emile served a brief stint on the Appeals Court of Orleans Parish, after which he was deferentially referred to as "Judge." With the rumblings of World War I in Europe, heedful of his heritage, Emile resigned from the court to join the Red Cross in his father's native land, France.

Upon his return, Emile resumed the practice of law and additionally served as secretary of Godchaux Sugars Inc.

In the latter part of his life, Emile moved to Pass Christian, Mississippi, an active shrimping and fishing port on the Gulf of Mexico, some sixty-five miles east of New Orleans. Years later, his cousin, my grandmother, and her husband, Albert, built the house on whose broad porch in the magical half dark I first heard stories about my great-great grandfather, little imagining what would lie ahead (*this book*!). In the end, everything connects.

Emile married twice, first to Mabel Goetter and then, after their divorce in 1901, to Mary V. Curtis. He had no children.

* * *

Albert Charles Godchaux (1870–1924). Leon's fourth-born son continued both the Exeter and MIT family traditions, but with a tonic twist: he played on the football teams of both institutions! After his university education in the east, Albert was trained at the store by his oldest brother, Paul Leon, and shown the ropes by such old hands as Joachim Tassin, Rosamond Champagne, Carl Wedderin, and Charles Steidinger. Albert eventually left the company to establish an insurance agency, Godchaux and Meyer.

Like his father and brothers, Albert was philanthropic and civic minded. He was instrumental in establishing what became the New Orleans Chamber of Commerce and served as its president. Quite a club man and civic activist, Albert assisted in establishing the Southern Athletic Club and served as president of the New Orleans Progressive Union, the organization that sponsored the 1899 Louisiana Industrial Fair, the last place Leon Godchaux visited before his death. As a board member, he advised the New Orleans Public Belt Commission that oversaw commercial railroad operations around the city. His multifarious club memberships included the Chess, Checkers, and Whist Club; Southern Yacht Club; Audubon Golf Club; and the Harmony Club, the premier Jewish social club in New Orleans, of which he was president. Albert was known to be genial beyond the norm and is said to have possessed an irresistible and unaffected charm.

Albert married Aline Meyer Zodiac in 1899. They had one child, Justin Albert, who was born in New Orleans in 1911. In time Justin followed the family tradition to Yale, where he was a member of that school's hallowed swimming team. Albert's athletic genes obviously persevered. Jane Godchaux Emke, Justin Albert's daughter, is a philanthropist and family stalwart who has been instrumental in reviving the Godchaux-Reserve house.

*   *   *

Walter Godchaux (1876–1952). Walter followed the Exeter-Yale route. He went on to initiate and to head the research department of Godchaux Sugars Inc., where he was a vice president. In that capacity, he was a pioneer in recyclables.

Walter developed new uses for several previously underutilized products. He found a profitable and sensible process to convert and reuse bagasse, the dry, pulpy fibrous residue, previously mentioned, that remains after the sugarcane stalk has been crushed. The product, which he patented under the name Servall, was a shredded, sanitized, reimagined form of bagasse, useful as animal bedding, poultry litter, and garden mulch. Servall eventually contributed to the Godchaux sugar business bottom line. He also invented—this time from dried molasses—the product Camola, used in animal feed mixes. Walter has been credited with being the first to plant soybeans as a cover crop in sugarcane fields. During his active career, Walter's driving interests remained animal husbandry and experimental agriculture, subjects about which he published many papers in professional journals.

Walter was also a major cattle breeder during the first quarter of the twentieth century, prominently featured in successive volumes of *The American Shorthorn Herd Book*. An esteemed member as well of the New Orleans Horticultural Society, Walter hybridized rare species of azalea and camellia.

Walter married Rosa Hyman in 1903. They had three children: Adele, Rosa, and Walter Jr. Walter Jr. was in the family management group working at Reserve when the sugar company was sold to the Zeckendorf syndicate.

*   *   *

Anna Godchaux (1862–1931). Anna was educated at Mrs. Cenas's Boarding and Day School for Young Ladies, a New Orleans day school near the family's Esplanade

Avenue home. She married David Danziger in 1880, a local public-school boy who went on to become a successful real estate investor in New Orleans. They had six children: Theodore Walter, Evelyn Ella, Leonard, Edna Gertrude, Miriam Martha, and Harold. Anna died in New Orleans in 1931.

*   *   *

Blanche Godchaux (1864–1941). Blanche married New Orleans real estate investor Leon Fellman in 1886. They had one child, May. Blanche and her husband, breaking with the family's hitherto uninfringeable attachment to New Orleans, made their home in New York, where she died in 1941.

*   *   *

Michelette Leonie Godchaux (1880–1957). Known as Leonie, she was the last of Leon's children, born when Justine was forty-two years old. She was named Michelette in tribute to Leon's mother and Leonie for guess who. In 1901, she married Augustus "Gus" Frank Mayer, who would go on to open his own retail establishment on Canal Street in 1927—the Gus Mayer Co. They had no children. Leonie died in New Orleans in 1957.

*   *   *

Black and Creole Descendants. There are some and perhaps many Black and Creole descendants who carry forward the Godchaux name, and surely many others who carry forward part of the Godchaux gene pool without the name. Over a period of a hundred years, generations of Godchaux men populated the family enterprise in the sugar business, spending between them a great deal of time in the south Louisiana countryside while their families were in New Orleans.

If long-circulating stories, familiar names, and visual evidence are to be believed, at one time or another, or possibly more often than that, men in Leon's direct genetic line found occasions to be intimate with Black or Creole women. Lion, of course, was out there as an unmarried person, itinerant peddler, and country storekeeper in his earliest years in America. He met Thérèse and who knows who else, and what became of those relationships?

Carrie Godchaux, Leon's granddaughter, wrote that her brother Paul Godchaux "had a carpenter who came to the house . . . a young colored boy . . . who looked so much like Paul . . . when they asked him his name, he said Leon."

Another more distant Leon Godchaux descendant, Terry Mecray, reported his experience in Morgan City, a hub in the bayou and oil country of south Louisiana. "We were having lunch there and a large black man came into the bar. . . . The bartender said, 'Leon Godchaux, I haven't seen you in a long time.' Mecray jumped up and asked the man, 'Is your name really Leon Godchaux?' He said 'yes.' Mecray then asked the man if he knew where his family had come from. He acknowledged that it was 'a sugar plantation up the river from New Orleans.'"

Then of course there is the six-foot-three-inch three-hundred-pound LSU graduate, currently well-known nose tackle for the New England Patriots, born in 1994 in sugar country, Plaquemine Parish, south Louisiana. This consummate professional Black athlete, Davon Godchaux, comes from an established line of Black Godchauxs who lived not far from the old Raceland Godchaux plantation complex.

*　*　*

Leon died in 1899, the year after Walter's graduation from Yale. By then he surely felt content that his family members would never suffer, as he had, from the painful inability to read and to write cogently. Just as he made his clothing operation into a heralded and notable success, and just as he managed to turn a failing set of sugar plantations into a top-class industrial business, he stopped the chain of illiteracy with which his French family had been saddled. Their underprivileged illiteracy probably prevented his grandparents and parents—going all the way back to the eighteenth century—from benefiting from the periodic relaxation of anti-Semitic dicta in France. In doing so, Leon joined his family with several premier educational institutions in America.

*　*　*

Looking over the onset moments of what became a veritable Godchaux dynasty in New Orleans, there appears what may or may not be a curious coincidence in the dates that Leon's children married. The first four children married during less than a decade between 1884 and 1893. The next six married either in the year that Leon died or within the next four years, each taking place, except for Albert's, in their birth order. Was it a coincidence that those last six marriages were consummated in a short four-year interval? Perhaps Leon's younger children, after all born to a woman thought of in those days as an older mother, might have felt at a loss being deprived of their powerful guardian father? Suddenly fatherless, Charles, Jules, Emile, Albert, Walter, and Leonie might have felt more susceptible to the lure of marriage than they might otherwise have been.

* * *

Leon and Justine ended up with twenty-one grandchildren, two thirds of whom, curiously, were born to their first three children, those married in the 1880s. Most of the grandchildren, like all but two of the original Godchaux children, continued to live in New Orleans. As recently as the 1950s, there were as many as eighty descendants of Leon and Justine living in New Orleans. Today, the number of direct descendants still domiciled in the city has dwindled to a handful. Moreover, in New Orleans, the surname Godchaux is carried by only two individuals, Alan Godchaux, Leon Godchaux's great-great grandson through the Paul Leon line, and Alan's daughter Sara Helene Godchaux. In the wider Godchaux family to this day, the names Paul and Leon among the men and Justine among the females so echo through the generations that sorting relationships can be a hopeless party game at reunions.

* * *

Appendix II

Time Line: Leon/Justine Godchaux, And Joachim Tassin

1717	Founding of New Orleans.
1781	Paul Godchot, Leon's father, born in Herbéviller, Lorraine, France.
1790	Michelette Lazard, Leon's mother, born in Lorraine, France.
1791	Emancipation of Jews in France.
1796	Anne Sarah Alexandre, Justine's mother, born in Vantoux, Lorraine, France, and dies in 1848 in Lorraine.
1803	Louisiana Purchase.
1806	End of the Holy Roman Empire. Napoleon defeats Francis II of Austria at the battle of Austerlitz. Napoleon, initially cordial to the Jews, promulgates pro-Jewish legislation.
1808	Infamous Decree (*décret infâme*) becomes law in France, hostile to the Jews.
1815	Napoleon is defeated at the Battle of Waterloo.

1817	Leon's eldest brother, Mayer Godchaux, born August 15 in Herbéviller, Lorraine, France. Mayer is the first of seven siblings: Henriette, b. 1819; Alexandre, b. 1822; Lion (later Leon), b. 1824; Lazard, b. 1826; Nathan, b. 1829; and Pauline, b. 1832. Mayer becomes Leon's partner in New Orleans.
1824	Lion Godchot born June 10 in Herbéviller, Lorraine, France.
1824	Johanna "Hannah" Levy born April 23 in Klingenmünster, Germany, dies in 1899.
1825	Jacob Wolf born in Dürkheim, Germany, dies in 1857.
1826	Julius Weis born in Klingen, Germany.
1830	Julius Freyhan born in Breslau, Germany.
1831	Paul Godchot dies in Herbéviller, November 22.
1832	Joachim Tassin born mixed race in St. John the Baptist Parish, Louisiana, to enslaved Black mother, Thérèse, property of Jean-Baptiste and Clarisse Tassin. Joachim is baptized at six months of age on August 18, 1832.
1835	Justine Lamm born April 8 in Ay-sur-Moselle, Lorraine, France.
1836	Lion Godchot leaves Herbéviller, sails from Le Havre for New Orleans on the packet ship *Indus*.
1836	Marie-Madeleine-Elene Coustaut, Joachim Tassin's first wife, is born.

1837	The first-ever newspaper with the name "Picayune" in its title is printed in New Orleans. Shortly thereafter, the name is changed to the *Daily Picayune*.
1837	Leon arrives in New Orleans in February. Documents in France support this date. Certain accounts and documents set Leon's year of arrival as 1840. For reasons outlined in this book, I believe he arrived in 1837.
1837–1840	Leon works in the Louisiana river parishes as a peddler.
1840	Leon opens a store in Convent, Louisiana.
1842	Daniel Henry Holmes opens his dry goods store on Chartres Street in New Orleans.
1844	Leon opens his first retail clothing store in New Orleans, "Leon Godchaux, French and American Clothier," at 107, 108 Old Levee Street (now Decatur Street). Leon lives above the store.
1844	Julius Weis emigrates from Klingen, Germany, to New Orleans or Natchez.
1845	Leon leases additional commercial space in buildings at 213-215 Old Levee Street.
1845	Leon renames his business Godchaux Frères, French and American Store, when he is joined in business by his older brother Mayer. Mayer remains Leon's partner until 1866.

1846	Marie Pauline Millon (or Milan or Muellon), Joachim Tassin's second wife, born in Bordeaux, France.
1847	By this time, Leon has leased buildings at 107, 108, 213, 215, 217 on Old Levee Street.
1849	D. H. Holmes department store moves to a larger establishment on Canal Street.
1849	Joachim, seventeen years old, purchased on November 26 by Leon and Mayer Godchaux at disposition of the property of Jean-Baptiste and Clarisse Tassin.
1849	Lazard Godchaux, Leon's younger brother, leaves New Orleans for California.
1851	Leon purchases Francoise on February 19.
1851	Leon Godchaux and Justine Lamm marry on May 24.
1853	Sarah Wolf born in Bayou Sara.
1854	Leon and Mayer purchase Eliza Guillaume and her twenty-month-old son, Frank, on February 20.
1854	Leon's probable first visit to New York City.
1854	Leon and Justine's first child, August, dies in New Orleans a few days after birth.
1856	Leon and Mayer sell Eliza Guillaume and her children Frank and ten-month-old Edgar.
1857	Joachim Tassin's emancipation contract signed June 8, 1857.

1857–1880	Justine and Leon have ten surviving children: Paul Leon, b. 1857; Anna, b. 1862; Blanche Emile, b. 1864; Edward Isaac, b. 1867; Charles, b. 1869; Jules, b. 1872; Emile Prosper, b. 1874; Albert Charles, b. 1876; Walter, b. 1878; and Michelette Leonie, b. 1880.
1857	Paul Leon Godchaux, first son, born April 17, dies in 1924, New Orleans.
1859	December 24, Leon arrives in New York City aboard the steamer *Baltic*.
1860	June 13, Leon, Justine, a servant, and two infants arrive in New York City aboard the steamer *Moses Taylor*. One infant is Paul Leon Godchaux; the other is their servant's child.
1861–1865	In New Orleans, Leon buys 81 Canal Street and subsequently 83 and 85 Canal Street. Leon opens manufacturing and wholesale operations at 81, 83, and 85 (near the corner of Canal and Chartres streets), which become retail as well in 1863.
1861	January 26, Secession Convention in Louisiana adopts the Ordinance of Secession by 113 to 17 votes.
1861	April 12, Battle of Fort Sumter. Civil War begins.
1861	Joachim Tassin enlists in the First Louisiana Native Guard.

1860–1862	L. Godchaux Frère & Co. operating in New York from 171 Duane Street, where Leon and Justine live.
1862	Early January, prior to the Union Blockade, Leon and his family return to New Orleans from New York.
1862	January 15, Union blockade begins at the mouth of the Mississippi River a hundred miles downstream from New Orleans. The port is shut to civilians.
1862	April 18, federal ships arrive at New Orleans.
1862	April 29, capture of New Orleans. New Orleans surrenders without a battle.
1862	May 1, occupation of New Orleans begins by Union troops. The city is occupied but not destroyed during the Civil War.
1862	July 19, Anna Godchaux, born in New Orleans, dies in 1931.
1862	September 22, preliminary Emancipation Proclamation signed by President Abraham Lincoln.
1863	January 1, Emancipation Proclamation becomes effective; Southern states are still in rebellion.
1863–1877	Reconstruction era in the United States.
1863	August 12, Joachim Tassin marries Marie-Madeleine-Elene Coustaut (or Cousteaut or Coustant) in St. Augustine Church, New Orleans, in the Treme neighborhood.

1864	July 15, Blanche Emile, born in New Orleans, dies in 1941.
1865	Henrietta Weis, daughter of Julius Weis, is born. She marries Paul Leon Godchaux in 1884.
1865	April 9, Civil War ends.
1865	December 6, Thirteenth Amendment to the U.S. Constitution abolishes slavery.
1865	Ku Klux Klan founded in Tennessee, with chapters across the South.
1865	Leon and Justine purchase the house at the corner of Esplanade Avenue and Liberty Street (now Treme Street), originally described as 840 Esplanade and is now 1240 Esplanade. The house was designed by Alexander Hypolite Sampson in 1854 for its first owner, Claude Tiblier.
1865	Joachim Tassin buys a house at 1031-1033 St. Ann Street (then 157 St. Ann Street).
1866	Mayer Godchaux exits the Godchaux retail business.
1866	Leon buys Sophie Boudousquié notes and mortgages on Reserve plantation in St. John the Baptist Parish.
1867	May 15, Edward Isaac, born in New Orleans, dies in 1926.
1868	Louisiana is readmitted to the Union.

1868	July 9, Fourteenth Amendment to the U.S. Constitution forbids states to discriminate and protects all persons, grants equal protection to all, and guarantees no deprivation of life, liberty, or property without due process of law.
1868	The Louisiana Constitutional Convention grants all citizens the right to travel on any public conveyance licensed by the state and mandates that state-supported schools be open to everyone without regard to color.
1869	January 8, Charles, born in New Orleans, dies in 1954.
1869	June 1, Leon takes title to Reserve plantation, his first.
1870	Leon closes stores on Old Levee Street.
1870	Marie Pauline Millon emigrates from Bordeaux to New Orleans.
1870	September 24, Albert Charles, born in New Orleans, dies in 1924.
1871	February 9, Leon Godchaux is naturalized as a U.S. citizen and recalls, probably in error, that he arrived in America in 1840.
1872	Temple Sinai is completed.
1872	July 11, Jules, born in New Orleans, dies in 1951.
1872	Morris Wolf becomes a partner of Julius Freyhan in Bayou Sara and St. Francisville.

1873	March 9, Mayer Godchaux dies at New Orleans.
1874	January 29, Emile Prosper, born in New Orleans, dies in 1950.
1875	March 1, Civil Rights Act becomes law, forbids discrimination in private places.
1876	Sarah Wolf marries Julius Freyhan.
1876	Joachim Tassin returns to New Orleans after six months in Europe.
1876–1885	Joachim Tassin leaves Godchaux's store and opens his own clothing store located between 1876–1881 at 241 Old Levee Street (now 933 Decatur) and 1881–1885 relocated to 205 Old Levee Street (now 819 Decatur).
1877	The Compromise of 1877 puts Rutherford Hayes into the presidency of the United States. Federal troops are withdrawn from the former Confederate states. Beginning of control of the South and soon the Congress by conservative Democrats.
1877	Onset of the Jim Crow period in the South.
1877–1880	Leon purchases Elm Hall plantation and Raceland plantation and surrounding places and builds Elm Hall Central Sugar Factory and Raceland Central factory.
1878	September 24, Walter, born in New Orleans, dies in 1952.
1878	Michelette Lazard, Leon's mother, dies in Herbéviller, Lorraine, France.

1880	March 7, Michelette Leonie, Leon and Justine's last child, born in New Orleans, dies in 1957.
1880–1885	Joachim Tassin lives on Old Levee Street (Decatur Street), perhaps above his store.
1880	By now, Leon owns fourteen plantations and other properties; first son Paul Leon takes over routine responsibility for the store.
1881	Albert Jacob Wolf born in Bayou Sara, Louisiana.
1884	April 18, Joachim Tassin's first wife, Marie-Madeleine-Elene Coustaut, dies of uterine cancer at forty-eight.
1884	November 6, Henrietta Weis marries Paul Leon Godchaux and becomes Leon and Justine's daughter-in-law. Henrietta dies in New Orleans in 1942.
1885	Fire destroys Joachim Tassin's store; he returns to work in the Godchaux store.
1885	Tassin moves out of the French Quarter and buys a house at 1471 North Roman Street, near Leon Godchaux's house on Esplanade Avenue, where he remains for the rest of his life.
1885	July 30, Carrie Godchaux, Paul Leon and Henrietta's daughter, born in New Orleans.
1880s	Leon's sons assume management positions: Paul Leon at the clothing store, Jules at Raceland Central, Walter at Elm Hall, Edward at Reserve.

1885	Morris Wolf assumes power of attorney from Julius Freyhan and takes operational responsibility for the business in Bayou Sara and St. Francisville.
1886	Joachim Tassin and Marie Pauline Millon marry.
1890	The State of Louisiana passes the Separate Car Act.
1890–1910	"Jim Crow" initial period in the South. Most Confederate states pass laws that disenfranchise Black people and some poor Whites.
1890s	Joachim Tassin claims to have married Marie Pauline Millon, a native of Bordeaux, with whom he lives, when mixed race marriage was legal in Louisiana. At the 1890s, Black and White cohabitation was a felony. Pauline is subsequently named as Tassin's universal legatee.
1892	Leon Godchaux has completed assemblage of Canal Street property.
1892	Homer Adolph Plessy boards a White-only railcar at the Press Street station in New Orleans and is arrested.
1893	The great Mississippi River crevasse at Reserve.
1893–1894	The new Canal Street Godchaux's building at 531 Canal Street is open at the corner of Canal and Chartres streets as a retail and office emporium.

1894	Narrow-gauge railway inaugurated at Reserve.
1894	Rosina Kahn Godchaux (wife of Mayer) dies in New Orleans.
1895	Morris Wolf and his family move to New Orleans and transfers Freyhan's power of attorney to Emanuel Wolf, who remains in St. Francisville.
1896	May 18, United States Supreme Court in *Plessy v. Ferguson* upholds the constitutionality of racial segregation in public facilities under the "separate but equal" doctrine.
1896	Tassin and Pauline travel to Europe.
1899	May 18, Leon Godchaux dies in New Orleans and is buried in Metairie Cemetery.
1900–1901	Justine Lamm Godchaux buys a house at 4007 St. Charles Avenue and lives there for the rest of her life.
1903	June 22, Morris and Emanuel Wolf buy the Louisiana property of Julius Freyhan outside of Orleans Parish (New Orleans). Morris is living in New Orleans, and Emanuel remains in West Feliciana Parish.
1904	October 11, Julius Freyhan dies in New Orleans.
1905	Justine Godchaux and her children donate $50,000 in honor of Leon Godchaux to the campaign to expand Touro Infirmary.

1906	December 29, Justine Godchaux dies at New Orleans and is buried in Metairie Cemetery next to Leon.
1906	Carrie Godchaux marries Albert Jacob Wolf.
1906	New Touro Infirmary opens with the Godchaux Memorial Pavilion entrance on Prytania Street.
1909	Julius Weis dies in New Orleans.
1910	May 3, Joachim Tassin dies in New Orleans and is buried in Square 2 of St. Louis Cemetery No. 2.
1910	Morris Wolf II (my father), son of Carrie Godchaux Wolf and Albert Jacob Wolf, born in New Orleans.
1911	Ruth New (my mother), daughter of Harry and Minnie New, born in Cleveland, Ohio.
1924	Paul Leon, Godchaux's first son who had served as store president, dies.
1924	Godchaux's store moves from 531 Canal Street to 826-828 Canal Street into the leased and renovated Macheca Building, erected at the turn of the century. Godchaux's remains in leased premises at this location until it closes permanently in bankruptcy. Godchaux's 531 Canal Street emporium is eventually demolished. The Marriott Hotel now occupies the site.
1933	Ruth New marries Morris Wolf II in Cleveland, Ohio.

1954	The U.S. Supreme Court in *Brown v. Board of Education* upholds the original intention of the Fourteenth Amendment, reversing *Plessy v. Ferguson*, bringing to an end the era of federal government–sanctioned segregation.
1956	January, private insider sale of Godchaux Sugars Inc. controlling interest to 52026 Corp., a wholly owned subsidiary of Webb & Knapp, a New York real estate firm controlled by William Zeckendorf.
1956	June 13, Godchaux Sugars Inc. calls "A Special Meeting of Stockholders" in which management reveals that control of Godchaux Sugars Inc. has been privately sold to interests controlled by William Zeckendorf and seeks proxies of unaware shareholders, effectively formally ending the Godchaux family presence in the sugar industry.
1956	June 25, special meeting of Godchaux Sugars Inc. takes place at the company's offices in New York.
1967	Morris Wolf II dies in New Orleans.
1968	Albert Jacob Wolf dies in New Orleans.
1974	Carrie Godchaux Wolf dies in New Orleans.
1986	The Godchaux flagship store at 826-828 Canal Street, along with the branch retail stores, is closed in a bankruptcy, ending the Godchaux family presence in the clothing business.

1993	September 7, Port of South Louisiana donates the Godchaux house at Reserve to the River Road Historical Society (RRHS). The house is subsequently renamed the Godchaux-Reserve Plantation House.
1993	September 25, Godchaux-Reserve Plantation House is moved by the RRHS back to the River Road facing the Mississippi at Reserve.
1993	November 25–28, Godchaux family reunion in New Orleans over Thanksgiving weekend.
1993	December 28, first meeting of the Godchaux-Reserve Plantation board, inaugurated in New Orleans by several Leon Godchaux descendants.
1994	The Godchaux-Reserve House is accepted to the federal National Register of Historic Places as "Godchaux-Reserve Plantation House."
1996	Godchaux-Reserve House Historical Society (GRHHS) is chartered in Reserve, Louisiana.
1999	Ruth New Wolf dies in New Orleans.
2018	Public celebration at Reserve of completion of phase 1 restoration of the Godchaux-Reserve House.

ACKNOWLEDGMENTS

I take pleasure in thanking the following individuals and institutions. Your assistance during the writing and production of this book is deeply appreciated:

Calvin "Bud" Trillin—my dear friend, for contributing the foreword.

Walter Isaacson, Nicholas Lemann, and Henry Lewis Gates Jr.—each a distinguished author, heralded professor, and acute observer of America's past—for their interest in and praise of this manuscript.

Richard Campanella—author, geographer, and senior professor of practice at Tulane University, School of Architecture—for his help in unraveling the myriad changes in street names and addresses in New Orleans during the nineteenth and twentieth centuries, and for his generous endorsement of the finished manuscript.

Lawrence N. Powell—professor emeritus, Department of History, Tulane University, and distinguished author—for his helpful edit of an early version of this manuscript, for his sharing of sources and visual material, and for his personal interest in the final version of this book.

Bill Goldring—who, like Leon Godchaux, has made in a single lifetime outsized and remarkable contributions as an entrepreneur and philanthropist, for his enthusiastic endorsement of this book.

Betsy Davidson—for her diligent review and critique of the final manuscript and for sharing her editing and publishing experience in ways that helped to bring this project to completion.

Carl Lennertz—for lending his vast expertise to the myriad aspects of promoting, marketing and distributing this book.

Christopher Lehmann-Haupt—(sadly, posthumously) for his constructive editorial suggestions after reading the first ideas that formed the basis of this manuscript.

Steven M. L. Aronson—for his editorial suggestions and work on the structure of this book at an early stage.

Joseph Olshan—for extensive editing and helpful suggestions about the viewpoint of the manuscript.

Deceased family members Paul L. Godchaux Jr. and Charles Godchaux McCarthy—for their hard work first collecting and then finding a format to publish genealogical data connected to our sprawling family.

The American Academy in Rome—for a much appreciated residency during which I was liberated from regular responsibilities to work on this project.

Jari Honora—historian and genealogist, staff member of the Historic New Orleans Collection—for his incisive research and generous collaboration about Joachim Tassin and his help with accessing and obtaining images at the Historic New Orleans Collection.

Cynthia Johnson Hebert—expert history researcher based in New Orleans—for her generous contribution of details, documents, visual material, and last-minute genealogical sleuthing.

Rebecca Smith—at the Historic New Orleans Collection, head of Reader Services and Technical Processing—for her generous assistance with obtaining rights and permissions.

Jennifer Navarre—senior research associate at the Historic New Orleans Collection—for documentary research about the Godchaux and Tassin families, as well as help with understanding the renaming of Liberty Street.

Leon Miller—head of the Louisiana Research Collection of Tulane University—for his guidance through the Tulane Research Collection and his persistence in seeking out elusive information.

Andrew Mullins III—staff at Tulane University, Louisiana Research Collection—for assistance in finding my way through records and with reproduction and digital initiatives.

Lori Schexnayder—Research Services associate at Tulane University Special Collections—for her retrieval of crucial nineteenth-century newspaper articles during the COVID-19 lockdown and for her deeply appreciated assistance once the collection reopened with locating visual material and technical help with reproduction of the photos.

Agnieszka Czeblakow—head of Research Services, Howard Tilton Memorial Library Special Collections—for her search through other possible sources and collections in New Orleans outside of the Tulane system.

Kyle Neff—Public and Research Services coordinator, LSU Special Collections, Louisiana State University—for his assistance with the university's archives.

Dorothy Weisler—for her many hours spent at the Historic New Orleans Collection and the New Orleans Notarial Archives Research Center that accelerated the discovery of visual material.

Ann E. Smith Case—Tulane University archivist—for her assistance at Special Collections at the Howard Tilton Memorial Library.

Vernon V. Palmer—Thomas Pickles professor of law at Tulane University and co-director, Eason Weinmann Center for International and Comparative Law—for suggesting useful colonial military legal source material.

Tom Strider—registrar of the Louisiana State Museum—for his help penetrating the maze of resources in his institution and for his hands-on engagement with finding documents I needed.

Michelle Brenner—assistant archivist at the Louisiana State Museum Historical Center—for easing my time at the mint by gathering documents and enabling the efficient processing of requests.

Mindy Jarrett—archivist and digital content specialist, Louisiana State Museum Historical Center, New Orleans Jazz Museum—for her invaluable assistance assuring my review of the Godchaux collections and for assistance with sourcing the files and folders I needed.

Greg Lambousy—director, New Orleans Jazz Museum—for facilitating my use of the Louisiana State Museum Historical Center archives.

Stephen Hales—Rex Organization historian and archivist—for managing to find helpful documents related to Leon Godchaux's membership in Rex, even though most of the early Rex archives have been destroyed by fire.

Shane M. LeBlanc—clerk of court at Convent, Louisiana, St. James Parish—for helping locate original documents that revealed Leon Godchaux's property transactions that extended over many years.

Florence M. Jumonville—former archivist at Touro Infirmary in New Orleans—for her diligent search through hospital archives and much-appreciated tracking down of the Godchaux Pavilion plaque.

John Lawrence—former director of Museum Programs, Williams Research Center of the Historic New Orleans Collection—for guidance through his organization's resources.

James R. Swanson—present owner of the Leon Godchaux's house at 1240 Esplanade Avenue—for his help in authenticating the location of the building.

Rhonda Sylvera—assistant to James Swanson—for unlocking the door and admitting me as I wandered on the street in front of 1240 Esplanade Avenue.

Brooke Robichaux—news editor at *L'Observateur*—for her help in obtaining photographs from Reserve.

Kimberly Williams Cook—a direct descendant of Lazard Godchaux living in Florida—for her helpful meeting at Reserve, where we discussed the trajectory of Lazard Godchaux's life in California and the subsequent evolution of his family.

Gail and Harvey Lewis—for ongoing interest, suggestions, and enthusiastic support of this project as well as deeply appreciated careful proofreading by Harvey of parts of the final manuscript.

Cynthia Dobson and Melissa Dawn Castanedo—staff at Lake Lawn Metairie Cemetery in New Orleans—for help in locating the tombs of Leon and Justine Godchaux.

Cathy Kahn—archivist for Temple Sinai and former archivist for Touro Infirmary—for assistance with details about those institutions.

Sally Sinor, archivist, at the Notarial Archives Research Center, and Siva Blake, deputy clerk, Office of the Clerk of Civil District Court for the Parish of Orleans—for their help in finding long-ignored commercial transactions and personal information certified in the nineteenth century by notaries in St. John the Baptist Parish and in Orleans Parish.

Derek Wood—for his skilled archival research in New Orleans.

Helen Williams—museum director in St. Francisville and director of the West Feliciana Historical Society—for her research assistance tracking the Wolf family during its early days in Bayou Sara and in St. Francisville, Louisiana.

Mimi W. Miller and Nicole de L. Harris—executive director and curator, respectively, of the Historic Natchez Foundation—for their assistance in locating archival documents connected to the family, life, and career of Julius Weis.

Edward P. Cohn—emeritus rabbi of Temple Sinai, New Orleans—for his research guidance and critical reading of parts of an early version of this manuscript.

Jane Godchaux Emke and Bert Emke—family stalwarts for their diligent efforts on behalf of the Godchaux-Reserve House—for commissioning in 1995 valuable private research about the Reserve property, for other research provided to me subsequently, and for their continuing interest in this book.

Dick McCarthy—for sharing family documents that came down through the Charles Godchaux line, accumulated by his grandmother Justine Godchaux, who married Richard McCarthy Jr. in 1934.

Judge Martin L. C. Feldman—now deceased—for his provocative questions that propelled me into further research.

Dr. Gerald Keller—vice president of the Godchaux-Reserve House Historical Society, resident of Reserve, former teacher, and Reserve School Board superintendent—for his informative books, interviews, ongoing engagement with this project, fact-checking, and introductions to helpful individuals.

Stephen Guidry—owner of a prominent contracting and maintenance business in Reserve and president of the Godchaux Reserve House Historical Society—for his visual material, and his inspiring effort and leadership in moving forward the restoration of the Godchaux-Reserve House.

Julia Remondet—former director of St. John the Baptist Parish Economic Development initiative and former secretary of the Godchaux-Reserve House Historical Society—for her contributions to my understanding of life in Reserve in earlier periods.

Gregory Beadle—former superintendent at the Reserve refinery—for his information about the unwinding of operations at Reserve, for his impressive unearthing of facts, and for sharing of his own research.

Margaret Cambre Cerami—resident of LaPlace, Louisiana—for the right to use photographs from the collection of Sidney Walter Cambre of Reserve, Louisiana.

Carol Mandel—for her insightful suggestions related to the presentation and marketing of the manuscript at a very early stage.

Ann Holcomb—for reading early parts of this manuscript and for constructive suggestions as to the direction of the project.

Marie-Jeanne Gwertzman—for her painstaking translation of archival documents from New Orleans, written in difficult-to-decipher nineteenth-century French.

Laura Renée Westbrook—for research presented in her 2001 doctoral dissertation, "Common Roots: The Godchaux Family in Louisiana History, Literature, and Public Folklore," and for her enthusiastic encouragement all through this project.

Roger D. Joslyn, CG, FASG—a professional genealogist—for his investigation focused on Leon Godchaux in New York.

Ilya Slavutskiy—reference service librarian, Patron Services, at the Center for Jewish History in New York—for his assistance with retrieving data connected to the Godchaux family presence in New York.

Moriah Amit—senior reference service librarian, genealogy coordinator, Center for Jewish History in New

York—for her assistance in tracking down information about the Godchaux family in New York.

Kevin Burke—senior story producer, *Finding Your Roots*—for his informed advice about genealogical research resources and for his introduction to helpful researchers and readers of the manuscript.

Brandon Fradd—exemplary amateur genealogical sleuth—for turning up more useful information in an hour than I could in a month.

Henri Gueron—perhaps a distant cousin—whose interest in Jewish immigrants from Alsace and Lorraine led to fruitful conversation and to deeply appreciated assistance in the translation of difficult-to-decipher pre–Civil War documents written in French, contained in the New Orleans Notarial Archives.

Renée Carl—for assistance in tracking down Godchaux documents in the National Archives, Washington, DC.

Edris New—for providing background information about the Harry New family in and before they settled in Cleveland.

Andrée and Eric Gerschel—mother and son, Godchaux descendants, who live in Paris and Neuilly-sur-Marne—for sharing genealogical information about the family in France. A happy consequence of working on this book has been being able to interview and to meet my French cousins in Paris.

BIBLIOGRAPHY

Advertisement for clothing by J. Tassin and Leon Godchaux. *Daily Picayune* (New Orleans). October 6, 1876.

American Jewish Yearbook, The. Philadelphia, 1899.

Anonymous. "Leon Godchaux Dies Suddenly." *Daily Picayune* (New Orleans). May 19, 1899.

Anonymous. *The Picayune's Guide to New Orleans.* New Orleans: Nichelson & Co., 1904.

Ashkenazi, Elliott. *The Business of Jews in Louisiana 1840–1875.* Tuscaloosa and London: University of Alabama Press, 1988.

Ashworth, Henry. *A Tour in the United States, Cuba, and Canada.* London: A. W. Bennett, 1861.

Baker, Raquel Derganz. "Leon Godchaux Descendants Visit Historic Reserve House." *L'Observateur.* April 6, 2016.

Barry, John M. *Rising Tide: The Great Mississippi River Flood of 1927 and How It Changed America.* New York: Simon & Schuster, 1997.

Bloch-Raymond, Anny. "Mercy on Rude Streams: Jewish Emigrants from Alsace Lorraine to the Lower

Mississippi Region and the Concept of Fidelity." *Journal of the Southern Jewish Historical Society* 14 (2011).

Bloch-Raymond, Anny. *From the Banks of the Rhine to the Banks of the Mississippi: The History of Jewish Immigrants and Their Individual Stories.* Santa Maria, CA: Janaway Publishing Inc., 2014.

Blue Band, The. Published by Godchaux Sugars, Inc. Multiple issues, "A Plant paper published monthly for employees of Godchaux Sugars, Inc., at Reserve, Raceland, Napoleonville and New Orleans, Louisiana . . . for publishing news and activities at Godchaux Sugars, Inc."

Bojs, Karin. *My European Family: The First 54,000 Years.* New York: Bloomsbury Sigma, 2017. First published in Sweden as *Min Europeiska Family,* 2015.

Boudousquié, Adolphe. *New Orleans Notarial Archives.* February 20, 1854. Purchase of Eliza Guillaume and her son, Frank, by Mayer and Leon Godchaux.

Boudousquié, Adolphe. *New Orleans Notarial Archives.* June 8, 1857. Vol. 13A, Act 144, Folio 285, and assorted other of his notarial documents.

Boudousquié, Charles. *New Orleans Notarial Archives.* November 30, 1849. Vol. 29, Act 275. Purchase of Tassin by Leon and Mayer Godchaux and assorted other of his notarial documents.

Brattain, Michelle. "Miscegenation and Competing Definitions of Race in Twentieth Century Louisiana." *Journal of Southern History* 71, no. 3 (August 2005): 621–658.

Bray, Steven M. "Analysis of Ashkenazi Jewish Genomes." National Academy of Science, 2010 and 2016.

Broyard, Bliss. *One Drop: My Father's Hidden Life—A Story of Race and Family Secrets*. New York: Bay Back Books (Little, Brown and Company), 2007.

Buman, Nathan. "Two Histories, One Future: Louisiana Sugar Planters, Their Slaves, and the Anglo-Creole Schism 1815–1856." Doctoral dissertation, Louisiana State University and Agricultural and Mechanical College, 2013.

Burnett, Walter Mucklow. *Touro Infirmary*. Baton Rouge, LA: Moran Publishing Corporation, 1979. Distributed by Touro Infirmary.

Butler, Anne. *Three Generous Generations*. Baton Rouge, LA: Claitor's Publishing Division, 2004, 2008.

Butler, Anne, and Norman C. Ferachi. *St. Francisville and West Feliciana Parish*. Mt. Pleasant, SC: Arcadia Publishing, 2014.

Butler, Anne, and Helen Williams. *Bayou Sara—Used to Be*. Lafayette, LA: University of Louisiana at Lafayette Press, 2017.

Butler, W. E. *Down Among the Sugar Cane: The Story of Louisiana Sugar Plantations and Their Railroads*. Baton Rouge, LA: Moran Publishing Corporation, 1980.

By Dawn's Early Light, Jewish Contributions to American Culture from the Nation's Founding to the Civil War. New Jersey: Princeton University Library, 2016.

Campanella, Richard. *Bienville's Dilemma: A Historical Geography of New Orleans*. Lafayette, LA: University of Louisiana at Lafayette Press, 2008.

Campanella, Richard. *Lost New Orleans*. London: Pavilion Books Company Ltd., 2015.

Campanella, Richard. "From Landmark to Parking Lot: The Original Temple Sinai Endured for 105 Years." *Preservation in Print*. October 2018.

"Canal Street on Saturday." *Daily Picayune* (New Orleans). January 9, 1866.

Carpenter, Frank G. "The Land of Sugar. A Visit to Louisiana's Biggest Plantation and Its Immense Sugar Refinery." *Los Angeles Times*. November 29, 1896, 13.

Christovich, Mary Louise, Susan Kittredge Evans, and Roulhac Toledano, with photographs by Betsy Swanson. *New Orleans Architecture: The Esplanade Ridge*. Vol. 5, Gretna, LA: Pelican Publishing Company, 1977.

Cohen, Michael R. "Cotton, Capital, and Ethnic Networks: Jewish Economic Growth in the Postbellum Gulf South." *American Jewish Archives Journal*, 2012.

Cohen, Michael R. *Cotton Capitalists: American Jewish Entrepreneurship in the Reconstruction Era*. New York: New York University Press, 2017.

Cohen, Rich, *The Fish That Ate the Whale: The Life and Times of America's Banana King*. New York: Picador USA, 2012.

Cole, Shawn. "Capitalism and Freedom: Manumission and the Slave Market in Louisiana, 1725–1820." *Journal of Economic History* 65, no. 4 (December 2005): 1008–1027.

Comeaux, Neal J. "The Life and Times of Leon Godchaux The Sugar King of Louisiana." Three-page entry, http// www.stjohnparish.com.

"Copartnership Announcement." *Daily Picayune* (New Orleans). June 6, 1860, 8.

"Copartnership Dissolution Notice." *Daily Picayune* (New Orleans).June 17, 1863, 3.

Dart, Elisabeth Kilbourne. "Working on the Railroad: The West Feliciana 1828–1842." *Journal of the Louisiana Historical Association* 25, no. 1 (Winter 1984): 29–56.

Davies, W. D., and Louis Finkelstein, eds. *The Cambridge History of Judaism*. UK: Cambridge University Press, 1984.

"Death Notice Joachim Tassin." *Daily Picayune* (New Orleans). May 4, 1910.

Dickens, Charles. "The French Market at New Orleans." *All the Year Round.* December 26, 1874, xiii.

Ellison, Sara Fisher, and Wallace P. Mullin. "The Case of Sugar Tariff Reform." *Journal of Law and Economics* 38, no. 2 (October 1995).

Evans, Eli N. *The Provincials: A Personal History of Jews in the South*. Chapel Hill: The University of North Carolina Press, 2005.

Everett, Donald E. "Free Persons of Color in Colonial Louisiana." *Louisiana History: The Journal of the Louisiana Historical Association,* winter 1966, vol. 7, no. 1, published by Louisiana Historical Association.

Eyraud, Jean M., and Donald Millet. *A History of St. John the Baptist Parish*. Marrero, LA: Hope Haven Press, 1939.

"Firm May Build 'New City' Between New Orleans, BR." *New Orleans States.* May 22, 1956, 3.

Gandy, Joan W., and Thomas H. Gandy. *Natchez City Streets Revisited.* Charleston, SC: Arcadia Publishing, 1999.

Gehman, Mary. *The Free People of Color of New Orleans.* 7th ed. Donaldsonville, LA: D'Ville Press LLC, 2017.

Gill, James, and Howard Hunter. *Tearing Down the Lost Cause.* Jackson: University Press of Mississippi, 2021.

Gleason, David King. With a foreword by Samuel Wilson Jr. *Over New Orleans.* Baton Rouge and London: Louisiana State University Press, 1983.

Godchaux, Elma. "Godchaux Began Humbly, Rose to Financial Peaks: French Boy Found El Dorado Through Tireless Effort, Human Understanding." New Orleans *Times-Picayune.* March 1940.

Godchaux, Elma. *Stubborn Roots.* New York: The Macmillan Company, 1936.

Godchaux, Leon Sr., Susan Godchaux, Walter Godchaux Jr., and Justine Godchaux McCarthy. "Friends of the Cabildo, Oral History Podcasts." No. 554–562; 626–627ff, 1978–1998.

Godchaux, M., Frères & Co. October 21, 1861. Receipt in "Godchaux, Frères & Co." file. Confederate Papers Relating to Citizens or Business Firms, compiled 1874–1899, Documenting the Period 1861–1865, National Archives Microfilm M346, roll 358, images on fold3.com.

Godchaux, Paul L., Jr. "The Godchaux Family of New Orleans." New Orleans, 1971. Unpublished pamphlet "compiled in tribute to my mother, Retta Weis Godchaux."

"Godchaux's Section." *Times-Picayune* (New Orleans). March 1, 1940, p 1ff/.

Goldring/Woldenberg Institute of Southern Jewish Life. *Encyclopedia of Southern Jewish Communities— Reform Congregations—New Orleans, Louisiana.*

Goldstein, David B. *Jacob's Legacy: A Genetic View of Jewish History.* No publisher found, 2008.

Gopnik, Adam. "Blood and Soil." *New Yorker.* September, 2015.

Gray, Christopher. "From Butter and Eggs to the Home of Haute Cuisine." *New York Times.* September 27, 1998, 7.

Green Fields: Two Hundred Years of Louisiana Sugar. The Center for Louisiana Studies, University of Southwestern Louisiana, 1980 (multiple contributors).

Greenwald, Erin. Quoted by Laine Kaplan-Levenson in *Sighting the Sites of the New Orleans Slave Trade.* Podcast, TriPod: New Orleans at 300, WWNO, New Orleans Public Radio. November 5, 2015.

Gyss, L'abbé J. *Histoire de la Ville d'Obernai*, 1866.

Halkin, Hillel. "Jews and Their DNA." *Commentary Magazine.* September 1, 2008.

Hall, Henry, ed. *America's Successful Men of Affairs: United States at Large. New York Tribune*, 1896.

Heitmann, John A. "Organization as Power: The Louisiana Sugar Planters' Association and the Creation of Scientific and Technical Institutions, 1877–1910." *Journal of the Louisiana Historical Association* 27, no. 3 (Summer 1986): 281–294.

Herbert, Cynthia Johnson. *Hooper-Godchaux House: 5700 St. Charles Avenue,* privately printed, New Orleans, 2021.

"Highest Water Mark." *Daily Picayune* (New Orleans). June 20, 1893, 1.

Historic New Orleans Collection, MSS 478 Godchaux Family Papers, June 30, 1839–May 14, 1895.

Honora, Jari. "Joachim Tassin—First Employee of Godchaux's," creolegen@yahoo.com, November 19, 2018.

Huber, Leonard V. With an introduction by Samuel Wilson Jr. *Landmarks of New Orleans*. Louisiana Landmarks Society and Orleans Parish Landmarks Commission, 1984.

Huber, Leonard V. *New Orleans: A Pictorial History*. New York: Crown Publishers Inc., 1971.

Kamins, Tony. *The Complete Jewish Guide to France*. New York: St. Martin's Griffin, 2001.

Keller, Gerald J., and Darroch E. Watson. *Images of America: Reserve*. Charleston, SC: Arcadia Publishing, 2011.

Keller, Gerald J., Lisa Keller-Watson, and Darroch Watson. *Precious Gems from Faded Memories: A Pictorial History of St. John the Baptist Parish*. Dexter, MI: Thompson Shore Publishing, 2007.

Klebaner, Benjamin Joseph. "American Manumission Laws and the Responsibility for Supporting Slaves." *Virginia Magazine of History and Biography* 63, no. 4 (October 1955): 443–453.

Korn, Bertram W. *American Jewry and the Civil War.* Philadelphia: Jewish Publication Society of America, 1951.

Lachoff, Irwin, and Catherine Kahn. *Images of America: The Jewish Community of New Orleans.* Charleston, SC: Arcadia Publishing, 2005.

Lemann, Nicholas, "Losing Our Religion," Liberties, Liberties Journal Foundation, Washington, DC, winter 2022, vol. 2, no. 2, 119–139.

Lewis-Kraus, Gideon. "Game of Bones." *New York Times Magazine.* January 20, 2019.

"Look Back in Time, A." *Sugar Bulletin.* 67 No. 12 (April 1, 1989).

Machlovitz, Wendy. *Clara Lowenburg Moses: Memoir of a Southern Jewish Woman.* Museum of the Southern Jewish Experience. Goldring/Woldenberg Institute of Southern Jewish Life. Jackson, Mississippi, 2000.

"Magnificent Gift, A." *Jewish Ledger* (New Orleans). No. 24, June 16, 1905.

McCarthy, Charles Godchaux. "Genealogy and Family History Descendants of Leon Godchaux and Justine Lamm." Prepared for the family reunion, Thanksgiving, New Orleans, 1993 (unpublished booklet).

Menand, Louis. "In the Eye of the Law: How White Supremacy Enlisted the American Legal System." *New Yorker.* February 4, 2019.

Meyer, Pierre-André. "Le clan Goudchaux-Berr-Wolff-Marx de Nancy et sa descendance." (18e-20e siècles.) Histoire et Généalogie. Paris, 2016.

Milberg, Leonard L., Adam D. Mendelsohn, and Dale Rosengarten, sponsor, editors, and curators. "By Dawn's Early Light: Jewish Contributions to American Culture from the Nation's Founding to the Civil War." Exhibition catalogue. New Jersey: Princeton University Library, 2016.

Mintz, Sidney W. *Sweetness and Power: The Place of Sugar in Modern History.* New York: Viking, 1985.

Montz, Quincy. "My Recollection of the Reserve Community Club Complex and Life 'the way it was' 1920s through 1950s." Reserve, LA: unpublished illustrated pamphlet, 1985.

Moody's Manuel of Railroads and Corporation Securities. Vol. 1, part 2, 1921.

"More Views in New Orleans." *Harper's Weekly.* March 30, 1861.

Moses, Clara S. *Aunt Sister's Book.* New York City, 1929.

New Orleans Press. Staff, *Historical Sketch Book and Guide to New Orleans and Environs.* New York, 1884.

New York City Birth Records, 1861, 8:154. Entry for Leon and Justine Godchaux, New York Municipal Archives, New York; FHL microfilm 1,315,313 and New York, New York City Births, 1846–1909.

"Notice of Appeal of Peter G. Treves and Irma S. Wachtel, as beneficial owners of stock of Godchaux Sugars, Inc., a New York Corporation, for a determination of the value of their stock." Supreme Court of the State of New York, Appellate Division, County of New York. Index No. 9592/56. September 17, 1956.

Obituary of Joachim Tassin. *Daily Picayune* (New Orleans). May 4, 1910

"Poor French Boy's Ambition Fruited into Big Enterprise." *New Orleans Item*. October 7, 1910. Part Second, 1, 21.

Powell, Lawrence N. *The Accidental City: Improvising New Orleans*. Cambridge, MA, and London: Harvard University Press, 2012.

Powell, Lawrence N. "Up from Slavery: The Angola Story." In *Grace Before Dying* by Lori Waselchuk. New York: Umbrage Editions, 2010.

Powell, Lawrence N. "Leon Godchaux." *Notable New Orleanians: A Tricentennial Tribute* by William D. Reeves. A publication of the Louisiana Historical Society. New Orleans, 2018.

Putzel, Judith. "Leon Godchaux—Sugar King of the South." Unpublished eighteen-page private essay, 2021.

Redard, Thomas E. "The Port of New Orleans: An Economic History, 1821–1860: Trade, Commerce, Slaves, Louisiana." Louisiana State University and Agricultural & Mechanical College. PhD dissertation, 1985.

Reeves, William D. "Overview to Title of Reserve Plantation." Private research paper commissioned by Jane Godchaux Emke, 1995.

Reeves, William D. "A Summary History of Godchaux-Reserve House." Private research paper commissioned by Jane Godchaux Emke, 1995.

Reeves, William D. "Title to Reserve Plantation, Plus Comparative Acts." Private research paper commissioned by Jane Godchaux Emke, 1995.

Reeves, William D. "Final Report to Jane Godchaux Emke." Unpublished report, New Orleans, 1995.

Riffel, Judy, ed. *New Orleans Register of Free People of Color, 1840–1864*. Baton Rouge, LA: Le Comité des Archives de la Louisiana, Inc., n.d.

Rodrigue, John C. *Reconstruction in the Cane Fields: From Slavery to Free Labor in Louisiana Sugar Parishes 1862–1880*. Lafayette, LA: Louisiana State University Press, 2001.

Samuel, Ray, Leonard V. Huber, and Warren C. Odgen. *Tales of the Mississippi*. New York: Pelican Publishing Company, 1992.

Schoenfeld, Samuel. *Sugar Down Through the Ages*. Lamborn & Company, Inc., 1932 and 1948. Delhi, India: republished by Pranava Books, 2020.

Simons, Andrew, and the Greater New Orleans Archivists. *Jews of New Orleans: An Archival Guide*. The Greater New Orleans Archivists, 1998.

Sitterson, J. Carlyle. *Sugar Country: The Cane Sugar Industry in the South 1753–1950*. Lexington: University of Kentucky Press, 1953.

Snowdy, Jack S. *Godchaux: The Life of Leon Godchaux 1824–1899*. An unpublished historical play dealing with the life of Leon Godchaux. Reserve, Louisiana, 1972.

Solnit, Rebecca, and Rebecca Snedeker. *Unfathomable City: A New Orleans Atlas*. Berkeley: University of California Press, 2013.

Sternberg, Hans J., with James E. Shelledy. *We Were Merchants: The Sternberg Family and the Story of*

Goudchaux's and Maison Blanche Department Stores. Baton Rouge: Louisiana State University Press, 2009.

Sternberg, Mary Ann. *Along the River Road: Past and Present on Louisiana's Historic Byway.* Baton Rouge: Louisiana State University Press, 3rd edition, 2013.

Sublette, Ned, and Constance Sublette. *The American Slave Coast: A History of the Slave-Breeding Industry.* Chicago: Lawrence Hill Books, 2016.

"Sugar Fields of Louisiana, The." *Southern Bivouac.* 2, no. 1 (June 1886).

Times-Picayune. June10, 1924.

Tompkins, John S. "Robert R. Young's Alleghany Corp Forges Close Ties with William Zeckendorf." *Wall Street Journal.* July 5, 1956.

Van Zante, Gary. *New Orleans 1867.* Photographs by Theodore Lilienthal. London and New York: Merrell, 2008.

Wall, Bennett. "Leon Godchaux and the Godchaux Business Enterprises." *American Jewish Historical Quarterly* 66, no. 1 (September 1976). Special Bicentennial Issue, 50–66. Published by the Johns Hopkins University Press.

Walvin, James. *Sugar: The World Corrupted: From Slavery to Obesity.* New York and London: Pegasus Books, 2018.

Weis, Julius. *Autobiography of Julius Weis.* New Orleans: Press of Goldman's Printing Office, 1908, privately published.

Welder, Kathleen, and Lisa Talma. "History and Development of the Godchaux-Reserve House." Unpublished paper, June 1999.

Westbrook, Laura Renée, PhD. "Common Roots: The Godchaux Family in Louisiana History, Literature, and Public Folklore." Unpublished dissertation, University of Louisiana at Lafayette, 2001.

Whitten, David O. "Tariff and Profit in the Antebellum Louisiana Sugar Industry." *Business History Review* 44, no. 2 (Summer 1970). Published by the president and Fellows of Harvard College.

"Will of Late Mrs. Godchaux Probated To-Day." *New Orleans Item.* January 10, 1907.

Wilson, Samuel Jr., Roulhac Toledano, Sally Kittredge Evans, and Mary Louise Christovich. *New Orleans Architecture: The Creole Faubourgs.* Vol. 4. Gretna, LA: Pelican Publishing Company, 1974.

Wolf, Carrie Godchaux. "Personal Family History of Albert and Carrie Wolf." Unpublished forty-page typescript. New Orleans, 1967.

Wolf, Jimmy. "History of the Wolf Family." Unpublished ten-page typescript. New Orleans, 1991.

Zakim, Michael. "A Ready-Made Business: The Birth of the Clothing Industry in America." *Business History Review* 73, no. 1 (Spring 1999): 61–90. Published by the president and Fellows of Harvard College.

INDEX

C

Cain, Chris, 214
Cambre, Sidney, 192
Canal Street, 64–65
cane (see also sugarcane), 26, 160–62,
    170, 187–88, 190, 194, 296,
    337, 384
Carpenter, Frank G., 234, 400, 432
Célestine (slave), 107
cemeteries, 282, 288
census, 130, 226–28, 289
Chaffe, W. H., 238
Champagne, Rosamond, Jr., 63
Champagne, Rosemond, 36, 46, 63, 76,
    164, 269–70
Chandler Vintage Museum of
    Transportation and Wildlife, 196
Charles (Sophie's son), 131, 134
Charlotte (Elma's daughter), 388–89
cholera, 17, 54
Chrysler Building, 327
civil rights, 142, 210, 216
Civil Rights Act, 142, 144, 216, 411
Civil War, xxi, 13, 25, 35, 56, 59, 62–63,
    67–69, 75, 83, 85, 87, 89, 95–96,
    100, 103, 105, 109, 111–14, 117,
    124–25, 131, 134–36, 142, 144,
    164, 169, 209–10, 213–14, 217,
    225, 230, 237, 241, 293, 306, 370,
    378, 380, 386, 407–9, 431, 437–38
Clark, Edward B., 67
clothing manufacturing, 58, 92, 137
Coinage Act of 1857, 69
Comité des Citoyens, 212–13
Commune de Paris, 178
competition, business, 32, 112, 206, 313
Confederacy, 95, 115
Confederate currency, 94, 113, 125
Confederate States Army, 95
Congregation Dispersed of Judah, 246
Congress, 110, 138, 210, 243, 411

Convent, Louisiana, 1, 15, 27–31,
    405, 423
convict leasing, 243
cotton trade, 107
Coustaut, Marie-Madeleine-Elene, 110,
    219, 288, 404
Creole Faubourg Marigny, 116
Crusades, 5
Crystal Palace, 137
Curtis, Mary V., 396

D

Daily Picayune, 65, 90, 104, 120, 123,
    129, 153, 201, 267–68, 287, 386,
    405, 429, 432–33, 436, 439
Darcantel & Diasselliss, 199
David, Anne, 51
Degas, Edgar, 167
Democratic Party, 210
Democrats, 210, 411
Denziger, Walter, 280
Depression. See Great Depression
D. H. Holmes, 64, 207, 304, 313
Diamond Plantation, 191
Dickens, Charles, 112, 433
Dillard's, 64, 313
Disney, Walt, 195
Disneyland, 195–96
Double Dealer, 388
Dowling, J. J., 214
Dreyfous, Felix J., 268
Duane Park, 93
Duane Street, 93
Duke of Clothing, 208, 263. See also
    Godchaux, Leon
Durrell, Edward H., 175

E

East Louisiana Railroad Company, 213
1853 Exhibition of Industrial Arts, 137
Eiseman, Ben, 358